BOTH SIDES

NICKLAS BENDTNER
BOTH SIDES

WITH **RUNE SKYUM-NIELSEN**

TRANSLATED FROM DANISH BY IAN GILES

monoray

First published in Great Britain in 2020
by Monoray, an imprint of
Octopus Publishing Group Ltd
Carmelite House
50 Victoria Embankment
London EC4Y 0DZ
www.octopusbooks.co.uk

An Hachette UK Company
www.hachette.co.uk

ISBN 978-1-91318-362-2

A CIP catalogue record for this book is available from the
British Library.

Printed and bound in Great Britain

10 9 8 7 6 5 4 3 2 1

CONTENTS

COOL DOWN

PROLOGUE – 2018

WE LAND on time. I chew a little harder on my gum. Swallowing until the pressure in my ears drops. It's getting close now. The uncertainty.

I've encountered it before – lots of times – just never when playing for my country. Even with minor injuries or when I'm not completely fit, I've been picked. That was how it was when Morten Olsen was calling the shots.

The atmosphere on the way home from Stockholm has been tense. Almost no one has been talking whenever I've looked down the rows of seats. Not even the players who should be dead-cert picks.

Nicolai Jørgensen and I are sitting at the very front on the right, and across the aisle are Kasper Schmeichel and Jonas Lössl. Those of us with the longest legs.

The lads who really are touch-and-go have isolated themselves as much as you can when you're travelling shoulder-to-shoulder. Andreas Bjelland is looking at his phone. Mike Jensen has his eyes closed and is nodding in time with the music. Probably something by Kim Larsen if I know him.

And then there's Viktor Fischer. He has been smiling non-stop since the showdown against Sweden last night. There's not much else to laugh about, but his whole lower face is beaming. He looks like someone who knows he's home. It's theoretically possible given that Fischer is pals with Simon Kjær, and our captain is the only

1

member of the squad who has the confidence of the coaching team.

You have to hand it to Fischer – he really does have the gift of the gab. Since his transfer to FC Copenhagen, he's been a fixture on the sports pages. Three months of regular starts were all it took to make it to the World Cup. It's not totally fair, but I'm rarely nervous and when I am I usually say it like it is.

FOR THE LAST time I do the sums. It should be straightforward. Today is Sunday 3 June. National coach Åge Hareide knows that I'll only be back to 100 per cent in four or maybe five days' time. He's known that for a week since I got injured with 18 minutes left of Rosenborg's final match ahead of the mid-season break for the World Cup. Nevertheless, he didn't drop me when he reduced the squad from 35 to 27. That has to mean something.

My groin – my bloody groin that's been hampering me since the car accident nine years ago – already feels better. The first scan was a positive surprise and if I manage to keep up my momentum, Hareide could bring me on in the friendly against Mexico on 9 June. On 9 June, there will be just seven days left until our opening game against Peru.

I only need to be ready to get on the pitch and score on 16 June – not a second before. It won't be a problem.

Ivan Marko Benes called as we were boarding. He's always worrying. Not every agent does their job like that, but it's Ivan's way.

'Why the fuck isn't Åge waiting until tomorrow? Like he said he would. Why isn't he waiting for your next scan?'

Ivan's dad is a Croat, and at his parents' home in Amagerbro you can really learn how to swear. But they don't talk bullshit. He's genuine – and that's a rare quality in our industry.

I don't know either. Why does Hareide want to trim his squad as soon as we arrive at the airport hotel at Kastrup? Why today instead of tomorrow when I'm due to be scanned? Personally, I think I'll get through no matter what. He doesn't need a scan to make the right decision.

ACROSS THE LUGGAGE belt I can see Bjelland staring at his mobile. I see Hareide approaching. They exchange a few words – not many – and neither of them looks happy. Then Bjelland's suitcase glides past on the belt. Our only left-footed centre-half grabs it and leaves without even saying goodbye. Hareide stands still for a long time, following him with his eyes.

Although it shouldn't, I feel the relief wash over me. Bjelland has been dispatched, but I'm still here. That can only be positive. Adrenaline is fizzing up through my body from my calves. I love adrenaline.

It's rough for Bjelland, and also kind of incomprehensible. But I don't have time to think about that now. Right now, all that matters is making it to the hotel and the players' meeting. This would be a bad day to dawdle and arrive late.

When I get to the conference room, most of them are there waiting. Nicolai Jørgensen, Viktor Fischer, Pione Sisto and Yussuf Poulsen are there. Martin Braithwaite and Andreas Cornelius. And Kasper Dolberg. There isn't room for eight strikers plus Christian Eriksen in this squad. It can't be done – not with the mindset Hareide and Jon Dahl Tomasson operate with.

Hareide still hasn't shown up, but Jon Dahl is already there. He catches my eye. 'Nicklas,' he says. 'Come with me. I just need you for a second.'

And I know full well what the score is. And just as I expect, Hareide is in the corridor outside waiting for me. His shirt is damp with sweat. It's dripping from the tip of his nose – completely freely.

'You're not coming, Nicklas. We don't think you can be ready in time.'

I feel dizzy. This makes no sense – absolutely none at all. When I moved to Rosenborg, Hareide promised…I feel like shouting at him even though I know that it can't possibly pay off. It's never done me any good to shout at my coaches.

'We'll have to agree to disagree. But it's best we leave it at that,' I say.

Hareide wipes his nose, and I stagger back into the conference room, and find a spare seat. I listen as he lists the four rejected players.

Me, Mike, Bjelland and Peter Ankersen from FC Copenhagen. Hareide's eyes dart around the room. Like a flickering torch that has no idea what it is looking for.

'Would any of you like to say anything?' he suddenly asks.

Mike shakes his head. I put my hand up. This seems to throw Hareide even more. 'Nicklas?' he says.

'I'd like to give a team talk,' I say. 'Best of luck to you all. I wish we could do this together, but that's not how it's going to be.'

There's a smattering of applause. Then everyone gets up. Hareide proffers his hand and we briefly shake hands. Nicolai comes over. We were supposed to have been fighting it out for the top spot, but now he pretty much has a free run at it. He shakes his head slightly.

'What a load of shit,' he whispers. I wrench myself free and hug people swiftly left, right and centre.

Someone taps me on the shoulder. It's Jon Dahl. 'Tough break, old chap,' he says. Gone from his face is any hint of annoyance. I've seen him on his way out too. We know things about each other. He doesn't bullshit me. I leave his outstretched hand hanging in the air and head out to find my suitcase. I need to get away from here.

DOWNSTAIRS in the lobby, Kasper Schmeichel and William Kvist ask whether we're still sharing a cab into the city. All three of us have apartments in the centre.

'Fine by me,' I say, getting into the front passenger seat.

Kvist has spent most of the spring warming the bench and must feel chuffed to have made the cut. I need to vent my frustration.

'I would have been ready for Peru. I'm dead certain,' I say.

They say pretty much the same thing. They definitely get it that I don't understand what's happened. But they don't say much else. They're both on the Danish Players' Association committee so it goes without saying that they can't play favourites. Footballers are so fucking terrified of saying something wrong, they prefer to say nothing at all. I hate that.

Heat is rising off the asphalt on the motorway. The air conditioning in the car sounds like my mum's vacuum cleaner. The one at 16 Otto Liebes Allé. They mention me on the radio. Most of the news bulletin is about me. That I haven't been picked. Four of us drew the short straw.

The taxi driver takes his eyes off the road and examines me. Maybe it's pity. What would I know? I don't think I've ever understood taxi drivers.

I google 'black screen' and post the black image as a story on Instagram. I'm speechless, but I feel like I need to give a sign of life to my 250,000 followers.

Then I message Philine. Tell her that I have to cancel our appointment. She probably saw it as a date – of sorts – even though I only just sent Reanin back to Los Angeles.

It's insane. We're barely halfway through 2018 but this has already been the most dramatic year for my love life – possibly ever – and I'm sick of all the drama. Including the drama I create.

'It's okay,' Philine replies. 'But you should know that I had lots of fun and delicious things planned for you.'

WE CROSS the Langebro bridge. I'm the first to be dropped off, and the symbolism is heavy as the taxi disappears out of sight into the sluggish Sunday traffic with the other two inside. When I get into the ancient lift in my building, it's like a sauna – but things are going to get even hotter. The fifth floor is boiling, and a wall of heat envelops me when I open my apartment door. I pull my T-shirt over my head and hurl it to the floor. Then I open the windows and head up to the penthouse via the stairs inside the apartment and open the door to the wine chiller. Cold vapour tumbles onto my chest and the new lion tattoo that wraps around my neck and shoulders. I end up standing there for a couple of minutes even though I've already made up my mind.

Downstairs in the kitchen I find a corkscrew and glass. There's nothing edible in the cupboards, but that doesn't really bother me. I'm not hungry. I'm thirsty.

In the middle of the round dining table the sweets in the bowl have all melted into a sickly-smelling mass. It's so hot that I give up on sitting down. Under the window facing the view of the harbour I find a draught. I sit down on the wooden floorboards, next to the iridescent bronze sculpture I paid through the nose for when I bought it from one of Caroline's artist friends. That was back when we'd just got together. The Amager boy and the baroness. The sculpture depicts a woman in a mermaidy pose. She's almost naked – but only almost. Back then, Caroline said it looked like her, and that was why I needed to snap it up.

I pick up the Montrachet. Domaine Ramonet is one of the best bottles of white wine in the world. Online it sells for three thousand pounds, but I'm connected and I can cut out the middlemen. It's the 2009 vintage. The year when everything changed for me and my career.

I knock the glass over and it rolls across the floorboards. I drink straight from the bottle. The alcohol goes straight to my head and after 20 minutes the Montrachet is all gone. I get to my feet. I don't notice my groin as I bound up the steps in five big leaps. The champagne fridge is kept at 7.0 degrees Celsius. The best temperature for storing fizz. I go for a Krug.

Once I'm back in position, I stuff so many pouches of snus tobacco under my upper lip that my gums sting. I pull out my mobile. It's been on silent since we were in the taxi to the city. Now I've got 67 missed calls, 200+ text messages and 100+ WhatsApps. I scroll through the texts. One is from Morten Olsen:

'Dear Nicklas. No words can comfort you right now. But then again – remember I made it to three finals after I turned 30.'

I don't know if it's that straightforward. My legs aren't what they once were, and maybe there are fewer years left in them than I dare admit out loud. Maybe my finals are behind me. Maybe this was the last one. If that's true, then it's an unbearable thought. There's no word from Arsène Wenger – of course there isn't. But if he could see me right now, he would grab hold of me.

'What are you doing?'

I can hear his voice right now. The thick accent. 'You have to be intelligent now. You have to focus on your rehab. What you eat! What you drink!'

And I know full well that he'd be right. He usually was.

Simon Kjær messages. Saying I'll be missed in Russia – both on and off the pitch. He finishes with a sad emoji and an offer to talk on the phone, but I don't feel like talking to anyone right now.

I can see that Ivan has deluged me with calls. The reporters who know my latest mobile number have obviously also tried to ring me. Many of my teammates – past and present – have messaged. Many of my flings from along the years feel sorry for me. Not a peep out of any of my exes. Not Julie, Amy, Reanin or Natasja. Natasja is guaranteed to be rejoicing. I don't know about the others.

Some blogger babe I've never met in real life invites me on an all-expenses-paid holiday to the Caribbean. No thanks. As they say in London, there's no such thing as a free lunch. At least not if your name is Nicklas Bendtner. It took some time, but I have learned that much. The hard way.

I GO AND splash cold water on my face, sit down on the bog and look around. Although I bought the apartment in 2013, there's still no proper finish to the place. It was my dad's mate's job – his responsibility. It went wrong – like everything else between us. Dad got weak when the money got big. And I became too fond of the lifestyle that came with the money. Once again, I have that desire. I want to go back in time and hit that young lad on the head with a hammer. Make him understand what a chance it is. That he has something special – something he has to look after.

My eyes begin welling up. All the bad stuff from over the last few years pops up in my thoughts. Random thoughts and memories keep coming into my head – like when I had my breakdown in the airport in Los Angeles.

The others are enjoying their last night off before the World Cup, while I'm sat on the shitter blubbering. I've been slogging away for eighteen months. I moved to a tiny town way up high in Norway to start over. And all along I saw the World Cup as my carrot. The thing that was going to make the slog worth it. It was the dream of Russia and the national shirt that motivated me to change everything. To stop taking shortcuts, to opt for the hard and unglamorous detour – the one that everyone could respect me for taking.

What am I going to say to people? To Nicho? To the ones who continued to believe in me? They must all be terribly disappointed.

This time I want to break into something red, but I'm so pissed I can't remember what the different grapes and vintages mean.

What do I know? I know I'll soon be done with another bottle. Tonight, it's all much of a muchness. But tomorrow, I think to myself, tomorrow you're going to make your mind up, Nicklas. You're going to decide who you want to be in future. Whether you want to go back to being the old Nicklas. The one you know all too well. Or whether you want to keep trying – trying to be the new Nicklas.

LIVE WIRE

1988–2001

MANY TEARS are shed as I'm dropped off at nursery. And it's my mum who is most affected. She thinks it's terrible to hand over her little boy to a group of total strangers.

'I didn't become a mother to give my children away.'

That's the sort of thing she says to anyone who bothers to listen.

Personally, I see things completely differently. As soon as I'm out of my snow suit, I leap out of the starting blocks. There's always something to be experienced. Toys that need to be tried out, climbing frames that need to be conquered.

I could crawl from the age of six months and as soon as I start at nursery I have my eye on the big kids. After a week I begin to do as they do. I stand up and start to walk. This is when I was just ten months old.

Nursery bored me. But then one day the door is open – wide open onto the rest of the world. None of the nursery staff see a thing, and when I reach the end of Gammel Skovvej, I make a right down Saltværksvej. I'm about to step into the road before someone calls my name. Well, calls and calls. It's my mum and dad – jumping and shouting and waving their arms on the other side of the street. The next day, a man comes and fits an extra bolt on the gate.

When I turn four and am in kindergarten I make my escape again.

Down to Saltværksvej, across the road, round the corner onto

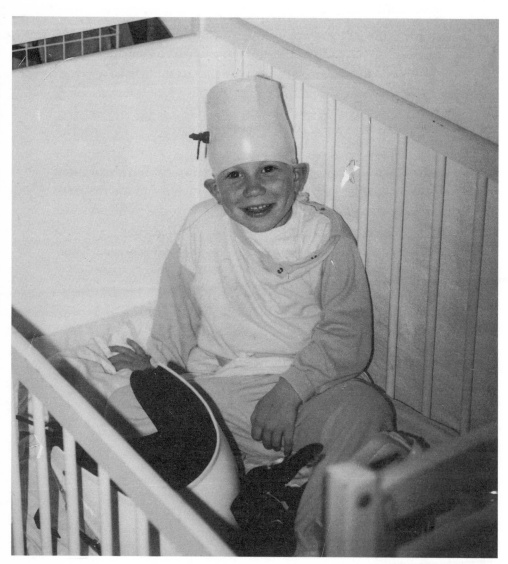

Me in the cot at Banevænget, circa 1992. (Private photo)

Banevænget and all the way to our house where I knock on the door. Mum shrieks when she opens the door. Of course, it all ends with someone installing a fence around the kindergarten.

I don't remember a single bit of this. But I've heard it so many times that a whole series of short films have been created in my head. It's my escape from nursery that particularly captures my imagination. Mum says she can't help telling everyone the story.

'When you set your sights on something, you do it,' she says.

For a few years my mum and dad hardly dare bring me along when visiting friends and family. If they let me out of their sight, I destroy one thing after another. They say I take everything to pieces. And that's how it is. I've got a rocket up my arse and I simply can't sit still. If something isn't happening then I make something happen.

When my mum takes me to Malaga, I get lost in the airport. When we go to LEGOLAND, they put out a call for me on the tannoy. Afterwards, my parents cancel a trip to visit friends in the USA. My mum is absolutely certain I will run away from them. And if it happens in the USA, then we'll be in serious trouble because of all the paedophiles on the loose. Perhaps Mum has a point given my chalk-white hair, blues eyes and winning smile that's never held back. They call me a charmer.

I take up handball, ice hockey and swimming, I learn roller hockey, basketball, diving and table tennis. And what else is there? I'm more or less the best and fastest at everything. By my third birthday, I'm skiing down a black run by myself somewhere in Sweden. Soon after, I learn to ski backwards. I ski as fast backwards as the other kids do going forwards. Even the Swedes are speechless.

It's hard to explain, and I'm fully aware that it sounds totally smug, but that's just how things go for me. Once I understand what others are doing, I can do it better myself. Generally without having to practise. At the open-air swimming baths, I perform somersaults off the 10-metre diving board on my first attempt – forwards and backwards – and my dad is so impressed that he simply stands there pointing at the other children and their parents.

'Did you see that?' he asks without really posing it as a question.

At home, the traditional Scandinavian traits of self-deprecation and not boasting – we Danes call it Jante's Law – are a no-no. A note is pinned on our fridge to remind us of this. 'The Bendtner Family's 15 Rules,' it says.

'You ARE to think you are something special,' reads the first rule.

'You ARE to think you can do what you want. If you can't then it is because you don't want to,' says number two.

I never get further – but the most important one is at the top.

When my mother falls pregnant and is expecting my little brother, the other grown-ups look at her with a mixture of surprise and awe. 'Just think,' they say, 'just think if you have another one like Nicklas.'

It doesn't happen, and my parents are pretty happy about it. Jannick is completely different – that much anyone can see. Once he is big enough, he moves into my room. It's not cool to have to share the space, but we get a bunk bed and I get to sleep in the top bunk. That's cool enough. I like it when new things happen.

On the first night Jannick falls asleep straight away. He keeps doing that. I lie awake for as long as I possibly can. Sometimes I manage to keep going right until it gets light again. Why I do this I don't know, but it doesn't help that my mum and dad look in on me and say, 'Close your eyes.' I open them wide. As wide as I can, for as long as I can.

In the darkness I can glimpse some green creatures. They stare back from the posters on the wall. I kind of like Batman and I'm totally crazy about the Ninja Turtles. I have all their trading cards and I've been given Raphael and Michelangelo costumes for my birthday. Every morning I ask to go to kindergarten in fancy dress. I'm only allowed during Carnival.

The Turtles say funny, cheeky things, they master every type of martial art and they can vanish right before the eyes of their enemies. Just like Batman, they have a kind of superpower and that ignites my interest. I'll never have superpowers. No matter how good I get at sport, there are limits and there will be those on the other side who you dream of emulating. The ones you can truly look up to.

It's only later on – much later on – that the penny drops about their names. Raphael, Michelangelo, Leonardo and Donatello are named after Italian artists. I come to appreciate that extra layer as an adult, but as a boy it goes straight over my head.

When Mum is cooking and Dad is in the workshop, we watch cartoons. She always knows when there is an ad break because she can hear Jannick screaming. He's doing that because I'm tickling him or doing something else to annoy him. I tease him out of sheer boredom. When I'm bored, everyone suffers. That's just how it is. I don't know if I'm actually an evil child, but I can't control it. I'm an expert in finding other people's weak points and drilling into them.

Jannick doesn't make it easy for himself. Even though I love him with all my heart – and believe me, I still do – we are night and day in so many different ways. He's quiet, I'm noisy. He's dutiful, I'm cheeky. He's disciplined, I'm unruly. He goes to Scouts, I bully him about it. And even though he learns karate and rapidly becomes the best person at it in the country, it's still me who promises to beat everyone up in the school playground. If they even consider hurting a hair on his head…No one gets to tease my little brother – that's my privilege, and that's how it is with my friends too. I'm allowed to tease them, but no one else is. And if they're taking a beating then I always step in and help out. It's a principle that will cause me quite a lot of trouble over the years.

MY MUM comes from the Kastrup neighbourhood. She's one of the most loving mothers you could wish for, and she has such a huge heart filled with love for us boys. Me, Jannick and my dad. Whether it's problems at work, conflicts in the family or anything else in the way, she always takes care of us. In her book, we're the centre of the world.

When mums like mine appear on TV, people probably think to themselves: Wow! I wish she was my mum.

My mum is that kind of mum. That's why she can remember all those stories about me. It means a lot to her, and I think it's also kind of the same when things go to shit for me too. Then it's shit for her as well, and it gives me a guilty conscience.

My dad isn't from Kastrup – he comes from Sundbyvester Plads in Amager. They met at the shopping centre in Amager in the 1980s. He invited her to his birthday party, and not long after they were eating shrimp sandwiches and drinking white wine at my grandma and grandpa's house. My mum says they were so nice that they made her feel comfortable with my dad. There had been a few stories going around about him – just like there are stories about me. That he was the black sheep of the family and a bit of a rascal. A womanizer, a hustler and nicknamed Mister Amager. But in a way, for her, his parents proved that he came from something good.

It's completely typical for people from Amager to get together and end up living on Amager. But that doesn't mean that the Amager natives are one big happy family. Seen from the outside, we're just the people from Shit Island, the place they decided to build the sewage works – but on the inside, we can be just as divided as anyone else. We talk about people from Kastrup, Tårnby, Vestamager, Amagerbro and Sundby. And then there's people from Dragør, of course.

My mum has never been able to stand people from Dragør. Out there where all the pilots and their stewardesses are too big for their boots. It's hardly likely to have been improved by the fact that my dad moved out there with a new woman.

Dragør is probably the only place on the whole island where I would dare leave an Audi for more than a couple of days in a row. Even in Kastrup or Sundby it might be gone in the space of a few hours. That's just how it is.

Out here we're a right bunch of reprobates. I know all about that. I was a scoundrel myself in my teens, and I was like that with my friends from way back when. Most of my friends are from way back.

I still hang out with more or less the same group of lads. We've kept in touch throughout the years and many believe that they should have stopped me. That it's their fault whenever I end up in a mess.

When people spout that kind of rubbish, they have no idea

what they're talking about. If you got to know me as a child, as a teenager and as a young man working abroad, you would realize that I make my own decisions. Even when they may seem totally incomprehensible to everyone else. And to me too – just a few minutes, hours or days later.

If you come from Amager, then you talk like people from the cobbled streets of central Copenhagen. I do in any case, and when Danes ask me where I'm from, I never say Copenhagen. I always simply say Amager. I love hearing myself say it, because most people I encounter think that Amager is the worst of the worst. When I say Amager, the tone of their voice changes. Nervous laughter while they check whether I'm joking, or what I'm on about. When they realize that I'm totally serious, the next thing they say is: 'But Amager is actually a pretty nice place, right?' It never fails. Very Danish.

I still like being proud of Amager. It's hard to describe exactly why, but as I remember it, we always backed each other up when we were running around making trouble. We looked out for each other. And a spade was a spade. I really miss that sense of community.

FOR MOST of the 1990s, my dad ran a shoe repair and key-cutting shop on Saltværksvej. My mum works in an office for Scandinavian Airlines right by the airport. She's been there since I first started at nursery. Before that, she was an instructor at the Form & Figur fitness centre on Frankrigsgade.

Since my parents became homeowners, money has been tight. Their mortgage eats it all up. This isn't me guessing – it's something I know, because they often talk about it. Fortunately, it's not downright misery – and they save hard to ensure they can afford both a summer and a winter holiday.

In summer, we stay in my grandparents' apartment on Gran Canaria. It's just behind Sunwing, a hotel that is really popular with the Danes.

Jannick and I love being on Gran Canaria – we love the big beach, the waves, the warmth and the pepper steaks at the Pirate.

The Pirate is the only restaurant I've ever been to, and I am barely able to speak of anything else afterwards. The sauce is thick and has a really special taste. If you really pay attention, you can feel it leave a tingling on your tongue.

Sometimes we borrow the Sunwing tennis courts. That's what Dad calls it: borrowing. He's found out that there's a Danish guy who stays in the same room year after year. The Dane calls himself Bamse the Bear and never uses the tennis court. We're pretty certain of it given that Bamse has only one leg.

If anyone from the hotel asks whether we're Sunwing guests, my father flings his arms about.

'Whether we're guests? I'm *Bamse*,' he says. It works every time.

I've no idea where my dad gets his information from, but that's him in a nutshell. I love him for it. Sparkling eyes and a big sense of humour – always smiling. That's his thing. He does favours and always finds where it's easiest to climb over the fence.

EVENTUALLY, WE ABANDON Banevænget. Jannick and me in the same room simply won't do – not any longer. My dad has found a bigger house over on Otto Liebes Allé. Just like Banevænget, it's a side road off Saltværksvej. Dad gets help from some handymen he knows, but he does most of it himself. He's pretty handy and is a trained heating engineer.

While the house is being fixed up, we stay with my aunt Gitte. She lives alone with her son, who is smaller than me, but bigger than Jannick. They have an apartment in a building just round the corner in an area called Vægterparken. Nowadays, some might describe Vægterparken as a ghetto, but what do I know? All I know is there are blue lights, robberies and fist fights every single night.

Our family moves into an 18-metre square room. We're all to live there together. The kitchen, toilet and dining room are shared with my aunt and cousin, and I really don't like it. I'm eight years old and I'm having a terrible time. I'm being nagged at constantly and I react – like I always do whenever I feel backed into a corner. I hit back and tease – and it's my cousin who suffers.

We're constantly coming to blows.

It lasts for ten long months, and when I look back it must have been rough having us foisted on anyone. Especially me. I'm really not made for so little space. Whether I'm on the football pitch or off.

When things almost can't get any worse, my grandma goes and dies. It's sad, and my mum and aunt are down in the dumps, and I've no idea what to do with myself given the glum mood.

When I can't and don't want to sleep, I eavesdrop on stories from the living room. The grown-ups are holding a wake night after night in memory of my grandma. My mum used to drink in moderation, but that's not the case when she's in her sister's company. Talk turns to my grandpa. He's been a big shot and has done some totally crazy things. During the war he was in the resistance movement and fought the Germans side by side with legends like Flame and Citron. They bombed ships in port, sabotaged trains and all sorts of other things that took real balls. Afterwards, he became a racing cyclist and participated in the Six Days of Copenhagen track event. He sounds like one hell of a guy.

Now my mum is worried about him. After my grandma's death, he's moved to the holiday apartment on Gran Canaria. He spends his days walking the dog, riding his bike and tossing back sangria. I expect it's probably tied up with his wartime trauma, but drinking is something my family does. Especially when something is bothering us, and especially on my mum's side. It's not something I want to dig into too much, but many do. Drink, that is. Including my parents at times.

The more curious I get, the higher in the cupboards I can get, the more I find. Spirits are hidden in all sorts of places. Like the day when I think I've found a bottle of apple juice. I unscrew the lid to chug it. I don't get far – it stinks of booze.

I decide I won't get into drinking. I remember saying this to myself, perhaps even on the day my grandpa died. He only outlives my grandma by two years before cycling off a cliff.

ALTHOUGH WE ONLY move a kilometre down the road, I change schools from Skottegård to Korsvejens School. This happens just before the summer holidays between first and second grade.

I spent years thinking I was kicked out of Skottegård, but it turns out I wasn't. It seems that my dad went to parents' evening and something went wrong. A teacher said that I had probably not 'got enough oxygen at birth' – and it leaves him seething. I can well understand him – how do you respond to something like that?

He doesn't realize that it's the kind of thing people say without meaning it literally. The kind of thing that shouldn't always be taken 100 per cent seriously. So he slams the door and takes me out of that school. No one is going to talk about his son like that.

Over at Korsvejens School, it doesn't take long for my unruliness to become a running theme. I'm sent home from a camping trip because I've been completely unmanageable. And I get the blame for something to do with a drawing pin on the supply teacher's chair. That's one I can't quite get away with given it was me who put it there.

I've no idea why I do such brain-dead stuff. Sometimes, it's a very short path from thought to action. Or as my Danish teacher always puts it:

'Nicklas, you don't think before you speak.'

She may be right about that, but what is she going to do to help me? What should I do with myself? I need a reaction, attention, fresh air – something. Anything. It's impossible for me to sit still for as long as is required of me.

When I turn eight, a man from the council comes to visit. He follows me around. At school, to football and at home at 16 Otto Liebes Allé. I quickly forget all about him, and after a few days he disappears again. My mum explains that the man is a psychologist and I'm being assessed for DAMP – or ADHD as the doctors refer to it. I've no idea what any of this means, but the psychologist doesn't believe that I am failing anything nor that I have DAMP.

'You're just a really lively boy,' Mum says to me.

She's become a member of the school board of governors and she remains one until I finish ninth grade. I'm not stupid enough for a second to believe that she has suddenly gained a passion for school politics and all the rest. Like so many other things, it's something Mum does for my sake – and quite honestly, it looks like a good investment. I don't feel in danger of being expelled from Korsvejens. Although maybe I should given that I'm constantly sent out of class. And as if that isn't enough, I also get sent to the headteacher's office. Her name is Grethe and she's a little old lady, but she's still sharp as a pin.

On one occasion, she gets her hands on one of my essays for my Danish teacher. It's about Little Ole the troll. The troll is always up to something, and sometimes crosses the line. For example, Little Ole calls the fire brigade even though there's no fire. When the firemen turn up, they can see that Little Ole didn't mean any harm and they roll around on the floor, laughing their arses off. But Little Ole's parents still ground him because they don't see the funny side of his practical jokes. After a week, Little Ole also prank calls the police. And that's a bad idea indeed.

'That's when things went really wrong,' it says in my essay. 'He was put in jail, released on 5 November at ten o'clock, and then he came back home to his mum and dad – and ever since that day he has never pulled anyone's leg.'

My mum helped me with the essay. We write it while I'm grounded. And I think that Grethe, up in her office, finds the essay to be extremely telling of my behaviour as a pupil, because she gleefully shares it later on when Danish reporters call up to ask about my school years.

However, unlike Little Ole, it's hard for Little Nicklas to give up his troublesome ways. It can't be fixed overnight.

OUTSIDE THE DOOR to our classroom, time is dragging. Usually, I climb up by the window on the other side of the corridor and scratch my name into the window frame. Other times I fall asleep because I've barely slept at night.

Occasionally, I pack my school bag and slip home to think more about my behaviour. Then I get sad and drag myself to my dad's shop to tell him what's happened. Dad knows all about being a live wire, and he generally feels sorry for me. It's nice to feel that he understands me in one way. And it's extra nice when he finds 30 kroner in the till and sends me out for two pizza sandwiches from across the street. Then we sit together and eat them and wait for the next customer to come into the shop.

When I reach sixth grade, Gregers figures me out. Gregers is a teacher, and it's a relief that people like him exist. This older dude with glasses makes me feel a little less hopeless.

At first, we only have him for PE – and PE is my turf. Once again, I know full well that it sounds arrogant or superior, but that's just how it is. No matter what we play – rounders or basketball – and who I end up on a team with, we completely outplay the others, and perhaps that means my classmates find it easier to put up with me the rest of the time.

One day our Maths teacher quits and Gregers takes over. It changes everything. For the first time, I'm paying attention in class of my own volition, and as soon as I'm restless in my seat and say some nonsense out of sheer impatience, he sends me out to do ten laps of the playground before I can come back inside. He just knows that I need to burn a lot of energy before I can get my head in gear.

Suddenly I'm one of the best kids in the class. Maybe not in Danish or English or History – I don't have superpowers after all – but at least in Maths.

I've never had any problems adding or subtracting – I'm pretty good at figures – but Gregers teaches me to use them for more than that. He teaches me division more or less overnight. And just like that...unbelievable! There it is. I'm a little taken aback, I must admit. But anyway...in many ways, Maths is something with gaps. Things that appear and can be filled in with the right shape or the right figure. I can picture Maths. I can't picture present-tense inflections. They're two different things.

Gregers is the first person not to treat me like a stupid boy. Instead he finds me as I am. He wants to get the best out of everyone, and I feel accepted as who I am. It's such a positive development that

School photo, Korsvejens School, August 2002. (Private photo)

I slowly learn to deal with being told off by him. When Gregers raises his voice – obviously he does – I don't get defensive. Then I pull myself together even more. He's earned it from me.

After a year, Gregers is replaced by a real sourpuss in Maths. The sort of person who is more concerned about teaching me the rules of calculation than how to count. I lose all interest in a flash.

Fortunately, Gregers continues to be our PE teacher. And he keeps being happy for me. But to be honest, in PE it's not hard to love me.

When I think back, he was probably a sort of taster of the coaches who I would later appreciate that I would do everything for them. The ones who understood that I can I figure out how to slog my way through and give it my all to the final drop of blood – that I'll play while injured if that's what it takes. Just so long as I don't feel wronged. On the other hand, if you just shout to get into my skull – almost before you've even looked me in the eyes – then that's another matter. Then I become difficult – and difficult is my middle name at Korsvejens. Not just in the classroom.

I DON'T DISCRIMINATE between people. If I want to tease someone, then in theory everyone is fair game. Even the kids from the older grades. Sometimes my little brother finds me haring round the playground tailed by a bunch of bigger boys. Sometimes three or four years my senior. First they surround me, then they give me a beating. But sometimes I get away. They can't take my speed from me.

I remember a handball competition in Amagerhallen where we played against other schools from the island. One team with a lot of foreign boys who were so bad at passing that I just end up standing there laughing whenever they're in possession. It ends with them calling their big brothers and suddenly I'm in deep trouble. I'm chased down the corridors and I have to get help hiding under some foam mats in a circle around the track. It's just before the final, and when the whistle is blown to start the game I emerge from my hiding place. We win the whole thing and we're handed medals and a trophy, while this raging bunch are baying and shouting that they're going to get me. It gives me a kick when there's a whiff of danger.

Personally, I've never been involved in that kind of thing – beating some randomer up for no reason at all. Where I'm growing up, fighting can be an okay way to solve some things, but if that's the way then it has to be one-on-one.

At school, there are some pretty mental people and they don't give a shit about fair play of any kind. One of the boys in another class in our year has a big brother who may only be 17 years old but is already on probation in a biker gang. When the big brother graduates at the end of tenth grade, his little brother gets so many beatings that there's barely time for them all. People have really been waiting – saving them up.

I've had his big brother on my back, so I don't get involved to help him. No one does. And that teaches me a lesson. If you want to cause trouble, remember to do it in a charming manner. Otherwise the hammer blows are guaranteed to follow.

MY PARENTS try to discipline me – but without luck. It all ends with my dad hitting me. Completely powerless, he gives me three paralysing blows – dung-dung-dung – while we're in his workshop one day. It leaves my shoulder more or less numb.

The shop is long gone, and the pizza sandwiches and comforting words have come to an end. I don't exactly blame him. I'm well past my 13th birthday and my problems at school just keep coming. My dad doesn't hit me to punish me – he hits me out of frustration. I deserve it.

A week later, we're back in the same place. I've been sent home from school and told not to come back until next Monday. This time, Dad doesn't hit me. His eyes are filled with tears and he begins to cry. This is the first time I've ever seen him cry about something bad.

'What the hell are we going to do with you?' he asks.

'I don't know,' I reply, and find myself crying too.

It's the first time we cry at the same time, and although it should be a bad thing it leaves an impression on me. That I mean so much to him that I can make him truly sad.

It's like I really get it and quietly adapt. Not that I become a model pupil or anything. I'm still lazy and constantly looking for my friends when we have homework to do.

Perhaps it may not sound like it, but my inner joker has begun to get serious. Ever so quietly. It's really moved me to see my dad cry. It occurs to me that other people also have feelings. That I'm actually hurting them. This is a new sensation.

VENT

1992–2002

MAYBE YOU KNOW how it feels? In front of you is this beach where the sand stretches so far that it seems like there's a sea of yellow before the actual blue ocean begins. Even though the waves are breaking, washing away, breaking again – the surf is trembling. From a distance, it looks like tiny fluctuations on a huge surface. That's what the beach in Gran Canaria feels like to me as a boy.

Many years later – long after my grandma and grandpa have passed away and their apartment has been sold – I return and realize that everything has shrunk. The beach seems many times smaller now.

Of course, that's not how it works. It's the other way around. It's me who has become many times bigger. That much I understand. And, of course, it's me who has seen beaches that are many times bigger than the ones in Gran Canaria. That much I also understand.

You name it, I've been there. The Maldives, Barbados, Bahamas, Cairns, Cannes, Venice. I've used every single possible holiday to travel. And while it may sound like a confession, I've also used every imaginable excuse to travel even more. Even when I've not had any holiday due but have been injured, I've travelled as much as possible. Getting out into the world and letting it distract me. I dare say I'm more curious than most other footballers.

Maybe it's about something more than just travelling. Maybe it's also about escape. When I'm far from home, I take less notice of it all. All the snide remarks, the articles and the thousands of geniuses filling online threads with comments about me and my career. It's absolutely incredible what people think they know about me – without knowing the slightest thing.

I've got used to it – it comes with the territory – but I still wish it didn't have to be that way. Maybe I could occasionally be allowed to enjoy something without simultaneously being reminded how much I've thrown away or how stupid I've been. There's always a 'but I heard that Bendtner…' or 'just think, if Bendtner had…' to be found whenever I go online.

It's as if my haters would prefer to forget how far I've got by being a really, really lively live wire. While I was still a teenager, I played week in, week out for one of the top ten teams in the world. And I've scored 30 times for Denmark in 81 internationals – including at the European championships and the World Cup.

So no – I've clearly not failed completely. But the opportunities I've been given were used far too poorly. And we should probably go back over all of that. What I want to tell you about now is the story of my early years as a footballer. About the very early years. I'm still very fond of this chapter in my life so I don't want to ruin it with too much negativity. Because what I remember most of all about myself is that I was a happy boy. Almost always happier than everyone else. Especially when I was surrounded by those white pitch markings.

That's why I don't want to risk having the same experience at Banevænget that I had on the beach in Gran Canaria. That's why I've stayed away – even though it was my home until I was almost eight years old. Even though it's only five minutes out of my way whenever I'm on my way into the city from the airport.

If I can protect just that last little piece of my childhood, there's still something to be happy about. Something I don't need to regret. Something that can't be taken away from me – no matter how wild I could be, and how much I struggled to sit still at school. I prefer it that way. And that's why I have to describe our back garden as I remember it from afar. I'm not going back to look at it through eyes that have aged 27 years. I don't want to contaminate it.

IT'S A SEPTEMBER day in 1992. Two or three months earlier, Denmark won Euro 92. Everyone at kindergarten is talking about it. The grown-ups are talking about it. Everyone is talking about it. In any case, I imagine everyone is. But that doesn't bother me because football means jack shit to me. I'm four years old and I'm mostly into the Ninja Turtles, Batman and mischief. Mischief is my speciality. On a trip that summer, I managed to cut the guy ropes on a whole bunch of tents making them collapse – we had to come home early.

This makes the adults laugh a lot. They have friends visiting and they're tipping back the G&Ts. The friends' kids want to play football. I just want to play, and if I can kick ass with a round thing at my feet then that's fine by me. We kick the ball about and tumble around in the back garden.

It's not long before Kim – my friend Chrille's dad – makes a suggestion:

'If Nicklas doesn't already go to football, you should hurry and sign him up somewhere.'

No one in my family plays football. My dad was a semi-serious go-karting driver over at Kløvermarken, and Mum used to play handball and volleyball. She was pretty damn good at it too. That's what girls from Tårnby are like when they're good at something – real contenders.

Anyway, as far as my parents are concerned, anything that might wear me out is something worth trying. They make enquiries and agree on Tårnby Boldklub, which is where Chrille also happens to play. Kastrup Boldklub is actually slightly closer by.

The coach is a woman and she's the mother of one of the other boys on the team. I don't normally pick up last names, but my mum uses it from their very first encounter. I think she kind of looks up to Anita Troest.

It's not long before Anita suggests I play with the five- and six-year-olds instead of with the other four-year-olds. Anita's youngest son is called Magnus and he's a year older than me. He is by far the best kid on the team, but then I get the chance to play as an attacker and I score constantly. It's not all that hard. The ball gets passed to me or I tackle for it, and then I run straight through the defence and kick it past the goalie.

It's straightforward, and it's insanely good fun. My team celebrates with me, and I receive almost no complaints about going it alone. Often, opponents end up blubbing – but as long as I'm not getting yelled at, it's good with me. I grow in the company of my teammates, and it feels natural. Everything makes sense. Football. It's the best game I've tried. Way more fun than ice hockey or handball. Simply beyond comparison.

When I'm not at training, I play with my friends. We pile up our jumpers on the grass and use them as goalposts. At home in our back garden, my dad puts up a set of goalposts for us. Just like that. That kind of thing is the easiest thing in the world for him. He also puts his own picket fence up. It's a hit and many of the other dads begin to copy it. He brags about it for a while.

TÅRNBY BOLDKLUB is also known as *Amagerkanerne* – the Amager-icans. It has a handful of grass pitches just off Gemmas Allé at its disposal. The club becomes my favourite place in the whole world. When I head off to training, I've often been bored by something or other at school – but as soon as I get my boots on, my worries disappear. Fifteen minutes earlier, I may have been really down in the dumps, but once I'm on the grass those dark clouds vanish. Like mist in the sun. Then I stand in the middle – together with the others. We're going to do something together. As a team against another team. A moment of unspoiled happiness washes over me. It's still like that.

On the pitch, I'm not *fucking impossible Nicklas* – on the pitch I'm useful. I'm worth something to the others. But for that to happen I need to be allowed to play, allowed to participate. Watching football from the sidelines or on the TV just isn't the same thing for me – and when that does happen I feel frustrated and out of sorts. It should be me running around out there.

My parents are relieved. They can feel it. Finally they've found something good for me – and they say my personality is practically transformed. While others go from being quiet and peaceful to being total thugs on the pitch, football has the opposite effect on me. Obviously, I complain about the referee and so on, but I don't kick people and I don't provoke people just for the sake of it.

The day before I began going to football, my grandpa had promised that he would give me five kroner for every goal I scored. It doesn't take long for him to call it off. It's not a good deal for him because I'm banging them in. Sixty to seventy of them every season.

Our team has loads of good players, including Magnus Troest and Niki Zimling, but they're all a year or two older than me. Even though we're a small club, we win against almost everyone. Except Rødovre. Rødovre has a really hot-headed – but also pretty talented – kid on the team. His name's Mike. I hate losing, and it's even worse against him.

In 1996, at the age of eight, we become the Copenhagen champions in minifootball. We also reach the final of the Donald Duck Cup. That's as close as you come to a Danish championship in the junior years.

That summer I attend the Danish Football Association's football school for the first time, and as usual I get moved up to play with the year groups above me. At the end, there is a penalty shootout competition for all 200 participants. I win.

I love taking penalties, and I almost never miss. A lot of people take bad kicks when it's for real rather than in training. I take better kicks when there's something at stake.

WE END UP seeing more and more of the Troest family. I like playing with Magnus and his big brother Jonas, but their sisters are too small to really join in. On a summer holiday in the south of France, one of them is completely obsessed with dancing and since all the others find it embarrassing to waltz with a little girl, I take over. We swirl around until it's way past our bedtime. Girls don't scare me – they can't embarrass me or make me feel uncertain. And I reckon they never will.

Our families travel a lot together. To campsites around southern Europe and on ski trips to the Swedish mountains and the Austrian Alps. Anita and her husband, Jørgen, have a positive influence on my parents. They eat healthily and barely drink. Occasionally, Jørgen sneaks in a visit to my dad to have a beer – but never more than one. That kind of impresses me and Jannick. Most of our parents' friends like to drink.

While Anita is in charge of football coaching, Jørgen looks after athletics. They're both on the board of the Amager Athletics Club, and my brother and I are signed up so we have something to do when we're not playing football or at Scouts. Mere weeks later we've smashed most of the club records. Jannick takes care of the long jump and high jump, while I'm fastest in the 60, 100 and 200 metres. In fact, I set a couple of national records for Denmark – albeit they're later outdone.

Jørgen shows me loads of things about points of balance and how my feet should touch the ground, and how my arms should be kept close to my body. This minimizes air resistance so that I can steam ahead even faster. I get the hang of these techniques and remain faster than everyone else – even when I begin to grow like crazy.

Just a few years later I begin scouring the internet for inspiration, though it's rarely for specific footballers I want to emulate. It's more about the amazing details. The ten best goals from free kicks, the ten best solo goals, the ten best passes. But there is one exception – because I have my first idol. Ronaldo. Brazil's Ronaldo!

To this day, I consider him the best striker in the history of football. Him and Messi.

Ronaldo is a trailblazer with his feinting, but it's not just that. It's the whole package – there's just something about him. I really like that he knows how to enjoy life and how he is constantly smiling so everyone can see his huge buck teeth.

At Real Madrid, Ronaldo pretty much straps a small suitcase to his belly, but that doesn't stop him from wiping the floor with his opponents. Or perhaps it does, because in the end it's injuries rather than defenders that stop him in his tracks.

Ronaldo's acceleration – the explosion when he zooms off with the ball glued to his boots – is verging on supernatural. He's like a superhero, and I start copying his feints. One by one.

Later on it dawns on me that I can never be like my idol. I have a completely different centre of gravity. I'm much taller, and my legs have grown far too long to pull off the tiny dance steps that he fools people with time after time. But some of the feints stick. That's how thoroughly I've swotted up. Despite everything else.

AT HOME we don't talk about football – at least not seriously. My dad isn't into it – nor is Jannick – but sometimes Mum puts on the Danish show *Sports Saturday* while she's cooking tea. It's also her who keeps a scrapbook of my many tournaments. There's a match every weekend and the whole family comes with me all over the country.

I carry on scoring lots of goals, and when several of the other boys on the team want to move to Fremad Amager, my mum suggests that I try a third option. My parents have spoken to Niki Zimling's dad, and he recommends KB. Kim Brink, the former Danish Superliga coach, is apparently setting up a new football school, and only the very best talents from KB and B1903 – FC Copenhagen's two parent clubs – are up for consideration. Even though we've beaten KB several times, they have the best youth teams in the country. Mum believes I should be coached by the best. She still regrets not switching to a better handball team – one off the island of Amager – before she became a teenager and got stuck in Tårnby.

I'm up for anything. Something new has to happen – and it does. On my 10th birthday – 16 January 1998 – we cross the Langebro bridge and head all the way out into the Copenhagen suburbs – to Peter Bangs Vej in Frederiksberg to be precise.

KB's junior team are playing Avarta, and I get my chance during the second half. At some point, there's a high pass across the pitch, and I don't have time to think about what to do. But somehow I get off the ground with both my legs. Once in the air, I scissor kick for all I'm worth. I strike the ball perfectly and am able to turn my head enough to see the ball sail into the far corner of the goal. I've scored a couple more goals like that since then, but never quite as perfectly as I did on my debut for KB.

Afterwards, the coach comes over to me. He's not someone's mum or dad – not like in Tårnby – and he's spent the whole match shouting all sorts of stuff, none of which I understood. Encouragement and suggestions, I think. He shakes my hand as if I'm a grown-up.

'If you've got the courage to move clubs, you're welcome here,' he says, introducing himself as Søren Belling.

I certainly would like to accept – it's all much bigger and that suits me. There should be enough space.

That same summer, Denmark are heading to the World Cup finals for only the second time in history. Brazil and Ronaldo are also in attendance in France, and my hero is going to play against Denmark in the quarter-final. In the previous round, Ebbe Sand scored a truly beautiful goal with an assist from Michael Laudrup's genius pass – and even I was cheering at home in front of the TV. Nevertheless, I'm not quite sure who I'm supporting more in this match. When Brazil score beautiful goals, there's no conversation to be had. Brazil always score beautiful goals.

Denmark lose, but it's close with a final score of 3-2 and I'm actually a little annoyed. On the other team, that boy Rivaldo is from a completely different planet, and he overpowers Peter Schmeichel on two occasions with cunning shots. When all's said and done, that's good enough. Rivaldo, Ronaldo and the other Brazilians have the chance to become world champions. I find it hard to imagine that happening for Denmark.

SØREN, MY COACH at KB, has moved me up through the age groups just like when I was at Tårnby. This means that my teammates are up to two years older than me. You can tell easily given that several of them are going through puberty, while I'm small and slender.

It's a rock-hard environment and I get a taste of my own

medicine from the school playground. In the showers, it's me the others are spraying with water and when they find out I'm wearing my female cousin's old jeans – a brand called Miss Sixty – they can't control themselves. I get called lots of things. A poofter, a homo, a baby doll, a princess and so on. Poofter is probably the worst thing you can say to someone at that age.

Suddenly, I'm no longer the naughty boy in class. I'm the one that others tease, and no one holds back. There are players from all over Copenhagen, and there's no positive special treatment – no protection. It's not like back home in El Dorado where everyone knows each other. Rich kids from Frederiksberg and Hellerup, refugee boys from Nørrebro, latchkey kids from the suburbs. And everything in between. There's a lot of troublemakers, and my face fits in a way that it usually doesn't. If anything, I'm outdone.

One day I come back from the training pitches and can't find my clothes to change back into. Eventually, someone shows me where they are. They've been stuffed in a bin bag, pissed on and then the bag has been knotted.

I drop the bag on the floor and run out of the changing room. When I catch sight of my mother in the car park, I'm already blubbing. She gets really angry and calls Søren right away. I sit in my seat beside her and dry my eyes while she shouts at him. It's not often that Mum gets worked up like that, and it makes an impression on friendly old Søren. At the next training session, he issues warnings to everyone who had anything to do with the pissing incident. He also calls their parents.

'If you so much as think about that kind of behaviour again, your days in my team are over,' he says to the other boys. 'Is that understood?'

It is understood. Several of my teammates are a bit sorry for me. Or at least they assume the role of my protectors. Especially on the pitch, where more and more of our opponents play using their larger physique.

THE LEADER in the dressing room is called Nino. He's our goalkeeper and totally on the ball. His family fled the civil war in Yugoslavia, and he has a giant nose and a giant dick that already has hair on it. Many years later when I am training with Denmark on Malmö FF's pitches, he turns up and taps me on the shoulder.

'Do you remember me?' he wants to know.

'You look just like you always did – of course I do,' I reply.

'Okay,' he says. 'You really have to fucking forgive me for that time. I hope you're not pissed at me or anything.'

I tell Nino everything is fine. I don't tell him that I know how he feels. But I do. How many of my schoolmates do I wish I could apologize to personally? Lots of them.

You don't gain any respect by snitching on other people. You get respect when you prove to be indispensable – which is what I resolve to be. I don't want to be known as a grass. I don't want to look like someone who can't go the full distance. In the dressing room, I'm just as cheerful and like a little brother as I've always been. And on the pitch I score more goals than ever.

I want to be the one that makes a difference – and for the next while I don't miss a single training session. One day when my mum is supposed to drive me, she is so late that I lose my patience. But I don't have any money to buy a two-zone ticket, so I jump on my bike and slog along behind the bus. Panting, I follow it through central Copenhagen and out to Frederiksberg.

It's the story of two-year-old Nicklas all over again. The one who escaped from nursery and made it all the way down to the traffic lights by Saltværksvej.

I PLAY AT my first Danish championships in Næstved in 1999. The eight best pre-teen teams are brought together and in the semi-final we play Brøndby. We're already 2-1 down before I can get started. I don't remember it in any great detail – only that I play an absolute blinder. I score four in a row and we end up winning the match 5-2. Three to four hundred spectators clap me off the pitch with five minutes to go, and the internal KB newsletter highlights me as a player worth keeping a serious eye on.

I also score in the final against AGF – dribbling around their goalie and putting the ball away with my left foot, which has never been as good as my right, but good enough to tame and control the ball.

That's enough to secure the winners' medals, and even though I was better against Brøndby, I'm given the player of the match trophy. The player of the tournament trophy is awarded to Danilo Arrieta, who just a few years later moves to play for Valencia.

On the pitch, I make a difference. The kind that causes a stir in a group of lads. Then you're more than a little shit from Shit Island. Suddenly you're totally okay.

My competitors for the two strikers' spots are Fosu Boateng and Mads Torry, both born in 1986. They're not half bad, and in terms of physique, there's no doubt that Torry is ahead of me. He's taller and he has bigger muscles.

At training, balls get pumped at us. Rock-hard passes, ten or 20 or 30 or 40 at a time. It's all about making yourself as wide and cliff-like as possible so you can tame the ball while you have a defender who weighs 15 kilos more than you on your back, get rid of the ball again, run into position and finish. I get pretty good at it, and in the big matches I keep delivering the goods.

The problem arises when the opposition is decidedly bad. Then I go completely AWOL. This turns Søren Belling's hair grey. He says that I'm making it hard for him. That he can't help me if I don't give 100 per cent. Every time. That it breeds envy when I get given a longer leash than everyone else.

I really like Søren, so I try to fix it – but I don't always succeed. I have to admit that teams like Vestia from Sydhavnen are a complete turn-off.

The further we travel, the more switched on I am. When we play in the Danish championships or in cup finals or at tournaments in Holland, France and Sweden, I've got goals in my boots and if there's any dissatisfaction with me then it's not something I truly notice. I come to feel more and more like a part of the gang. Even off the pitch.

At the age of 13, we head to the Gothia Cup in Gothenburg.

We take the tram from the hostel to the pitches, and on the seats next to me there are some Norwegian girls who are a bit older than me.

English isn't exactly my forte, but that doesn't stop me.

'Why don't you come home to my...*lejlighed*?' I ask them, trying to invite them back to my flat.

The whole team is bursting with laughter, but one of the girls actually takes the bait and begins to write long declarations of love to me. Many years later, Søren Belling still finds the opportunity to remind me of the occasion. For me, it's more or less business as usual. For as long as I've been interested in girls, I've reached out to them. On some occasions more successfully than on others. That's just how it is.

MAYBE MY persistence is because my dad was a shoe repairer. I'm sick of patched-up football boots. I want them to always look like they're brand-spanking-new. One day, Puma come out with a model that's not black but green. Green like the Ninja Turtles. Frankly, this is just about the best idea ever. I simply have to own them and I nag my mum until she gives in.

I'm becoming style conscious. I need my clothes to be Evisu or Le Coq Sportif, and my hair changes style and colour on a monthly basis. Dreadlocks, highlights, patterns. Black, red, white. I give most things a go.

After a tournament in Jutland I'm named best player. The prize is one of Brian Laudrup's Ajax shirts, but I just don't like it. I can't bring myself to wander around in something so awful, and I end up taping over his name so that only the number ten is visible on the back.

Brian Laudrup is a decent player – no doubt about it – but he doesn't inspire me. The idea that I should admire a player simply because we come from the same country...It just seems stupid to me. It's probably about several other things too. I've become a true FC Copenhagen fan. Sunday after Sunday I troop into the lower half of the Carlsberg Stand at Parken Stadium together with Morten from KB. When we're there, we chant lines like 'It's Sunday, the time is quarter to kick, I put on my FCK strip, and even if my slag is begging for a Sunday shag, I say no, it's time to go!'

I love that song, I love the club and I love the community. And that's why it's simply impossible to wear the shirt that Brian Laudrup left FCK for – without ever having sacrificed himself.

In my bedroom at home the only footballers on my walls are foreigners. Totti, Ronaldo and Romário. And obviously Thierry Henry and Robert Pirès from Arsenal. Henry is a goal machine, and I have just discovered Pirès. He's from France and is basically a jack-of-all-trades in the midfield. His flow – the way he moves – looks utterly effortless. I really want to be able to move the ball forward like Pirès does, and if I weren't a striker I would play with his ease.

Another of my walls is plastered in pictures of Pamela Anderson and all sorts of other women that I've found in porn mags or have printed off the internet. Some of them are completely naked – the real McCoy – and they solicit lingering looks from my dad. One evening, he comes into my room with small yellow Post-its. One by one, he puts them over the women's privates. Pure censorship.

'You just can't make your mother looks at these kinds of things,' he says.

We both laugh ourselves silly. I totally get it. It's not on. My mum doesn't deserve this.

When I get confirmed in church, my parents give me Pirès's original Arsenal shirt. Number 7. His autograph is even on it. It's been conjured up by Benny Nielsen. Benny Nielsen is a retired footballer and now he's a talent scout. Including for Arsenal. I really like Benny, because he doesn't act like a know-it-all when he turns up to watch our matches.

He and my dad talk a fair bit. My old man has become our team leader at KB, and to be honest he's not bad at it. It's as if Dad has finally found his place. As if he knows full well that he's no great football expert. That's left to Søren Belling, while my parents take care of all the practicalities. Transport, changes of clothes, bottles of water and so on.

Sometimes, the opposing teams' dads shout at me. Then I shout back. 'Shut your big mouth!' and stuff like that. My dad's totally fine with that. Sometimes he even yells at them too. 'Yeah! Why don't you shut your mouth!'

That summer – the summer of 2002 – a new Danish hip hop duo make their breakthrough. Nik & Jay, who don't give a shit about the Law of Jante and rap about success before they've really achieved it. I think their music is okay – no more, no less. But all my mates say I should be the third member of the group. And in one way they're probably right. I also don't give a shit about the Law of Jante's tall-poppy syndrome, and I say as much. I wear the clothes I want to. And I've made my mind up that I'm going to be a star. That's definitely the plan.

AMAGER LAD

2002–2004

ØST NIGHTCLUB is on the corner of two streets – Rådhusvænget and the long Kastruplundgade, which runs all the way from the motorway in the south up to Saltværksvej. A land of milk and honey for poptart girls and rowdy boys. It's around a mile from Otto Liebes Allé – give or take – and when its Friday-night disco closes at 2am, that's where I need to head. I can run the route in five minutes, and I do so slightly too often around the ages of 13 to 14.

The DJ lets me out the back door. From there, I steal across the dark playground and as soon as I reach the streetlights I pick up the pace. Running along hedges, criss-crossing through the cosy suburb filled with detached houses. I don't have any choice. If I end up hanging around out front, they find me on their mopeds or in their cars. And then I get a beating.

Øst is the place to be in our corner of Amager. It goes without saying that a possible thrashing lingers in the air. People smuggling in clenched fists or beer bottles.

The ones who want to fight have driving licences and are possessive about some girls who are older than me but young enough to have to come to Øst. Under 18, in other words. Personally, I'm too young to be there after midnight. Once the clock strikes twelve, you have to be over 16 – because after midnight you're allowed to drink alcohol.

The guys are after me because I don't hold back. It just so

happens that I sometimes kiss the wrong person. Sometimes it's someone-or-other's girlfriend – or some babe the guys had planned to get their hands on.

We're talking about 2002, and I've been busy running. Including to football. By the time junior training gets started, we've parted ways with Søren Belling. I miss him already – the new coach has his own way of getting us in gear. He takes us over to the Damhus Lake and sets off the stopwatch. It's five kilometres all the way round and I hate it. Back at the athletics club, I found it fun to run over short distances – but I don't go to athletics any more. I stopped doing that when I moved to KB. This concept of moving without the ball appeals to me less and less. I'm sure many people will laugh at that because no – I have never been (and never will be) known as the keenest pressure player.

The coach doesn't like my body language. His name is Jonni Larsen, but he's known as the Chimney Sweep because that's what he does when he's not coaching football talent. He mucks out chimneys and he's not afraid to voice his opinion so everyone understands.

But I pretty quickly come to like the Chimney Sweep. He has swagger and he's direct. A real grafter – a bit like my dad. And he is totally authentic. What you see is what you get.

It goes without saying that my respect is far from diminished when I encounter his tasty bit of stuff who comes down to watch us play. She's blonde and has an enormous rack. We talk about her a LOT in the dressing room.

Over by the Damhus Lake, the Chimney Sweep is always taking shots at me. All. The. Time. Shot. Shot. Shot. Small nudges to my chest.

'What's up Nicklas…Why's your arse so slow?' he wants to know.

'No reason,' I reply.

One day, I catch sight of an unopened bottle of cola sticking out of his holdall. The moisture has condensed on the bottle – it looks like it's in an advert.

'What's it going to take for you to pull your finger out and run as fast as the others?' the Chimney Sweep asks.

'What's it going to take for you to give me that cola?' I ask, pointing.

'You beating the others – fair and square.'

Two minutes later when we're dispatched around the Damhus Lake, I position myself behind Mathias and Jakob. They say that Mathias is the fastest player at KB, but with 200 metres to go I overtake him and pull ahead. I win narrowly.

The Chimney Sweep has no idea whether to laugh or cry. That's what I'm like. I need a carrot to perform. But not a real carrot. I need a cola – or something else sweet. And I think the penny drops for the Chimney Sweep. Right there and then is when it happens.

NO DRESSING ROOM is without hierarchies. The strongest boy is still Nino – the goalie with hair on his dick. But the ones who pissed on my clothes also have something to say. And they've let me in. They are Jamil Fearrington from Vanløse, Benjamin Seker and Kim Tandrup from Husum and Danny Mirabel from Frederiksberg. Those last two are tight. Danny is the quiet sort, Kim is a wild one with a rough childhood behind him.

Back in Tårnby, we were all blonde. Potato Danes, as some foreigners might say. At KB, there's a real mix and I quickly realize I have no problem with people who come from other places and look different to me. I thought maybe I would given that's what I've grown up with.

My dad and his labourer mates have never spoken particularly fondly about foreigners and immigrants. And that's just how it is. If you mostly hang out with people who know just as little as you do, you can very easily build up the wrong ideas. That's something I know a great deal about since there are a lot of people out there who get me wrong, day in and day out. They write things that are wrong – and about things that have never happened.

THE FIRST TIME you step into our dressing room the tone seems harsh. Almost too harsh. Like when one of us is caught with skid marks on his pants. They get hung up on a peg so that everyone can have a good laugh.

That's just how it is – those are the rules – and you get used to it. Very few of us mean any harm by it. We're just lads – all looking for a place in the group. Everyone wants to feel like they belong, whether that's at the bottom or the top of the hierarchy. The worst thing is feeling like an outsider.

The Chimney Sweep calls us the Italian posers. Me, Danny and Kim. He thinks we spend more time in front of the mirror than is good for us – and he's not far off the mark. I've changed my haircut ten times in two years. At the time, we have hair down to our shoulders and we smooth it down with body lotion and those small hair bands that came into fashion when the Italian team wore them at the World Cup. The Maldini, Totti and Inzaghi style.

'Are you sure you've got it right? What a bunch of girls,' says the Chimney Sweep, shaking his bald head.

The fact that everyone on my team is a year or two older than me suddenly means I'm ahead of my time. My classmates don't drink alcohol – not yet – but I do with my football mates.

Jamil is often home alone at his parents' house in Vanløse and he throws some sick house parties. As a rule, I usually warm up with Kim in Husum. I make my own way out there. It takes me an hour and a change of buses, and although we've never really talked about it, I think my parents are getting suspicious. We're partying hard. They've otherwise tried their best. Instead of a blanket ban on alcohol at home, they've taught me how to drink in moderation. One beer with dinner – that kind of thing. But it goes off the rails in no time at all.

I throw up pretty early in the evening. That's no bad thing – it's a good investment. As soon as my stomach's empty, my head feels so fresh I can keep drinking as if nothing happened.

Kim has a cousin who is a hotshot in the world of Copenhagen nightlife, and when I'm 15 years old I sneak into an adult disco for the first time. Not somewhere naff like Øst or A-bar down by Rådhuspladsen, but a real place where we show fake IDs and the average age of those inside must be well into the 20s.

I'm the first one onto the dancefloor – totally unpractised. By 1am, I'm sleeping like a log on a couch and it goes without saying that the others have a right laugh about it when we get to training on the Monday. But I also notice something else in their tone. I can tell they took care of me.

Back in Amager, I let rip all the stuff I've heard the KB boys use. Girls still don't scare me – not one bit – and one night at Øst I score with a girl from the tenth grade at Korsvejens School. A few days later I'm sitting on a bench in front of the gym at school doing nothing much with Alex and Nick when she comes walking by. She's got curves and wears bold make-up, so her eyes are visible from a distance. She's practically a woman already.

'There's my girl,' I say.

'What are you talking about?' they say, laughing daftly together. They simply don't believe me.

'She totally is,' I insist.

'If that's your girlfriend, run over and snog her,' says Alex.

'Okay,' I say. And then I do it. I tap her on the shoulder, stand on my toes and tongue-kiss her.

They can't believe their eyes. And to be honest, it must have been an insane sight for Alex and Nick. Neither of them has even reached puberty.

I act way bigger and more experienced than I actually am. Before long, when we end up at home on her parents' bed, I've no idea what we're up to. I lie on my stomach and finger her because that's basically all I've heard about in the dressing room at KB. Suddenly she turns me over so that I'm lying on my back.

'Now I want something,' she says and she mounts me.

Pop goes my cherry.

I GET pretty caught up with the opposite sex. Before the end of ninth grade, I manage to have sex with at least five of the girls in my class. And in addition there are the ones who are older than me. Like the day when I was 13 or 14 and two older girls knock on our door. I'm not at home, but my mum opens it. The girls have brought stuff for me. A bag with Lynx deodorant, two pairs of their own knickers and a love letter signed by them both. I've probably met them at Øst or at a football tournament – I can't remember any more – but nevertheless, my mum sends them away and confiscates the gifts. Especially the love letter, which she still guards carefully some 16 or 17 years later.

It's not just my teammates I go out with. Chrille – the one from my back garden at Banevænget – and Nevers, who lives in Sundby and has moved to KB from Fremad Amager, are also in on it. As we trudge home from wherever we've been – a party or Øst or a trip into the centre of Copenhagen – we do idiotic things. We kick wing mirrors off cars and throw stones through windows. If we happen upon roadworks, we change the signs around so that motorists are led to a dead end. That last one still brings a smile to my face. The others aren't all that good.

We also muck about a fair bit with fireworks. If we have six big fireworks, then that's goodbye to six post boxes. Preferably out in Kastrup where they don't know us the same way they do in Tårnby.

On one occasion, Nevers and I decide to swap girlfriends. The girls are up for it, but it's not a good deal because my bird is hot while Nevers' is second-rate. It's like getting a Skoda in exchange for a Ferrari – but you've got to be a mate.

The boyish pranks intensify. The worst one is probably when we break into the school IT room. We're standing there holding the computers before we get cold feet and flee empty-handed. Shortly afterwards, I land a work experience gig at the Sportmaster branch in the shopping mall where my parents first met – the Amager Centre. Together with a friend, I plan a major heist. I'm going to sneak North Face coats out of the window and round the back where he will be waiting in the alleyway to receive them. I manage to do my bit before I spot the CCTV cameras. Naturally, I panic and hurry to retrieve the coats. Instead I steal a pair of trainers.

'You seem to have got new shoes,' Mum says to me when I get home. 'Where did you get them from?'

I can't remember what I told her, but she accepts my cock and bull story. I don't think she wants to admit to herself that I might be thieving.

We also nick bikes when we get the chance – basically everyone does in Denmark – but one night I'm involved with the hijacking of a crane. It's me, two girls and this bad boy that I don't really know. I seriously can't remember how we came to find each other. On the other hand, I will never forget how he smashed his right hand through the cab window.

We cruise around in the crane until we hear sirens and hide in a flat in Vægterparken. It belongs to the parents of one of the two girls we're with. The guy sits there and prises the shards of glass out of his hand. He's bleeding like hell and I end up wondering to myself, What the fuck are these two sweet girls doing with me and a psychopath who just smashed his own hand through a window? All just to drive around in a crane? It's totally stupid.

In the summer of 2003, my family, the Troest family and Chrille's family go on holiday together to a campsite in the south of France. Chrille, Magnus and his big brother Jonas aren't all that fond of me, and I feel weirdly on the outside. I tell them to piss off – or maybe I do so myself. I don't mind being on my own. That'll change later, but as a boy I love it – being alone on an adventure.

I sneak off to the beach for a swim, and when I stagger back I end up dripping water on a speaker that's playing music on a towel.

'Be careful, that's Bang & Olufsen,' one them huffs. A Dane.

I turn around and catch sight of a boy and girl of my own age. Let's call them Christina and Silas. We fall into conversation, and I apologize about the speakers. They're best friends, not boyfriend and girlfriend, explains Christina.

We hang out for the remainder of the holiday and when we return home to Copenhagen, Silas and I stay in touch. Silas' dad lives in a mansion, and I frequently go to visit. We quickly become new best friends and talk on the phone almost every day.

Sometimes we get up to some pretty over-the-top stuff. Like renting a limo to cruise around in. Silas' dad spoils his son and Silas is more than happy to flash his cash so that everyone can see how rich he is. He is clearly trying to impress me – but it doesn't work.

Not properly. I think it's almost the other way around. It impresses him that I'm not impressed.

It's not the Asger Jorn painting (which I obviously don't recognize), all the money or the big gestures that mean I like spending time with Silas. But rather I'm curious by nature, and he shows me a new world. It's as if my days with Silas put me in mind of something. That there is something else out there. Something other than Amager, and something other than football.

AT KB, we keep winning, and even though the Chimney Sweep threatens me with the bench, I never seriously feel in any danger. Most of the time, I'm passionate about football – and when I'm like that I'm second to none.

The game has begun to get more brutal and physical, while technique and tactics matter less and less. In training, we're pushed completely differently and during matches the opposition teams work hard to embarrass me. Pushing from behind and kicks to my ankles and shins become my daily fare. Even when the ball is nowhere to be seen.

I'm up for a scrap, but I'm drowned out by my dad. He's still the team leader, and he is getting more and more involved in the game on the pitch. Maybe he feels he has seen enough to know what he's talking about.

If I come in for criticism, he's always on my side. Always. It's always the other side's fault. Never mine. And if people don't agree with him, then it's they who are total idiots. The whole lot of them.

He means well, my dad, but many years later when I look back I gradually begin to see that I let myself be influenced by him and his strong protectiveness. Unconsciously, I learn that you can benefit from blaming just about anyone else when things fuck up. I get pretty good at that.

It's never my fault – whether I'm at school or on the pitch – and everything is on my terms. And by my terms I mean 110 miles per hour. Rarely does anyone – not even my mum and dad – ask me to dial back my big dreams. If I want to be the greatest footballer in the world, then I just have to go for it. That's the message I get. And probably the only message I bother to take in. I can do what I want. Just like Nik & Jay.

The feeling of knowing best – no matter what – still haunts me. Even at the age of 31. And sometimes these situations arise... Situations where I end up being a fool and have to admit that it's actually me who is wrong. I've got better at doing U-turns and saying sorry. But it's something I'm still working on – because it doesn't come naturally to me.

I get picked to play in the Copenhagen select teams. We play against other Danish regions in a few competitions, and they're pretty fun. At the gatherings for Copenhagen's top talents, we practise stuff that we otherwise don't focus on. Small technical details, finishing with our left foot, running into free space. That kind of thing.

I'm waiting to be picked for the first time for the Denmark youth team, when almost exactly as I turn 16, it happens. I'm picked for an U16 tournament in Portugal.

In the first match we beat the hosts, in the next one we lose to Spain. I've still not scored and I beat myself up about it. But then in the final game against Armenia something happens. I put us 2-0 up, and then I score to make it 4-0, then 5-0, and one of the goals is a solo effort. Everyone tells me:

'You were totally incredible, Nicklas – totally, totally incredible.'

This has no effect on me personally. After all, it was just a match and I would have preferred to score in the first two games rather than against Armenia.

When we get back home to Otto Liebes Allé, our answering machine is flashing like crazy. The tape is full of greetings from all sorts of people speaking English. And while I don't understand it all, there's no two ways about it. The messages are from talent scouts inviting me to visit. Manchester United, Barcelona, Chelsea, AC Milan, Roma, Feyenoord and a whole string of other clubs. We're talking about more like 20 than ten.

My dad talks about putting his new job on hold. Just for a

while so we can take this seriously. In the middle of all this, Benny Nielsen calls. He's been in touch with the head of talent at Arsenal. One of his other scouts was in Portugal.

'They want your lad,' says Benny.

It's a pretty crazy thing to just throw out there – and it changes everything. I don't know why I'm so into Arsenal – are you even supposed to know why your heart beats more for one thing over another? I don't know why. I just know. I'm a massive Arsenal fan.

IN MARCH I fly to London. My dad and Benny come too. It's my first visit to the capital of England. Outside Denmark, all I'm familiar with are pistes, beaches, campsites and football pitches – and that's about it. So the pulse of the big city knocks me sideways. All the people, all the energy – so many people coming and going. The tempo here is my tempo. Here, I don't look like someone fast-forwarding through a frozen landscape. London. I feel at home here.

We land ridiculously early in the morning, but it's so far to Arsenal's training centre that it's mid-morning when we finally arrive. It's a wild place.

I'm almost never impressed, but the conditions are just completely unlike those at the Danish clubs I've been visiting every other weekend as a KB player. The whole thing is extremely stylish and the pitches are like the greens on a golf course. Perfectly cut, no blade of grass longer than any other.

The dressing rooms are so new they sparkle and the food in the canteen is more akin to something in a restaurant. The whole thing has been designed in the head of the manager – Arsène Wenger. Everything has to be connected, because every age group is expected to be able to play the same dominant, on-the-ball type of football.

It's been agreed in advance that I don't have to undergo a trial. Of course, the club still try to make me have one. My dad says 'No, no! No, thank you!' but it doesn't affect me. I've got nothing to hide. How could it ever hurt me to show what I've got? I can't think why not, so I happily get changed and head out onto the pitch with Arsenal's reserve coach, Neil Banfield.

With just me, Banfield and a goal, I start dribbling. First with my left foot, then my right. Then I have to make long deliveries. Then I have to shoot for goal. Finally, headers and control.

After 15 minutes, he waves me over. When I'm within a metre, he nods and maintains eye contact – then nods again. That's it. I'm approved. We belong together – Arsenal and me.

It's not just in my head. We've been invited to lunch upstairs in the canteen, and the first person to come over is Wenger who offers his hand. He seems extremely friendly and is smiling. He tells me how much he is looking forward to working with me. Then a jet black, broad-shouldered figure appears at our small table. It's Patrick Vieira. I recognize him at once. Arsenal's captain – the world champion in 1998. He pats me on the shoulder.

'Welcome. I hope we'll get to see more of each other,' he says before leaving.

I assume this must be normal. I've since wised up and I'll never forget Vieira for pulling off that stunt. He has class – top calibre.

THE RUMOURS fly around KB. Maybe I blab a little too – just like Danilo Arrieta did when he left for Valencia. Even though Danilo is on the bench in Spain, it doesn't worry me. I'm determined to put KB in my past. I know I'm ready to take the next step.

But then – out of nowhere – FC Copenhagen's director of football wants to talk about the future. I don't know Niels-Christian Holmstrøm – and I only meet him again a few years later – but my dad says it's time to make demands. They need to come up with something that makes it attractive to stay.

He's talked to some of the other dads and the salary as a member of the KB talent squad is barely worth mentioning. If you're 16 years old, a youth contract pays about £400 a month, if you're 17 then it pays £450, and if you're 18 then it pays £500. Only when you turn 19 do you get an adult wage.

My dad goes to see Holmstrøm with our demands. At first,

I'm to be paid £2,250 a month. Then I'm to be paid £3,000 a month. And finally, I'm to be paid £4,000 a month. And I'm to train exclusively with the first team.

When Dad comes back he's all het up.

'That Holmstrøm fell off his chair,' he says.

It sounds as if Holmstrøm got back to his feet again. In any case, he's told my dad some home truths.

'Best of luck to you all. It'll all go to shit for your son!' and 'He'll never make it in England. No Dane ever has. It's madness!'

Stuff like that. My dad seems shaky. For me, it has the exact opposite effect. Of course I need to leave, and no matter how many times my mum begs, it isn't up for discussion.

It's Nicklas escaping from nursery all over again. No one can hold me back if I have already made up my mind.

Holmstrøm's revenge is a little childish. I spend the rest of the season at KB on the bench. I haven't tried that before – not properly – and I don't care for it at all. I belong on the other side of the touchline. I need to leave. It can't happen quickly enough. I need to step up and work with the best.

THE ACADEMY

2004–2005

ARSENAL have made it crystal clear. Parents are to stay away for the first couple of months because otherwise the new academy players won't learn independence. So we say goodbye at Copenhagen Airport. Mum and Dad wave and cry as I head up the escalator. I feel something too and I'm taken aback. I think it's just a shade of sadness of some kind. That a good chapter in my life is ending.

But it's no worse than that. For me adventure awaits. Something to be conquered. For my parents, it is farewell. And doubt – growing bigger and bigger. Is sending their boy away really the right thing to do?

At least they know what awaits me at the other end. During the summer holidays, we visited the people I'm going to live with in Winchmore Hill in north London. They're called Anna and Clem Cattini, and they seem like really nice people. Over the years, they've put up a lot of members of the Arsenal academy – more than just a handful – including players like Jérémie Aliadière, Justin Hoyte and Jermaine Pennant, who are now all in the first team.

Before the contract was signed, Liam Brady – the almighty Academy Director – had flown to Copenhagen to watch me in action. He had also taken the journey up through the system himself. From immigrant teenager to first-team player. He travelled from Dublin to London as a 15-year-old and pulled on the Arsenal shirt 235 times.

As a general rule, foreign academy pupils are housed in pairs.

That means they can keep each other company – but Brady thinks I'll benefit from living alone. That I need the most secure framework possible.

He wants to present us with a couple of options, but when we meet the Cattini family I've seen enough.

Anna and Clem are both in their late 60s, have Italian roots and live in a terraced townhouse on Blenheim Close – a small cul-de-sac. Their own daughters grew up and moved out long ago, and they're really too old to play happy foster families. But I think they can't help it. They love opening up their home. That's how it feels.

The kitchen is on the ground floor, on the first floor my bedroom is next door to the TV room, and my hosts sleep on the top floor. Even though Anna cleans my room, I've not ended up in some luxury setting. The mattress on my bed – which is far too short – seems totally clapped out, and I fear that former academy pupils have made shameful use of it before my own arrival.

At the foot of the bed is a 14-inch TV. Apart from a small desk with an old PC on it, that's my only piece of furniture. When I'm not playing on the PlayStation, I use the console as a DVD player and watch a hell of a lot of films. That's all I've got the energy to do when I get home from training and lessons. For the first couple of months, I'm running on fumes because we're being pushed really hard. We do that from day one.

It's obvious that Anna and Clem want me to succeed at Arsenal. Clem asks concerned questions if I get home exhausted, and if he's going to the training centre then he drives me. Otherwise I have to take two buses and the tube and get off at Cockfosters. A handful of us get picked up there by minibus to do that last stretch.

The training centre and academy is on Bell Lane in London Colney, just north of London, and there's usually 30 to 40 pupils at any one time. Arsenal's youth set-up is one of the best in England, but the major success stories are still few and far between. It's almost never the case that a player goes all the way from the juniors to Highbury Stadium and the big scene – but sometimes the club does catch a talent at my age and guide him through to regular play in the Premier League. The most recent example to secure a regular berth on the first team like this is Francesc 'Cesc' Fàbregas. He's only a year older than me, and it's good to see that it can be done. On the other hand, he's considered a completely incredible talent – and competition in midfield is also slightly less tough than it is up front.

Bergkamp and Henry are the team's biggest stars. They would start for any club in the world and be hard to beat. No doubt about it.

I DON'T UNDERSTAND my contract – not from top to bottom. But it's easy to work out I'm not here at the academy for the money. Until I turn 17, I'm paid £290 per month. Once I turn 17, my pocket money until I'm 18 goes up to £390, and once I'm 18 I'm paid a one-off lump sum of £100,000 – less the wages I've already received. Only once I turn 19 will Arsenal make a decision on whether I'm worth investing in.

The English clubs do whatever they can to help their players. Tempting youth players with adult salaries is not allowed. A minor cannot sign a full contract.

Nevertheless, I'm guaranteed £100,000 for attending the Arsenal academy for the next two and a half years – and after a while it dawns on me that this is pretty special. Most academy pupils at other English clubs don't get handed a massive bonus on their 18th birthday. Most of them get their redundancy notice as a birthday present.

You can see it a mile off. The others have more to fight for, more to prove – and a hell of a lot faster. That's why they give each other wedgies and consider each other competitors.

Training is at a high level. We learn everything about tempered passing, directional taming of the ball, playing each other onto the correct foot and how to communicate on the pitch. It's pretty nerdy and well thought through. If everyone actually did what we're told, we would never lose the ball. Never ever.

As a striker, I have to learn to protect the ball. The coaches constantly bring up Alan Shearer. The old poacher of Blackburn

Rovers and Newcastle United. When he was seriously injured and came back slower, he recast his playing style and made it impossible to take the ball off him. I need to be able to do the same thing. If I control a long pass and then let the ball run away from me, I get the world's biggest bollocking. It's just not good enough, because losing the ball stops the entire team moving forward. A poor finish is what can happen – screwing your team over in the middle of a phase of play is out of the question.

It's as if I've arrived on another planet. It's overwhelming, and I have to get used to no longer being the best in my own age category. All of a sudden, there's lots of others bidding for top spot.

Tuesdays and Thursdays are the worst. Every Tuesday and Thursday afternoon we have lessons, and it's just like being back at Korsvejens School. We have lessons in every subject imaginable. Press Management and Financial Management. I thought I was done with this kind of thing, and – if it's possible – I actually hate it more now than I did back in Amager.

One day I bunk off. From my hiding place in the ladies, I can hear them running around shouting my name like madmen. When Brady catches sight of me later in the queue in the canteen, he pulls me aside:

'What are you playing at, son? Where have you been?'

He's heard some story about me hiding under a table. It's not true, so I tell him as much – my conscience clear.

'Honestly, Mr Brady, I've not been hiding under a table. This is all a big misunderstanding.'

More clashes follow. Directly below Brady in the hierarchy is David Court. It takes a couple of months before I get under his skin – but then there's no doubt about it. Court, a stocky hot-headed man, can't stand me. He simply can't conceal his disdain. Like the day I turn up at the clubhouse wearing a baseball cap. He tears it off and sets about jumping on it with both feet. He's like something out of a cartoon, and slightly against my will I end up sniggering. Then he shouts and screams and jumps some more. When he's finished, I pick up the cap and carry on towards the dressing room.

Court is probably just trying to put me in my place. I need to get it into my skull that I don't mean shit – I'm nothing while I'm not on the first team. For as long as I'm at the academy, I still haven't made it. That's his message.

But there is no uniform required and for as long as that remains the case no one is going to tell me I'm wrong. It can never be my problem that other people prefer sports gear while I go around in camo or whatever. We are dressed similarly enough on the pitch.

When the first team play at Highbury, there is a dress code. All the academy pupils have to wear suits and I do so without protest. In my inside pocket I have a notepad and pen to be used for homework. My task is to study Thierry Henry's patterns of movement closely. I generally learn more by doing things myself, but even if I only manage to write down a couple of lines, I slowly begin to see how much Henry does right. For example, he conserves his energy before suddenly exploding so that no one can keep up. That's how I want to use my own speed. I'm also impressed by how good he is at finding his teammates. Henry is a beyond outstanding finisher, and he is also one of the best providers of assists in the Premier League.

IT DOESN'T HELP my fighting spirit that I'm light years away from the first team. I'm not even close to training with my heroes, I only see them when they play at Highbury or when they leave Bell Lane.

The team are known as 'The Invincibles'. It sounds a bit like a league of superheroes – and that's not far from the truth. The record of 49 league matches without a defeat only comes to an end in October 2004. Undefeated in 17 months…That's some serious shit to follow in the footsteps of.

The closest I get to people like Bergkamp and Pirès is their muddy boots. At the academy we're tasked with cleaning them. It's a tradition and everyone has to do it, so I put up with it. No protests either. But it doesn't motivate me – if that's supposed to be the point of it. And I can't be bothered to clean my own. I simply don't have the energy.

In front of Highbury Stadium, January 2006. (Photo: Morten Langkilde/Ritzau Scanpix)

On the whole, the first few months feel like a lonely affair. It's very hard to make friends on the U18 team where everyone treats everyone else as a rival.

Brady has cottoned on to the fact that I'm not some language genius, and they rustle up an English teacher for me. A guy called Callum. He's extremely sweet and lovely, and has these little effeminate hand movements that convince me he must be gay.

Callum recognizes that I don't thrive in the classroom. For me, I prefer learning by doing – on the move – and we take long walks through the neighbourhood while he points at this, that and the other. Callum explains the difference between a house and a building, and teaches me that what I know as a road sign in Danish is in fact called a street name sign in English. That kind of thing.

MAYBE CALLUM isn't some raving homosexual. Maybe it's me who has become super attentive to people's sexuality. And I'm pretty sure I know why it has begun to occupy me so much.

After I've been at Anna and Clem's for a couple of months, Silas comes over during the autumn half-term. We've agreed to hit the town with some of his London friends, but I don't know much more than that. Silas asks me to take the tube to Piccadilly Circus and wait in front of a red phone box. It's a Saturday, late in the afternoon, and my ride turns up in some sort of old-fashioned car. It says Rolls-Royce on the back. Inside it's the size of a living room and Silas is accompanied by two men. One is perhaps Chinese, while the other is a Brit. He's really nice and a little chubby. He introduces himself as Alexander.

We soon arrive at the Chinese man's huge apartment.

'What's all this?' I ask Silas.

It's the sight of a butler in white tie and tails that makes me sit up and react. He's carrying around a silver platter of drinks. It's as if it's from an old movie.

Silas fills me in on a few things. Alexander's last name is McQueen and he's one of the world's leading fashion designers. We're going out with him – to a seriously fancy nightclub. I might as well start looking forward to it, according to Silas. And of course I do. I mean – I'm 16 years old and I'm going to party like a VIP.

The place is called The Shadow Lounge. And to be completely honest it is utterly unlike anything I've ever seen before. The dance floor is alive – built out of video screens that are constantly changing colour and pattern – and all the way around it there are small booths with leather sofas and thick velour curtains.

At first I think we've turned up in the middle of a fancy dress party. Lots of the women are in ball gowns and many of them are wearing hats. Some of the men have bare torsos and are wearing feather boas.

I look around a bit – I want to see if there's anything worth going after. There is. A girl appears beside a pretty good-looking guy. He looks like Joey from *Friends*, and the girl is more than pretty. She's phenomenal. Insanely beautiful.

I think to myself that I'd like to get off with her. We get talking at the bar and things are going pretty well. Even if I do say so myself. But then in the middle of it all, I notice a hand slide slowly down my forearm. Eventually, we hold hands – braiding our fingers together. Only then do I discover that it's not the girl's hand I'm holding. It's the guy's – the one who looks like Joey. The penny finally drops. The Shadow Lounge is a gay club. I've no idea how to deal with this kind of thing and I tear my hand away.

The next thing I remember is the Chinese guy's apartment. We're back at some after-party and apart from me and Silas it's mostly grown-up men there.

I stagger into the kitchen and throw up in the sink while someone caresses my back and hair. The alcohol is no longer providing any relief and I end up a little terrified. How on earth is this all going to end? I sneak into a bedroom and find a duvet that I wrap around me – as armour in case someone wants to keep groping me while I'm asleep. Then I open a large wardrobe and lie down on top of the shoes. Finally, I manage to close the door from inside.

When I wake up it's morning and I sneak back into the kitchen, which has been cleaned since I was last there. The rest of the group are slowly stirring and it transpires they're a really sweet gang. They ask where I've been and whether I'm having a shit time. 'Definitely not,' I reply. 'But thanks for asking.' I'm not uncomfortable any more and feel good about having experienced something that few people my age ever get close to. In fact, it's awesome.

Back in my room, I Skype with my parents and Jannick. We do this almost every day, even if it stutters and the live video keeps freezing on the PC. As usual, Jannick says it's too quiet and boring without me in the house. My mum says she misses me and to begin with the feeling is mutual, because I feel lonely and isolated. I've still not made any friends on the U18 team where everyone is fighting for their place, but it'll come. Or perhaps it won't. Maybe I need to get used to Arsenal being a career, while KB was a social thing?

But today I'm laughing so much I can't stop. My whole family is. The story about my encounter with London's gay scene is so crazy, especially the bit about the wardrobe, that it becomes a recurring anecdote. Whenever my family gets together, it still gets brought up.

CLEM CATTINI is a lovely man and a huge Arsenal fan. A real Gooner. And he's a retired rock and roll drummer. He's made hundreds of recordings and almost 50 of them have reached number one in the UK charts. He's made music with Paul McCartney, Tom Jones and Nirvana. It's completely crazy to think about.

After we've finished dinner and Anna is clearing up, he and I end up on the sofa upstairs. We start talking about what to watch if there isn't a match on. Clem prefers English shows – especially *Midsomer Murders* – but as soon as he nods off I switch over to something else. And as soon as he demands the remote back, I vanish into my bedroom.

I can't keep living like this. There must be something more out there, and I begin going down to the shopping centre to pass the time. There's a cinema and a burger bar. Sometimes I hang out with Fabrice Muamba and Johan Djourou from the academy, sometimes I'm on my own. I spend a lot of time talking to girls, and one night I invite one of them home.

The next morning, Clem is not happy. We've kept him and Anna up, he says. I'm also reminded that they were both raised Catholic. My conduct is completely unacceptable.

'You're banned from ever having your girlfriend to visit again!'

The girl isn't my girlfriend – just a kind of fuck buddy – but I don't manage to say that before Clem slams the door shut.

Instead, I take my scores to the Holiday Inn right by the shopping centre. But when you're staying in a hotel once a week, apprentice wages quickly run out. In hindsight, that's a good thing because it means I barely drink over the course of my first couple of years in London. Or, well…Obviously I do occasionally, but only when others are buying. I'm also too young to get served in the pub.

IN NOVEMBER 2004 my problems loom large. Literally. Over the past couple of years, my body has shot into the sky and I'm no longer one of the smallest players. On the contrary, I'm over 6ft 2in and still growing steadily. My back is protesting because it just can't keep up. There's some issue with my lower vertebrae, which means lots of rest.

I begin to score some goals for the U18s, which means more football agents begin putting in offers to represent me. One of them comes to visit at Blenheim Close, and when he sees my rather tragic bed he insists on buying me one that is longer and wider.

Back home, my dad reminds me that we shouldn't sign up with the first person who comes along – but hey, if the man wants to give me a 6ft 8in bed, then he can get me a 6ft 8in bed…It's only a few years later that I understand what the English mean when they say there's no such thing as a free lunch. Everything comes at a price. It's true for football.

Steve Bould, our U18 coach, says I'm extremely talented. Other times, he gives me a proper telling off. In the early months, it was particularly bad and I had to learn a few things the hard way – for example, never stay lying down when you're tackled. Not even when it actually hurts.

'Get up, stop whining!' he would shout.

Playing with someone who is pretty much my own age doesn't feel like progress, and I would prefer to be taking the step up to the Arsenal reserves. They play better football, people know their roles, the passing is accurate and the finishing more refined.

Occasionally, I get selected and brought on as a sub for the reserves, but for the time being they are more invested in Arturo Lupoli. He's a small Italian with a strong dribble. There's also the Dutchman Quincy Owusu-Abeyie, who was said to be in great shape at the time. They're both a year or two older than me, so I kind of feel like I'm probably going to make it after that.

One day I'm called into Liam Brady's office. It doesn't occur to me that something bad might be afoot. Why would there be when Arsène Wenger has praised me several times during first-team training. I'm wrong.

'Sonny boy,' says Brady. 'I don't think you understand what's at stake here. How many lads would give their right arm to have the chance you have right now. The chance to be in your shoes. I just don't think you're ready.'

I get a long speech. About how I was a big fish in a small pond back in Denmark. How I think football is something I'm automatically the best at. How I shouldn't be thinking about big cars, flash watches and supermodel girlfriends. How you have to earn that kind of thing. And that can only happen through hard work on the training pitch.

His gaze doesn't shy away as he speaks to me. Not an inch. And I try to stare right back. Show him I'm strong. But I also notice there's water welling into my eyes.

My mouth opens and I can hear my voice. It admits he's right. Although I've by no means fallen by the wayside, I've still got the potential to be outstanding.

'I know you saw a different player when I played for Denmark. But don't cut me. It'll come,' I say.

Brady studies me with this calm, piercing gaze.

'I'm not so sure, Nicklas. And it's no good being uncertain. Not at this level. You're going back to Copenhagen,' he says.

'No, I'm not,' I say and I begin to cry.

It's the first time I've ever cried in front of anyone other than my parents. Suddenly I notice how much I want this. Arsenal is my dream and I'm smashing the only plan I've ever had for myself into pieces.

'I promise you I'll change my attitude. You'll see the real Nicklas Bendtner. I promise.'

That's the kind of thing he wants to hear and we end up making a compromise. I'm to go home to Otto Liebes Allé and rest my back for a week. And I'm to have a long, hard think about whether I'm willing to make the necessary sacrifice. Not just in matches but in training too.

When I return to London, my mum comes along like some sort of cheerleader. Clem and Anna find it strange that she would prefer to sleep on a mattress next to me rather than stay in their charming little guest room, but that's just how it's always been in our family. I notice it lifts my mood to have her around. The same thing happens when my dad and brother come to visit. It gives me an energy boost and I give more on the pitch. It matters to me that there's someone on the sidelines who wants the best for me.

We're scheduled to play Aston Villa in the U18 league. The club is renowned for its youth section, but we beat them 4-0. I score three goals and provide a single assist. Afterwards, Brady comes over and greets my mum.

'*There* was the player I simply had to have six months ago. Finally!' he says, laughing. 'Just tell me, Mum, why it's taken him so long?'

She simply shrugs her shoulders and agrees with him. Because Brady is right. I've finally understood the seriousness of the situation. No club at this level has the time to have some clown running around taking up space. If I don't want it enough, it can all stop tomorrow. I hope it's sunk in. It should have.

I'M SENT off to Copenhagen for two weeks over the Christmas holidays. With me I take a letter addressed to my parents. It says

I'm making progress with my English, but it would still be a good idea for me to do homework daily.

I find it hard to motivate myself. My priorities are a little different. For example, there's loads of friends to be seen after four months in London.

Silas is throwing a New Year's party at his dad's mansion, where all sorts of mad stuff happens over the course of the evening. There's a lot of us drinking and getting hammered on strong liquor, and at one point Silas takes me to one side. He takes a CD case out of a cupboard with some white powder on it.

'Want to snort it together?' he suggests.

'What the hell are you up to?' I reply, my voice taking on a completely different, squeaking sound. Silas admits it isn't cocaine but only crushed caffeine pills. That it's all just to play it cool.

That kind of thing probably impresses any other 16-year-old, and I still think that's what Silas likes me for. That somehow, even if I can be totally crazy as well, I see through his bullshit and keep him down to earth.

Much later that night I know better. It turns out Silas likes me for several different reasons. Ever since we got to know each other, we've slept side by side in the same bed. It's never been a problem, and Silas has seen me with several girls already. He knows full well I shoot straight. Even so, I wake up to find him wanking off over me.

I react like any heterosexual teenager would. Not by hitting him or anything – but I shout like crazy. And maybe I'm a bit harsh, because he must be really, really confused by the whole situation. I just don't know how else to react. I rush to put my coat on and hurry home to Amager.

After that night we never see each other again. We don't speak, we don't write. But now Silas is living the jetset life and he's more or less in the closet. His life is full of lies and false people, and I've been there. Nowadays, it matters less to me than I'm sure people would think. I prefer to be true to who I am. True to the people I grew up with. And to dare to say it aloud. I've never been able to blindly fit in. All sorts of people want me to be something other than who I feel I am deep down.

IN MAY 2005, I can take stock of my first year in an Arsenal shirt. Since Brady threatened to terminate my contract, it's been non-stop progress. I've scored 12 goals in 18 matches for the U18s, while I've netted five times in 14 for the reserves – but of those just four games have been starts.

Of course, the most important thing is that the boss – Arsène Wenger – has more confidence in me. For the first couple of months, it seemed like an extremely slim chance, but gradually I join the first team for training on a weekly basis. The boss thinks I have a good eye for the game, and he thinks my first appearance as a substitute is on the horizon.

Maybe I'll make my debut in the Carling Cup. But first I need to have got used to the tempo. Although I'm constantly trying to facilitate – to run around like mad and pass the ball to someone who can do something better with it – everything goes insanely fast. Unless I'm concentrating fully on my control, someone manages to steal the ball from me. It's relentless. But if it has to happen then it's pretty cool to get skinned by some living legends.

Off the pitch, most of the club's stars – people like Kolo Touré, Sol Campbell and Patrick Vieira – treat me really well. Better than even the players my own age treat me. That's usually the case. The players who have made it are generally more willing to open their arms and welcome new people in.

Sometimes I forget that I'm only on trial with the big guns. During one training session, we play a match with some rather unusual rules. It's 11 on 11, but each player can only make a maximum of two touches at a time. I'm in a position to see Henry touch it three times.

'Three touches,' I shout.

Pat Rice, Wenger's red-faced assistant coach, shouts at us to carry on.

'Play on, for fuck's sake!'

But Henry has heard me. He turns in my direction with his index finger pressed to his lips. 'Sssssssh.'

Not long after, I do the same thing. First, the ball hits my heel, then my toe, then I make a pass. Even though it's all in the same movement, it's not a clean touch and a free kick is awarded against the academy pupil. Of course, I've got no problem with that. Not. I don't think. I just complain – big time. I snap that there should be equal treatment for everyone.

Henry tells me to shut it, but this time with a whole load of profanities. Looking back now, it's all pretty good advice. But I don't take it. I shout back that it's him who should shut it.

Then he strides over to me – right up in my face – and tells me to piss off. Completely indifferent to the fact that the game is still going on around us. Ashley Cole and Sol Campbell get involved:

'Move along, Nicklas, go, go, run along and shut your fucking mouth!'

So I do. I become unusually quiet. When one of the world's best strikers is stood there shouting at you, you react automatically.

But it doesn't end there. After training, Henry comes over and grabs hold of me. We end up talking – first in the dressing room and then in the players' lounge. I didn't know he had so many words in him – but he does. He delivers a two-hour monologue. About everything it takes to get to where you want to be.

I take it as a pat on the back. An honour. It's really decent of him, and definitely not something he has to do. In mid-flow, he mentions he's heard about me.

'They say you're a huge talent but you still need to learn a few things. Like respect and humility. Remember that, Nicklas. Respect and humility. When you're playing with the big boys, they're the ones in charge. All you should do is listen.'

I listen for all I'm worth and it ends with us hugging.

Naturally, I assume that's that. But it isn't. The next month I don't train with the first team. Not once. Maybe it's Henry's doing – he holds a lot of sway at the club. But maybe Wenger thinks I need to be put in my place too. Wenger is so discreet that you don't always notice him. But he's almost always there. He's hands on with everything, so of course he's also taken notice of our little disagreement.

Six months later, I'm about to kick up another to-do. This time it's Gilberto Silva I come to blows with. The Brazilian shouts at me to pull my finger out. Silva is probably the nicest man in the world, but in the heat of battle I forget that. Instinctively, I think to myself that he needs a taste of his own medicine, that he should just shut his face, but fortunately I manage to stop myself. I can still hear myself:

'Shut the fu— Yes, yes, Gilberto!'

THE RESERVES

2005–2006

WHEN I'M 17, I make my debut for the first team. It's 25 October 2005 and I get 90 seconds plus stoppage time against Sunderland in the third round of the Carling Cup. It's all over before I know it, so I don't count it as a big thing.

But without a doubt, the late appearance as a substitute should be seen as recognition of me and my fabulous start to the season. With nine goals in nine games for the reserves, and seven in five for the U18s, it's getting harder not to notice me. Steve Bould and Neil Banfield also say that 'people higher up in the system' are keeping a close eye on me. People higher up in the system…That could only be the boss himself.

My next first-team appearance is also my debut at our magnificent home ground, Highbury. It's almost sold out and I can hear the sound of 36,000 spectators. Arsenal's fortress since 1913 is packed with history, and when you set foot on the perfectly manicured pitch it feels as if the crowd might tumble down onto the grass at any moment. The stands are so close to the pitch that you can hear what's being shouted at you, and it's not always especially charming – but then again: I've already heard almost all of it in Danish.

I'm grateful for the small opportunities – but I don't think my fortune is made. As a member of the reserves, getting a few dying minutes in the Carling Cup is nothing out of the ordinary. Nor as a teenager. That's just the club's philosophy being followed to a tee, and even though I am making progress and overtaking the people around me, I'm still behind Arturo Lupoli in the reserves' internal pecking order.

I won't go around calling myself a first-team player until I actually am one. I need to be making starts and playing in the Premier League and the Champions League before I'm a genuine first-team player. And to feel like one. My goal isn't to be on the fringes – my goal is to beat Henry, Bergkamp and van Persie.

The football agents smell blood even more. They all want to 'represent my interests' as they put it. Basically, make sure I don't get cheated. Give me the optimum conditions for growth.

Some of them are completely desperate. As if they're head over heels in love or something. Not that I would know what that's like.

I ask them to call my dad and make an appointment, and before long they come to pick me up from Anna and Clem's in Winchmore Hill or at Bell Lane after training. You've got to give it to them – they make the effort. The guy who bought a bed for me is still pretty eager – and the same goes for Henry's agent.

In training, Henry and I are often paired up by Wenger, and we understand each other's running patterns. In terms of height and weight, we are more or less the same – but he is absolutely still a better player. Far better. I don't expect it to last for ever – but for now, he has some extra form.

'One day, you and me are going to play together at the top,' Henry says, and I nod and laugh, before saying: 'For sure, mate.' I'm picking it up. You have to say what the big lads want to hear you say…

The arrogance everyone always likes to talk about has disappeared from Henry. He's a nice guy, and his agent is probably phenomenally talented. But I'm leaning more and more towards a guy of Indian descent. David Manasseh. Ashley Cole puts in a good word for him, but that's not what makes the difference. It just feels right to work with someone who isn't always preaching about common sense and seriousness and my career in the long-term. The kind of thing I get plenty of at the academy.

Manasseh, who is said to have turned down a career in first-class cricket to sell football players, stands for something else. Even though there must be an age gap between us of at least 20 years, he's really friendly. Has an eye for a bit of skirt and he's a funny texter – that kind of thing. Always game for a laugh. I need those kinds of people in my life. Especially in London.

Although I've made a couple of friends on the reserve team – Fabrice Muamba and Johan Djourou, who both have African roots – it's nothing compared to my time at KB. People aren't as warm-hearted here. They're mostly thinking about what might get in the way of their dreams. Instead of living their dreams. That's my big goal – even though it's still some way off.

Manasseh has expensive habits and it's a lovely change of scene when he picks me up in his huge Bentley and drives us to some of the best eateries in London. He knows all the spots I hear about in the first-team dressing room when – completely against the rules – I sneak in after training.

The more I listen to them, the more tempted I am. When I still lived in Amager, I didn't care about that kind of thing, but now it's beginning to mean something.

Our first chat takes place in the most expensive hotel in the nearby city of St Albans. And with the greatest of respect, the hotel restaurant has a few tricks up its sleeve that are somewhat beyond the pepper steaks served at the Pirate in Gran Canaria.

Manasseh says a lot of things that sound right. Things I of course don't mind hearing while I'm still fighting to make my breakthrough.

'You've got everything it takes,' he says. 'No one else in England has your potential.'

I like the guy and his flamboyant arm gestures. When we sign our first contract, he invites me to Nobu to celebrate the deal. The Nobu chain is the new hip spot. Japanese and French fusion cuisine, and late in the evening the restaurant transforms into a bar and nightclub.

'It's the place to be,' as Manasseh says.

I don't know if that's my agent's job. But if he's looking out for my best interests, then it doesn't seem all that smart to introduce me to hangout spots like Nobu, given that a few years later when I come into some money I'm there constantly. Or perhaps it's a smart move by Manasseh. Maybe he's showing me the good life so I can get hooked. Hooked to a big income. Hooked to him and his company. Its name is Stellar Group.

The number of first-team stars dropping down to the reserves is basically equal to the number of reserve-team players lining up in Carling Cup fixtures. During the course of the 2005–06 season, we get visits from Robin van Persie, Emmanuel Eboué, Sol Campbell, Ashley Cole and Abou Diaby in the FA Premier Reserve League South. They get tested in the reserves when they return after time out through injury, and they rarely strike an impressive figure. Now I understand why. No one wants to get injured again just from playing in a training match.

All the same, it suits me down to the ground because it means I'm the one that gets noticed. Now, I've overtaken everyone else in the academy and the new kids that arrived over the summer don't really scare me. Maybe except for Theo Walcott, who is a year my junior and already headed for the England team.

Eventually, I end up training permanently with the first team, and several of them seem to be stand-up guys. We borrow PlayStation games off each other, and sometimes Fredrik Ljungberg and Sol Campbell give me a lift home from training.

Campbell is two completely different people on and off the pitch. In training, he's mercilessly pushing into my back. Kolo Touré, Pascal Cygan and the rest of them in the backline all do the same. They start applying pressure the moment I try to control the ball with my first touch. I try to back up, but instead I get shoved forward hard. To begin with, I'm not strong enough or brave enough to stand my ground and keep the ball at my feet.

They toughen me up. I have to dare to turn my back on people who want to cause me harm. Arsenal's opponents will try to bully me. That's what I'm being prepared for.

The harsh treatment is necessary. I quite clearly lack the

physique to stand up to the biggest guys. And sometimes I still lack the respect I'm expected to give. Still. Like the day I'm a smart ass in training and almost immediately need to be carried off the pitch. I'm bleeding from two wounds where the studs have gone through, and it's hurting like mad.

I'm in no doubt about what it's about. It's payback. When you're 17 years old and earning £390 per month, you don't nutmeg your direct opponent. If you do, you get skinned.

THINGS ARE going so well for me on the reserves that I come to the attention of a fan channel. They've pulled together my best moves in a long TV package, and apart from my English, which gets ribbed during the interview, it's pretty blistering to watch. In most of the segment, I first dribble past a couple of direct opponents or I play a one-two with someone before I put the ball in the back of the net.

There's an ease to my running that takes most defenders by surprise. Perhaps they expect a lad of my height to be slower than I actually am.

After a couple of months it's clear I have to contend with Lupoli – the dribbling, utterly selfish Italian – for the position of top scorer. When we beat Portsmouth 5-3, I score a brace and it would have been perfect had my rival not snaffled a hat-trick on the same occasion. Two of his goals are a result of my hard work, and when Neil Banfield picks Lupoli as the penalty taker and subs me with 15 minutes to go, I boil over. I lob my drinks bottle at the wall behind the substitutes' bench.

Once the final whistle has gone, Banfield gives me a bollocking that can be heard across most of London. The spittle is spraying out of his mouth and I'm tempted to dry my face with the back of my hand. But that would only provoke him and I don't want to do that.

'That's not how you behave! Not towards the team, not towards yourself!' he shouts. 'Especially not when you're winning and you've had a massive game!'

In one way, he's right. But in another, he's not. After all, my frustrations haven't appeared out of thin air. They're the result of the mathematics that Gregers opened my eyes to back in sixth grade. The maths is simple: almost no striker goes all the way from the academy to the first team, and I'm not going to succeed if Lupoli is successful at the same time. There's only room for one of us, which is why he needs to be taken down a peg or two. I'm done handing over sweets when he never pays back.

Just like I tell the guy from the fan channel, I've not come to the academy to use it as a springboard to a career somewhere else. I'm only interested in Arsenal. That's where I want to make my breakthrough. I'm a Gunner, and when Dennis Bergkamp hangs up his boots, I want to take his place. It's probably not that simple, but that's what I'm after.

We also talk about being a target man. Or rather: I have to explain to him that I'm more than that. That my height – by now I'm 6ft 3½in – doesn't mean that I can only stand around up front and finish. That would also be completely idiotic. I can dribble, and I can see the clear spaces from further away than my colleagues in attack. I've always been able to, and it's clear as day in the TV package. How I often choose to pass over taking the shot myself. And how that often helps my teammates to score. At Arsenal, it's a virtue to be unselfish. In the academy, they drum it into our heads. 'That's the Arsenal way,' as they keep saying.

IN NOVEMBER 2005, I get a first sniff of the North London derby between Arsenal and Tottenham Hotspur. There are a lot of football clubs in the city, but there's no other rivalry like it.

Even though it's just the reserves playing, the air is full of contempt. Not so much on the pitch, but in bucketloads in the stands.

During the second half, I run up the pitch with the ball at my feet and two opponents on my back. The defenders are sloppy in their attempts to pull me down, and I steer the ball into the far corner – unruffled. It's well received by the Gooners who have turned up.

It's after the return leg against Spurs at Meadow Park – the home of the Arsenal Reserves – that I make my first acquaintance with the English police. A month earlier, in January 2006, I turned 18 and Arsenal have paid me a nice, juicy lump sum. I spend most of the money on buying a summer cottage in North Zealand with my parents, but I've also got enough for an Audi A4 S with tinted windows and to get a tattoo – something my parents have long forbidden. When my mum sees it's her, my dad's and Jannick's dates of birth written onto me in ink, tears fill her eyes. Then everything's okay after all.

I also pass my driving test. That's the easiest one of all. I need almost no driving lessons because my dad has taught me the basics. He did it in the leafy streets of Tårnby when I was 15 or 16.

After the reserve derby I drive myself home from Meadow Park. I'm absolutely famished and I decide to pull over by a fast-food joint. I'm still in my kit and I walk straight into a pack of Spurs fans, who immediately start yelling ugly things about me and my shirt. They must have been at the reserves match, because they recognize me pretty quickly. There's no body contact or anything like that, but they still seem threatening. Shouting, yelling, spitting on the pavement in front of me.

As soon as my chicken burgers are ready, I hurry back out to the car, crank up some Kanye West and set off without putting my seat belt on. I often forget to do that. I also forget to turn on my headlights.

I notice a car following me in the rearview mirror. It shadows me closely for the next three-four-then-five minutes. I've no idea how long it lasts for, but it's making me fucking nervous. It stays right behind me at a red light, and I can see that there are four men inside staring in my direction – I decide to flee.

I put the A4 in sport mode and floor it. My wheels spin, rubber screeches on the tarmac, and in the space of a few seconds my pursuers are dust. I keep speeding, even when the road splits in two and turns into Blenheim Close.

There's still nothing in the rearview mirror, and I'm all but certain I've shaken them off. I parallel park in peace and quiet outside Anna and Clem's at number 15. Just as I'm finishing, three police cars come tearing up the road. Sirens and flashing lights, completely out of the blue. They block me in and uniformed officers jump out. The loudest one shouts at me while pointing a gun at me.

'Turn off the engine, slide your keys out of the window, and put your hands on the wheel where I can see them!'

It feels like I'm in *The Fast and the Furious*, but obviously I do as I'm told. Including when the door flies open and the voice from before tells me to step out with my hands folded behind my head.

Only then do they find out I'm just some snot-nosed, confused kid with pimples and wearing an Arsenal tracksuit. I don't exactly look like a hardened criminal on the run from the cops. They hide their firearms, but it's already too late. I'm in shock, and I can't find any words.

'What the hell happened?' one of them asks. 'Why were you driving like a psychopath? Why didn't you turn on your lights?'

I explain I've just come straight from a match. I was scared I was being followed by hooligans and forgot all about my lights and seat belt. That I didn't know the police drove around in unmarked cars.

One of the other officers runs some checks on me. The station confirms my story. It's good enough. There is a young Dane who plays for Arsenal. And all of a sudden they've all heard of me. The talented striker.

It all ends happily and I avoid any further charges. I've been driving recklessly in a built-up area, but they don't fine me or anything. It's a lucky escape – no doubt about it. I mean…it would never have worked out like that in Denmark. Regardless of whether I played for KB or Tårnby Boldklub.

WITH ONE reserve game to go, I've scored 16 goals compared with Lupoli's 17. But I've taken four more matches to score them. Even though I've got lots of assists, several of them leaving the honours to Lupoli, it's not ideal. Manasseh says the same thing to me:

'You need to finish the season first on the list of top scorers,

Nicklas. It will make everything easier.'

So I go into the final match of the season having made a promise to myself. Something I've never really thought before: I will finish everything, no matter what.

We're playing against West Ham away. They're a long way down the table and we're in third. During the first half I serve up a right sitter for Sebastian Larsson – despite the agreement I made with myself. I've not mentioned him yet, but Seb is the academy's friendly neighbourhood Swede – really calm and totally different from me. However, I soon get my own chances and it ends up working out. I score twice and overtake Lupoli to the finish line.

I've just turned 18, and I'm top scorer in the Arsenal reserves. It looks good on paper, and the Danish media cover the success as if I were playing in the first team. The team that's just played in the Champions League final. As it happens, I was actually on the bench for one of the group games against the Swiss champions FC Thun, but I don't even have so much as a 90-second share of that place in the final.

So naturally I'm not going to Paris to play Barcelona at the Stade de France. I'm off to Brøndby Stadium to play for the Denmark U21s. The team's usual striker, Morten 'Duncan' Rasmussen, has picked up a minor injury, and I've been called up by Flemming Serritslev.

I'm not sure I would even have been on the radar had it not been for an interview I gave to a Danish newspaper. This journalist dude called and asked why I wasn't in the squad for the U21 European Championships that summer, and I gave an honest reply. I said I hadn't heard anything from the Danish Football Association (DBU), and that I was a little surprised. I said that Denmark must be the best U21 team in the world if there wasn't room for a player like me.

So when we beat West Ham and I score my two goals, Serritslev is in the stands. After that, there's probably no way round it. I'm selected for the friendly against Spain – an opponent that Denmark is supposed to find particularly challenging. That's how all the journalists brand it. I don't care. It doesn't concern me. The past is pure statistics, and what previous generations have struggled with can never become my problem.

The second youngest player in the squad is two years older than me and most of them are three, four or even five years my senior. The new Liverpool recruit, Daniel Agger, was born in 1984. And that's what my dad latches onto. He only measures me against the star.

As the clock is running down at Brøndby, Arsenal are in big trouble at the Stade de France. Barcelona have not only equalized but have gone ahead in the Champions League final. But that can't completely ruin my evening. Because in the first half, I wrong-foot my marker and catch the goalie out of position, and during the second half, Thomas Kahlenberg delivers a perfect ball to my head. We end up beating Spain 2-0, and it's quite simply me who scores the goals. A couple of pretty good ones.

The next day the press go wild. The others on the team seem satisfied too. In training so far, they've just been sizing me up, but now I get hugs and I get welcomed and stuff.

But I can still sense it. I'm to remember that it was them who qualified. It's not me who got us into the European Championships for the eight best youth teams. That coolness seems familiar. It reminds me of the atmosphere at the Arsenal academy. And I really don't like it.

DEBUTANT

2006

THE FRIENDLY against Spain is only just over when a journalist wants to ask me something. Do I see myself as a contender for the Danish starting eleven when the U21 European Championships get underway?

'If I don't start all three games, I'll be disappointed,' I reply. 'I'll only accept it if we're through after two games and I get told I'm being rested for the third against Ukraine.'

My statements don't do the atmosphere in the squad any good. The others perceive it as an insult to Duncan, and things are only going to get worse. In our first group game we draw 3-3 with Italy, but I struggle to find chances. My teammates consistently choose other passing prospects, and I don't manage anything by myself either.

Against the Netherlands it's the same story, and of course it plants the seed of an idea – that the others are somehow boycotting me. After 60 minutes, Flemming Serritslev takes me off. Duncan comes on – but he's unable to score either. The match ends in a 1-1 draw and the reporters throw themselves at me. They want to know what I make of it all.

I'm not at all pleased, and I don't choose my words well.

'Duncan just stands there,' is one of the things I manage to say.

Afterwards, I know full well this may cause problems for me. So I find Serritslev and confess.

'You'd be better off talking to Duncan's face. And we'll see how bad it looks in the papers tomorrow,' he says.

The journalists give it all they've got. To be perfectly honest, it looks totally shit in print. It's not much better on TV or radio. Everyone must have been standing by with their microphones and cameras when I gave that interview. The story is all over the place.

I suddenly wish I'd taken the media training at the academy seriously.

The worst thing is that I don't even look down on Duncan. In the box, he's a dangerous guy to have running around. Unorthodox, uncouth and with an outstanding nose for a goal.

After the morning training session, Serritslev seems stressed. It's no longer enough for me to apologize to Duncan. Now I need to apologize to the whole team. Daniel Agger and Leon Andreasen also get hold of me. Leon, who is good friends with Duncan, is unsurprisingly the most pissed off of the two.

'That's not how we do things on this team. We stand together and look out for each other. Understood?' he asks without really posing a question.

Then we're called together and I do as we agreed. I prostrate myself. And that surely ought to be that.

But it isn't. Several of the journalists continue stirring the pot and develop the story further to suggest that in actual fact I'm criticizing Serritslev.

In a way, they're right – because I don't really get it. Why sacrifice a guy with my qualities for a guy with Duncan's qualities when we still had 30 minutes to turn things around? There was no need for Duncan – not at that stage in the game. What there *was* a need for was a striker on point with the skills to decide the game by himself. What was needed was me.

Nevertheless, the story blows up out of all proportion. And it results in my parents and little brother feeling frozen out in the Danish camp. None of the other families deign to even look at them because I've said something unfortunate. They think I've gone too far.

We can still reach the semi-finals. If we beat Ukraine, it'll all be okay. But we don't. We completely collapse as a team, and it's pretty clear that my apology has not helped one bit. The others still see me as an arrogant wanker. And fair enough – I probably was one. Thinking back, I wish I had expressed myself more diplomatically. But I also think the DBU completely shirked its responsibilities. The people who were supposed to be looking after an inexperienced player like me – an 18-year-old lad, new to the group – were caught napping. I was thrown to the wolves – who were ravenously hungry because the rest of the team had already learned their lesson. Keep your mouth shut.

ON THURSDAY 3 August 2006, Arsène Wenger summons me to his office.

'There's still something missing,' he says. 'You need to up your tempo before you're ready for the starting eleven. I'm proposing we send you out on loan.'

As I leave, I'm dumbfounded. I hadn't seen that coming. But if that's what the boss wants, there's little else to be said. You don't contradict the Arsenal manager if you want a long life at Arsenal.

Shortly after, Manasseh calls. I smell a set-up, because he already has a few options lined up. Most of the Championship apparently want me, but he only recommends one club – Birmingham City. The club has money, is investing heavily on promotion, and the coach is apparently really great at looking after his players.

On Friday we dash up to sign the contract. I know that Fabrice Muamba, my good friend from the reserves, is also going to Birmingham, so that's a start at least. And when I see the numbers in the contract, there's no doubt about it. I accept on the spot. I take no time to think it over, I have no follow-up questions. They are offering me what is definitely an adult wage.

Afterwards, we're sent to train with our new teammates. In the dressing room there's a package waiting for me. It's from Nike, who've expedited a shipment of football boots to me. Bright blue, just like the jersey, and I like them. I also really like that the people at Nike are such quick thinkers. More than that, I like that they've thought about me at all.

On Saturday the league gets underway and I start on the bench. Just before the summer holidays, Birmingham were relegated and the requirement now is for no mistakes. We must finish in the promised land of the top two that get automatically promoted to the Premier League.

But before that, 46 games in the Championship await. In a busy week that means two matches per week. The first game is against Colchester United – an opponent that takes no prisoners. No one in the Championship does – it's 50 per cent rugby and 50 per cent football.

I come off the bench with the match at 1-1. There's 34 minutes left and we're under pressure. Shortly after we also get a red card. But then one of the midfielders sends the ball to me. He boots it over and I receive it with my chest, turn my back on my man-marker and put it in the far corner.

The next thing I remember is a huge eruption of noise. The crowd – all 25,000 spectators at St Andrew's – go completely barmy. My games in the Carling Cup for Arsenal are incomparable with this, and in that moment I feel at home at my loan club.

IT'S NOW Monday and I'm on a quick trip back to Winchmore Hill. To pack my final things and say farewell. Anna and Clem deal with the sudden parting of ways at arm's length.

'We've done it before,' as they say.

I just about have time for one last trip to the cinema with Fabrice and Johan Djourou. Johan is staying on at Arsenal to fight for his chance. It's not the first time that our trio sits there in the darkness, but it is the last. I never quite get used to that bit. How life as a footballer consists of break-ups and parting farewells. We're like glorified nomads, told we're special, but rarely in control of where we settle – we don't always stay where we love, and risk being sent somewhere we can't stand.

The movie has been running for only a couple of minutes when my mobile rings. I almost always forget to turn it off, and I check whether it's anything important. Maybe it's someone from

Birmingham. I don't recognize the number or the country code, and my curiosity gets the better of me.

'Hallo?' I say, a little annoyed.

'Hallo!' the voice at the other end practically shouts. 'It's Morten Olsen!'

'Sorry?' I say.

I am perfectly able to hear what the man is saying – I just want to be absolutely certain.

'It's Morten Olsen! I'm calling from Belgium!' he bellows. At the time, I am unaware that the Danish national coach is a little hard of hearing.

'Just give me a sec – I'm at the movies,' I whisper, hurrying into the foyer.

'I'm selecting a squad and I'd like you to be in it,' he says. 'We're playing Poland in six days' time. Yes. On 16 August.'

I'm not exactly hyperventilating. My legs don't shake or anything like that. But something happens in my body, and I'm forced to take a really deep breath. Perhaps, more than anything, I'm surprised. Morten Olsen hasn't been put off by the U21 fiasco.

He's hung up. But it was definitely him. I'm almost 100 per cent. This feels real – like a really big moment – so I call my parents.

'You'll think I'm lying, man, but I've been picked for the national team! The real national team,' I say ecstatically.

'Shut up!' my dad says. 'Shut the fuck up. That's so cool!' That's all he says. Quite a few times. 'Shut up, man! That's so cool!'

In the background I can hear my mum getting worked up. She gets so emotional when things get big. She can't quite handle it. Suddenly I remember Johan and Fabrice.

'I'm actually at the pictures,' I say. 'I'll call back later.'

I LAND at Kastrup Airport on Saturday afternoon. There's four days to go until the match against Poland, and I feel like I'm flying.

Since the end of the summer holidays, the successes have been lining up. Picked for my country, put up at a classy hotel with ten times as much space as I had at Clem and Anna's, a proper grown-up wage…It's crazy to think about. Two years ago, I was going up the escalators to airport security, while Mum and Dad waved goodbye. I would love to see Niels-Christian Holmstrøm's face now. Maybe he regrets not letting me train on a permanent basis with the FC Copenhagen first team. I expect he probably does.

Anyway. On Wednesday, we are scheduled to play Poland at Odense Stadium, and the squad are due to gather early tomorrow morning at the Hotel Marina in the town of Vedbæk. But before that, I've got something else I need to do. A friend from my year at Korsvejens School is turning 18 and she's invited me to her party. It turns into something of a celebration for me. Everyone is completely electric. I left as the black sheep and here I am returning as a member of the Denmark squad. A budding superstar.

I try to control myself and I drink less than the other 30 to 40 partygoers. That goes really well – at least for a couple of hours – but then some guy passes me an unopened bottle of Fisherman liqueur.

'Chug, chug, chug!' they shout.

I take a pretty big chug. The next time I remove the bottle from my lips, it's empty. I feel invincible. As if nothing can go wrong for me – so why not? Not long afterwards I'm rather worse for wear, and after that I don't remember a thing. Everything from here on is stuff I've been told: that I pass out and get lifted into a wheelbarrow. That some of the boys push me home to Otto Liebes Allé where my 14-year-old brother opens the door. That my parents aren't home. That I'm carried to the upstairs bathroom and abandoned with Jannick. That I'm so far gone that I both shit my pants and piss all over the floor. That the black, sweet and sickly fluid takes days to get rid of. That I somehow manage to lock the bathroom door so that Jannick can't get in to me. That he tries to kick the door down.

That he eventually calls our uncle who's married to my mum's sister. He's a firefighter and he comes over and assesses whether I need my stomach pumping. If it gets that far, I'll have some serious explaining to do. Fortunately, it turns out the worst has passed. I just need to sleep it off.

I THINK it must have been my mum or dad who drove me to the Hotel Marina – but I can't remember. I'm still completely out of it, and I don't remember a single thing about my first day training with the real national squad. Apparently I got off scot-free without being found out. Something else I'll come to develop a talent for.

By Monday, my head has cleared. And that's when I get a feel for a special coach. In order to understand Morten Olsen, you also have to understand his career. While most players reach their peak from when they're 26 until perhaps 30 or 31, Morten Olsen just kept raising the bar. He was still world-class when he hung up his boots at the age of 40. That was in 1989, and after Franz Beckenbauer's retirement he was considered the best sweeper in the world. He was confident with the ball in a way few defenders ever are, he could pull off offside just by wrinkling his nose, and when it made sense he ran with the ball from box to box without anyone being able to take it off him. Naturally, he was also a leader – and with the captain's armband he controlled his teams: Anderlecht in Belgium, Cologne in Germany and the Danish national team. No one even dreamed of challenging his leadership.

Even during his playing career, Morten Olsen thought about football around the clock, and it's helped to make him extremely successful as a football coach. First with Brøndby, who in 1991 were just a minute away from making the final of the UEFA Cup. A frankly unimaginable performance by a Danish team. Then he continued his coaching career with Cologne and Ajax. But just like at Brøndby, he worked his players hard so they helped to get him sacked. That's what they said. That he was such a perfectionist that players couldn't stand the pace. The passion disappeared, even if the results were there.

That's exactly why Morten Olsen and the position of national coach were an almost ideal combination. When he was appointed in 2000, he could suddenly take joy in shouting, instructing and honing his squad over the course of seven or eight gatherings a year.

Instead of being trained to breaking point, they were so inspired that they delivered beyond their means.

Denmark qualified for the World Cup in 2002 and the Euros in 2004 with a team that had to learn to live without the Laudrup brothers and Peter Schmeichel. A team without stars. But also a team where everyone knew their place and their opponents down to the finest detail.

By the qualifiers for the 2006 World Cup, the era of miracles had passed. Despite the easiest group in living memory, we were cheated by Ukraine and the clinical finisher Shevchenko.

That's where – in the wake of a fiasco – my own Denmark career begins. Next up are the European Championships and the first stop on that path is a friendly against Poland. Well, 'friendly' is putting it mildly – I don't think there's any such thing as a friendly match. Not in Morten Olsen's world at any rate. There are test games. And the one against Poland is to be used as preparation for Northern Ireland, Sweden and Spain – the three major competitors in our group.

The Monday training session with the national squad is probably the toughest training session I've done to that point. Although we have just returned from the summer break and there is nothing major at stake, everyone is under constant pressure. The level of discipline is completely different to that in England. As soon as a player makes a mistake on the pitch it's noticed, and I must be on the receiving end of something like ten reprimands on the first day alone. But it goes without saying that no one gets special treatment – whether positive or negative – and if you do as you're told then that's also noticed.

During training, the country's top scorer Jon Dahl Tomasson picks up a minor injury. And with Morten Skoubo and Søren Larsen not even in the squad, I can see where things are going. It looks like a place in the starting eleven. If that's how things end up, I'll become the second youngest debutant for the senior Denmark team ever, behind only Michael Laudrup. That's what the papers are saying.

It's my first visit to Odense Stadium. The crowd from the island of Funen know how to keep singing throughout. I feel a shiver go down my spine when I hear the national anthem roaring from the stands. On either side of me I can hear my teammates humming along. I probably chew extra hard on my gum because I don't know the words, and to be completely honest I've never tried to sing along to the tune. Why, I don't know. But it's just not me. I've not tried since I caught myself screeching it in the shower once upon a time long ago.

FOR A WHILE it's a fraught affair. The Poles are playing good football and they really should be one up. But their guys up front still seem to be on their summer holidays. Completely unrefined in front of goal.

After half an hour, I gain control of the ball with my chest. I'm a few yards outside the box and pass it to Martin Jørgensen, who finds Dennis Rommedahl who immediately sends Thomas Gravesen down the right flank. He runs towards the goal line, and blasts a firework of a cross into the box catching the Poles napping. I've seen it coming and get ahead of the goalkeeper, who parries my shot. The ball bounces back, hitting my stomach and flops over the line. It's an ugly goal, but the build-up is exemplary. Rommedahl throws himself onto me, and the others quickly catch up. I've scored on my debut – just like Michael Laudrup – and the old boys seem pleased for me.

Five minutes later I am seriously unmarked. Nevertheless, Martin Jørgensen opts to pass to Rommedahl who fires it into the side netting. I end up gesticulating. I would have been one-on-one with the keeper right in front of goal.

During the second half the Poles press on. And once again Gravesen does something almost bordering on genius. His pass to Rommedahl must be around 100 feet, and it shatters their defence. Rommedahl dribbles round Dudek, leaving just him and me. He puts it away himself.

When we get back to the dressing room, I catch up with Rommedahl.

'You should have played me on,' I say.

Discussing press-ups with Thomas Gravesen in Vedbæk, September 2006.

(Photo: Lars Møller/Ritzau Scanpix)

'Are you thick?' he says laughing. 'I'm not letting you steal all the limelight!'

I like him.

EVEN THOUGH there are several strikers to choose from, I'm also picked for the next two internationals. We're scheduled to play Portugal at Brøndby Stadium and then we're off to Iceland to play in a European Championship qualifier.

The first training session has barely got started before I end up in trouble. As part of the warm-up, we are playing one-touch football. The ball has to be kept in the air, and two players chase around while the rest stand in a circle around them. If you throw the ball away, you have to do five press-ups as your punishment. Then you go back into the middle and race around.

It's obviously an old custom that newbies do the press-ups – no matter who actually fucked up. So when Thomas Sørensen thumps the ball half a metre past me, Gravesen orders me to the ground.

'Bendtner! Press-ups!'

'I'm not having that one.'

'What makes you think you're above the rules here? Down and give me five.'

'It wasn't my fault.'

It's probably only a couple of seconds. Then Gravesen is right up in my face and threatens me with a walloping.

'You're the youngest – so do what you're told!'

Suddenly it's become a matter of principle. In a way, Gravesen is acknowledging that it wasn't my fault, but I still need to be punished. Because I'm only 18.

I don't like that kind of thing. It's not a level playing field. I don't want to end up like Jesper Grønkjær, the nice man who always gets scolded. We all remember the photos from the 2002 World Cup when Gravesen and Stig Tøfting poured water down his trousers in front of the Danish press pack?

'I don't give a fuck – it wasn't my fault, so I'm not doing them,' I repeat.

It all ends with Thomas Sørensen doing his press-ups and the atmosphere is pretty uneasy when Morten Olsen shows up and starts whistling.

I've seen the same thing a thousand times over the years. It's about hierarchy. The others need to put the newbie in his place. Humble him. It happens all the time in professional football.

In the evening, I'm a bit worried I may end up being frozen out again like I was at the U21 Euros. But if that's what's going to happen then it's not of Gravesen's doing. That much is certain. He doesn't hold a grudge. Quite the opposite. It seems like he actually kind of likes it when someone does something unpredictable. He jokes around with me, unscrews the cap on the salt shaker – so that my pasta is completely inedible – and gives me a dead leg. But I'm never in any doubt: it's his way of welcoming me. It's meant with affection.

I'm also invited to join the card school. Or the Mousel Team, as they call themselves. Mousel is a pretty simple game in which each player is dealt four cards and a trump is chosen. The aim is to take as many tricks as possible.

They always play for cash, and the bets can easily reach £450. If there's six participants, we end up playing for almost £3,000 at a time. Apparently Morten Olsen is unaware of all this. I'm game and think it's a smart way to make some new friends.

Around the table are all the adrenaline junkies on the Denmark team. The gamblers. Peter Løvenkrands, Jon Dahl, Daniel Jensen, Søren Larsen, Stephan Andersen, Jesper Grønkjær and Thomas Kahlenberg.

Rommedahl is just hanging out and fetches coffee and cake for anyone who wants it. He keeps us in high spirits and seems like a really nice guy.

I ask him if he's going to join in. He declines and the others laugh conspiratorially. Later on I find out why. On one international outing, Romme ended up losing big time. From then on he put himself in the sin bin.

FOR THE GAME against Portugal, Jon Dahl is fit again. This means I'm back on the bench. From there, I watch him and Kahlenberg score for Denmark. Carvalho equalizes our lead twice. The Portuguese reached the semi-finals at the World Cup and are fourth in the world rankings – so we are up against a class act. Still, we're the better team on the pitch. Thomas Sørensen saves a weak penalty kick from Cristiano Ronaldo, and I come on for Jon Dahl with 20 minutes to go. Martin Jørgensen scores after an attack in which we play through the Portuguese defence. It's weird to be part of it. Our opponents are stronger in every position – on paper in any case – but we are better as a unit. Better in purely tactical terms. Morten Olsen is far more spectacular than most people, including me, realize.

In stoppage time, I get the ball on the halfway line. I pass to Daniel Jensen, lose my marker and step on the gas. My ability to pull away seems to surprise him and when I get the ball back he can't catch up with me. The finish goes hard between Ricardo's legs. It's a seriously cool goal.

I'm not called upon in Reykjavik, but for the third match in a row Gravesen delivers a phenomenal assist. Although he no longer plays for Real Madrid – my favourite club outside England or Denmark – he's still a magnificent footballer. He's clearly the best we have to offer. Unfortunately, that assist becomes the last thing Gravesen does for Denmark. A week later, he's had enough.

Graver had grown tired of everything required of him simply because he was more offbeat and outspoken than the rest of the team put together. It was hard work being an entertainer off the pitch and the focal point on it.

At the time I didn't understand it at all. Now I do.

JOINING THE GROWN-UPS

2006–2007

AFTER SPENDING a week at a hotel in Birmingham, an apartment's available. It's Jermaine Pennant's old one. The winger who was also at the Arsenal academy. He was on the fringes of the first team when I arrived at Bell Lane two years ago, and since then he's received attention for the wrong reasons.

In 2005, he was convicted of drink driving and during his release on probation he played a Premier League match for Birmingham while wearing an electronic tag. Steve Bruce's idea was to back up his player no matter what.

Now Pennant has become some kind of footballing nomad. He's just been sold to Liverpool – his fifth club in five years.

The penthouse is part of the deal that Manasseh has cut for me. Including the outdoor space, it covers well north of 3,000 square feet on the 17th floor at Centenary Plaza. The place is exactly as it was left. The living rooms are furnished with white leather sofas, I've got a fully stocked bar and there's a jacuzzi too – naturally. Hanging on one wall is the latest, most space-age Bang & Olufsen sound system that money can buy.

The building is one of the tallest in the city centre and I can see the stadium of our arch-rivals Aston Villa from my terrace. In the bedroom there's a gigantic, circular bed, although if I would prefer to sleep in something with four corners then all I have to do is use one of the other bedrooms – there's a total of three, all en suite.

If you are still harbouring any uncertainty, without a doubt this is a full-on playboy mansion. If Bruce Wayne had slightly gaudier taste, he would do his place up like this. In the dressing room the apartment gets described as 'the shag pad'.

In many ways I'm starting from scratch. Completely from scratch. I've never tried cleaning or cooking, and I won't for as long as I live here. On one corner there is a sushi restaurant, and on the other a decent Italian. I make a deal with them. I can turn up and order food at any time, including when the kitchen is officially closed.

The club sets me up with a cleaning company. Three ladies come in shifts and keep things in order. They wash my cars and cook food for me when I choose to eat at home.

I've supplemented my Audi A4 S with a Range Rover Sport, but strip clubs like Legs 11 and Spearmint Rhino are what seriously loosen my purse strings. It's the done thing when playing in Birmingham.

I think we're behaving like they used to at every English club. At least until the end of the 1990s when managers like Arsène Wenger arrived and changed the culture where booze and football used to go hand-in-hand. It wasn't just the fans who went to the pub. The players did too.

For us players, the strip clubs are a brilliant concept. They're open every evening, whereas nightclubs are only open at weekends. That's why a lot of us blow off steam there when we have time off in the week, a group of us from the squad. We sit there and watch girls taking off their clothes, and then if that gets too tedious we order lap dances for £20 a go. It might not sound like much, but over the course of a long evening it all adds up. Often, the girls want to come home with you and get it on. But they don't get paid for that. In Birmingham, there's status to be had in fooling around with the city's footballers.

TAKING INTO ACCOUNT various bonuses – starting eleven, scoring, securing three points – my wages are £35,000 a month. After tax. That kind of money quickly grows wings and disappears without a trace.

Of course, my parents have no idea how much I'm burning through or what exactly my wage is, but they sense that things have got a little out of control. One day they discuss with Manasseh whether I should put a little bit aside. They come away feeling that if my career carries on like this, I'll earn so much money I simply won't be able to spend it all.

And to be perfectly honest, things are going so well that they have nothing to worry about. As September turns to October, I've established myself as the top scorer on the team and I'm a permanent starting fixture up front.

Unfortunately, nothing goes right for me when we play Derby County in October. Nor for Arturo Lupoli. He has also been loaned out by Arsenal, and he is scoring even more at Derby than I am at Birmingham. He remains a talented striker, but his sort finds the defensive rocks in the Championship difficult to deal with.

It's a league that hardens you. I've played five matches in two weeks and am sore all over. Every day I find new bruises. On my feet, arms, legs and back.

Some of my goals are obviously better than others. But what particularly pleases me and the coaching staff is the physique they're being handed. I can stay on my feet no matter how hard they hit me.

I begin to appreciate the rough and tumble existence at Bell Lane and beam thoughts of gratitude back to Arsenal's tough customers. They've taught me to take a knee and a fist in the balls without immediately throwing myself to the ground. You don't pull those kinds of stunts in the Championship if you want to survive. Manchester United's Portuguese player would get slaughtered for his diving down here.

ALL OF A SUDDEN, I am reaching the ball higher up than my man-marker in response to crosses on the pitch. My timing has improved. The same applies to my first touch. Like when Sebastian Larsson finds me with a pass halfway down the pitch. The ball slams down onto my boot and with a targeted cat's paw I edge around Plymouth's goalkeeper and score goal number ten of the autumn. Number 12 if you include goals for Denmark.

Only once do I end up with my own team against me. I try to take a penalty kick that Gary McSheffrey has earned as a result of my through ball. The others are not happy with me.

Still, it feels as if I have slid up to the top of pecking order. I think my goals demand respect, but it's just as important that I've become part of the group. It's been easy enough because we all more or less share the same interests. Football, clothes, women and nightlife. It's not that we go out with the intention of getting hammered, but alcohol is automatically part of the mix. In a way, it's like being back at KB. I'm just three or four years older and earning my own wages. Plenty.

Not everyone lands quite so steadily on their feet. I only see Sebastian Larsson and Fabrice Muamba at Wast Hills, the club's shabby training centre. The other two Arsenal loanees are not as jovial as me, which makes it harder for them to take part in all the social stuff.

I don't think I've ever seen Fabrice drink. And that just doesn't cut it in that setting. You need to be game for anything here, and lots of the guys are. If a teammate needs a little private time with a woman other than his wife or girlfriend, then it's quite common to ask the youngest man on the team for a couple of hours shelter. Then they're ringing the bell as if I'm running some sort of whorehouse.

Wherever I've lived, my apartments and houses have always been open for business. Guys have asked, and I haven't been able to find a way to say no. Because I understand completely. As a footballer, it's nice to go under the radar.

That didn't stop until I got to Rosenborg. In Norway, we could hardly break wind before someone started talking about it.

At some point I begin to miss my friends from Amager. I suggest they buy plane tickets at my expense to come over, and there are several of them who are up for it. And suddenly my shag pad is transformed into party central. I invite everyone who likes to party, while spoilsports have to stay in Copenhagen. I need to burn off some energy, I need to have fun, I need to share some of all the good things that have come my way. I don't need finger pointing.

If we only have a match on a Saturday, then we're off until Wednesday. That means I can hit the town on Saturday, Sunday, Monday and Tuesday. Four days in a row isn't unusual, and to be completely honest it takes over. I can see that clearly today.

During the Danish autumn holiday, my family are coming to stay – but I've forgotten all about it. When they call me from the airport, I pretty much panic and dispatch a bunch of my friends who are staying over out of the front door. The apartment is overflowing with pizza boxes and empty bottles. The shit hits the fan – and it's completely impossible to hide it. My dad has a fit as soon as he steps through the door. What the hell am I thinking – what kind of welcome is this?

I don't want to hear it – so we end up arguing. After a while, he leaves in a rage and threatens to go straight back to Copenhagen. I can't deal with him and neither can my hangover. I'm in the sort of mood where nothing's my fault, and it ends up being my mum's job to pick up the pieces. She finds him down in a café somewhere, completely pissed off.

But then Dad does want to stay after all. He loves everything else about my new life, and he's easily persuaded.

Mum has since reminded me about that fight, and what she thinks it meant. How it was a kind of turning point between me and Dad. That I'm the master of my own house and can do as I please. That I get let off too easily from behaving unreasonably. That it was from then that things started to go wrong. On so many levels.

STEVE BRUCE has been the Birmingham manager since 2001. He spent the first season taking the club up to the Premier League, where the Blues finished higher than their local rivals Aston Villa for the first time since the 1970s. The next two years they fought to avoid relegation, and in their fourth season it was no longer avoidable.

Between 1987 and 1996, Bruce played more than 300 games as a central defender for Manchester United. A stocky commander who was a natural in the captain's armband. I guess he was the same kind of footballer as he is coach. Bruce swears by a direct, uncomplicated form of football. His repertoire isn't huge, and I hope I'm not offending him when I say his leadership skills are greater than his technical expertise.

We play a long and medium-long ball game, and when we're in trouble the ball gets hoofed up to me. Then I have to pull it down and get it set up for some friendly boots. When we score, it's rarely the result of rehearsed moves and set pieces. It's more a case of overpowering our opponents. All of a sudden, our four offensive players isolate their back line, but before we get that far, Damien Johnson and Stephen Clemence have turned the sun black in the midfield. And once we've moved up field, it's me and McSheffrey up front while Sebastian and the other winger come storming in.

There are a few other things Steve Bruce excels in. He has the rare skill of injecting fighting spirit and camaraderie into his squad. Everyone goes to war for everyone else – always.

I really like the man and his way of treating us. He senses what each individual player needs in order to perform at their very best. How some need space, while others can only handle a short leash and direct instructions about more or less anything. That kind of distinction between players is something Steve Bruce handles to perfection.

If you deliver, he rewards you with praise and trust. If you wobble, he seeks an explanation. If he hears something, he gets to the bottom of it. And believe me, our manager hears all sorts of things. He has ears all over the city.

Some time that autumn, he calls me up to his office. Once I'm inside, he slams the door with a boom. He's already in the red mist – strawberry-red in face. My thoughts gallop away –

I speculate like mad. What does he know? What am I going to be held accountable for?

'I've heard you were out on the town on Sunday, Monday, Tuesday and Thursday! What the hell are you playing at?'

I take a deep breath. Then I ask for permission to speak.

'I'm afraid that's not quite right, coach. I was also out on Wednesday.'

Bruce stiffens. First he needs to make sure I have said what I have just said. He opens his mouth, but no sound comes out. Perhaps he's having a heart attack. He begins to splutter and ends up with his head on his desk. Roaring with laughter.

I think one of my problems is I simply don't like lying. I do stupid stuff sometimes, but not to be cunning or to hurt anyone. That's why I'm also completely honest when I get the chance to be, although it's an entirely different matter with people I can't stand. But if you already have my respect, then I won't beat about the bush. And I accept it if you think my mistakes should have consequences. Arsène Wenger and Morten Olsen can already attest to that.

Steve Bruce has my respect. He would rather straighten me up than destroy me, and although many will probably think that he should have taught me a lesson that I wouldn't forget – that it would have been a good investment – I now know it wouldn't have worked. Not as intended, at any rate.

INSTEAD, I end up with a warning and over the next few months I dial back the partying. I no longer fire it up week after week. Now I fire it up every fortnight. That's down to someone rather close to our manager.

Like so many other things, it begins in the dressing room. People are banging on about Steve Bruce's daughter. They have been since day one. How she's not only damn hot, but she's also immune to footballers. The very fact alone that she is the apple of the manager's eye makes Amy Bruce incredibly attractive in the eyes of most of the team. One of the older players compares it with the forbidden fruit in the Bible story of Adam and Eve. But for me, it also brings to mind *Youngblood*, an ice-hockey movie from the 1980s in which the protagonist scores with the coach's daughter and has to learn how to fight to survive on the ice.

It sounds as if most of the squad have tried their luck but that no one has even come close. So one day I tell it like it is. That I'm not daunted by their failures. That I've been in need of a challenge like this. They all find it epically funny – all of them – and suddenly I've bet £1,000 with people like McSheffrey, Clemence and Johnson, who's our captain. It's going to be expensive if she's one of those people who can't stand me. And, let's face it, there's quite a few of them around.

A week later we're playing West Bromwich Albion at St Andrew's. Afterwards, there's a sponsor event in the lounge area. Someone points out Amy to me, and I hurry over to say hello. She's good looking and friendly in a slightly cool way. She's probably also a year or two older than me.

I mention I'm meeting up with my Danish pals for something to eat later in the evening. They've just landed and have come to watch the game.

'You're welcome to tag along,' I say.

'I'd like that,' she replies. 'Maybe I'll bring some friends.'

'Okay,' I say. 'So it's a date.'

It's a pretty short and discreet conversation, and none of my teammates have a clue. Quite the opposite. They think I've been rejected, and I'm happy to let them think that.

We meet at the Italian restaurant. The one just round the corner from Centenary Plaza. Drink has already been flowing. My friends are plastered, and after a couple of hours Amy says she's never seen anything like it.

'You Danes are completely crazy,' she says.

I look at them and see them yelling at each other. Jesus – she's right. Jesus, us Danes can really drink every other nationality under the table. I've never really thought about it, but we can. Even the English have a backstop of sorts because the pubs close before midnight on weekdays. We don't have to worry about that kind of thing. We have a shag pad just round the corner. With a full fridge and a view of the city. Closing time is for mortals.

When Amy and I part ways that evening, we kiss. We agree to meet again the next evening, and after that follows one date after another. I think we see each other every day for a whole week, and suddenly I've forgotten all about the bet. It's only when the lads demand their winnings that I reveal how great their defeat is.

Completely against the plan, I've only gone and fallen for Amy. Fallen harder than I've done for a girl before. And several things play their part. She's not only unusually attractive and sweet. Her other assets appeal to me too. Her friends are likeable – the kind of people you'd actually want to spend time with. And thanks to her dad and big brother – Alex, who is also a footballer – she knows what my job is. She understands when I need to concentrate on playing a match or if I need to get to training on time.

Perhaps it also appeals to me that I can live two lives and have two separate lifestyles. When she's visiting, we're one of the football couples and there's a bit of calm. At the same time, I can be a single guy running at top gear when she's back in London at uni.

IT DOESN'T take many weeks for the old man to cotton on to the fact that his pride and joy has got herself involved with the club's young bad boy. But if that's a problem then he hides it well. When I visit the family's home a little outside Birmingham, I'm treated like an extra son by Steve and his wife Janet. They've been married for more than 20 years and are completely made for each other. They finish each other's sentences, put up with each other's eccentricities. Give each other space.

I eat, watch football with and chat a lot with Alex, who's a really great guy. After a few years on the bench at Birmingham, he's now playing in central defence for another club in the Championship.

I think to myself it must be a mixed blessing to be Steve Bruce's son. On the one hand, it must be great to have a dad you can discuss football with at such a high level. But it must also be hard to know you're so passionate about something that everyone knows that your dad was better at.

Perhaps I seek a sense of security with the Bruce family. I wouldn't go so far as to say that they're my new foster family, but it has a definite whiff of it. They offer a base that I benefit from. Everything happens at a more elegant pace with them. A pace it's impossible to slow down to when I'm on my own and invite everyone round to Centenary Plaza. To this day, I still don't have a bad word to say about them. Not a single one. They're decent people, and that decency isn't something I find elsewhere. So I try to look after it for as long as possible.

Between Christmas and New Year, my own family come to visit. This time I've managed to get the cleaning ladies to come over beforehand. My mood gets an extra lift from seeing my mum bustling about in the kitchen. She's cooking the traditional Danish festive feast of roast pork, red cabbage and Danish brown sauce.

We're playing matches every three days. On 23, 26 and 29 December – and then on 1 January. The day before Christmas Eve and the day after New Year's Eve, we're expected to be on the pitch giving it all we've got. I'm not crazy about it.

A photographer and reporter from the Danish newspaper *Politiken* also stop over. I've been named 'Find of the Year' in Denmark. Of course I'm happy, but it's not something that overjoys me. I would be happier if someone had named me Denmark's Best something or other. But Find of the Year? I don't feel like a find – I feel like I've already been around for a while.

My mum explains to me that it's across all sports and a pretty big deal. That Daniel Agger won the prize last year, but that otherwise it's been a long time between footballers. The Laudrup brothers didn't win it. It's not something Agger and I ever discuss with each other. But we've also not grown up with newspapers as a major or essential part of our lives.

In Birmingham, I've got other things on my mind. Results have begun to fail us and after a draw and two consecutive defeats, there's talk of Steve Bruce being in the danger zone. Managers must be growing on shitting trees in the Championship, because I've literally never heard anything so stupid. We're still high in the table, and no one on the team wants to get rid of him. But the danger is real enough, and as we're away at Colchester for our next match I get seriously nervous. With half an hour to go, we're behind and my girlfriend's dad looks like he's been turned to stone. For a few seconds, he simply sits and stares at his big, rough hands. Then he leaps into the air. Like a jack in the box. He runs to the touchline and gives us a bollocking.

The message manages to fizzle round, but nothing comes of it. Not until Stephen Clemence decides to take matters into his own hands. Our midfield warrior hoofs the ball from way too far out, and the goalkeeper is able to track it with his eyes. Right until it hits a leg on the way and arcs beautifully towards the far corner.

I celebrate as if the goal is my own, the opponent is Real Madrid and we have won the Champions League. It's one of two or three moments from my time at Birmingham I will never forget. That's how relieved I am. The thought of losing Amy's dad as my manager is strangely unbearable.

IT'S A MORNING I only faintly remember. Still, it has stuck with me. It's done so because it says something about the high jinks I get away with at Birmingham. Some of what takes place would have been completely unthinkable had I been under the wings of Liam Brady and Neil Banfield at Arsenal.

It's a Wednesday or Thursday and it's seven o'clock in the morning when a taxi drops me off at Wast Hills. I've come straight from my night out and reckon I might get an hour and a half's nap before the others get to the dressing room.

That's almost what happens. At eight o'clock, Clemence shakes me. He keeps doing so until I wake up and come to. I'm sitting in the huge bath and I'm still wearing some of my clothes. Clemence is one of the seasoned lads. He's been in the game for years and seen it all. So of course he knows what's up. I stink of booze and I guess I must have been a pitiful sight.

'Mate, you go home and I'll cover for you. I'll say you came in but you were sick,' Clemence says.

By the end of February 2007, things are no longer going as smoothly as they were for Birmingham's Danish wonder boy. I've been overtaken by McSheffrey as the club's top scorer, and it's not because he's been unstoppable. I've stalled. One glorious goal since the start of December is all I've managed, and the crowd that loved me on day one have begun to jeer when I finish in vain or miss the ball. For them, my assists don't count. They see the numbers in black and white: zero goals in the last 13 matches.

This is my first goal drought as a footballer, and I've no idea how to handle it. But something dawns on me as I'm lying awake in the evening unable to fall asleep. It's not a happy realization, so I try to come up with some other explanations, but I just can't. It must be my lifestyle – everything I'm doing off the training pitch has caught up with me. Even though my body recovers at record speed – the doctors describe my physique as unique – and two hours of sleep can deal with the worst of the booze, I've not improved since Christmas. I've been used to developing month-on-month, year-after-year, but suddenly it's going the wrong way. I've got a bit worse. Less sharp and a couple of notches slower over the first few strides.

At the Arsenal academy, I sometimes had discipline issues, but I actually prioritized football over everything else. I'm not doing that at Birmingham. It's all become sidelined. Football and Amy on the one hand, strip clubs and partying on the other.

And I'm more or less allowed to behave like this. No one on the team is grabbing hold of their teenager and giving him a ticking off. But then again, why would they? We're still on course for promotion, and it's some of the older guys who have more or less shown me the way in the wild lifestyle off the pitch.

The only one who's seriously concerned is our manager. My girlfriend's dad. He asks me to focus and rarely punishes me with the bench.

'This is something every young player goes through,' he says. 'There are periods where you fall through. It's inevitable. But you just have to keep going.'

And I try to until I'm tempted into yet further trouble. That's how it always goes. A few days of concentrated effort, and then I give in to temptation. All it takes is for someone to call me with a fun suggestion.

It doesn't help either that one of my ankles has swollen massively. It's so pronounced it has to be taped so my right foot is held in place during training and matches. I really ought to take a long break, but I'm way too hungry to get back to scoring goals and play down the issue if anyone asks. The team doctor has given me some anti-inflammatories that relieve the pain. But it's not something to be shouting about. I actually dismiss it out of hand when a reporter calls around a bunch of footballers to ask about our use of Voltaren, as the drug is known.

IN THE MIDDLE of my goal drought, Andy Cole, who is surplus to requirements at Portsmouth, comes in on loan. This is the same Cole who was part of the legendary strike duo with Dwight Yorke at Manchester United. The Cole who was one of the best attackers in the Premier League during the 1990s. He's now 35 years old and has lost some of his pace, but there's nothing wrong with his football brain. He's still a quick thinker.

It's a big deal for me to play right in front of Andy Cole. He's the first offensive superstar I've really been partnered up with. There's no one on the Danish team who even comes close to his level of class or list of achievements. Not Martin Jørgensen or Jon Dahl Tomasson, who may well score their fair share of goals but are simply not as talented.

Bruce's matchmaking pays off. Cole can deliver passes I can work with. He can see the gaps, and he knows that I can too.

Between training sessions, I ask him for advice about various things. Ever since the autumn in 2006 there have been rumours about Manchester United. The club is supposedly interested in me, and Cole says good things about Alex Ferguson and his whole set up. But it doesn't make a huge impression on me. I've not got it into my skull that the biggest club in the world is my prospective suitor. All I'm dreaming of is a comeback at Arsenal. I've still not broken through into my favourite team, and for as long as that hasn't happened, nothing else is of interest.

Against Southampton, I snap up the ball and play a one-two with Cole. He knows I need something to accelerate on, and the pass is so perfect I am able to run straight onto it. One on one with the goalkeeper, I do something I've picked up from Preben Elkjær. The goalkeeper storms out towards me and widens his body, but instead of dribbling or finishing, I nudge the ball to the right and run to his left. Even though I've got twice as far to go, he doesn't have a chance of getting there first. I give the ball a final touch and it rolls over the goal line. That's 2-1 and three crucial points in the table.

Earlier in the match, I'd squandered two big chances, and back in the dressing room one of our defenders tells me he closed his eyes. He was so convinced I was going to kick it past the open goal. But I've not yet got that bad. I'll never get that bad. I seriously can't even imagine it.

The victory takes us closer to automatic promotion. And a few days and two matches later I am round at the Bruce family's house when it will all be settled. If Derby are held to a draw, we can't be caught. In the end they lost.

I watch the match with my girlfriend's dad in his outdoor bar. We hug under the heat lamps, and when the coaching staff turn up, Amy sends me into town to celebrate with the rest of the team. With the lads. That's how they do it in England. She knows better than anyone.

THE FIRST TEAM

2007-2008

IT FEELS GOOD to be back. The pitches at Arsenal's training centre are so well-groomed that the ball never makes a lopsided bounce, and I'm now officially allowed in the first-team dressing room. It's a big changing room – many times bigger and better equipped than the one in Birmingham.

A new set of rules apply too. Like taking off your outdoor footwear before coming inside. That's one that Emmanuel Adebayor is really into. I've been given a locker right next to him because I've been given squad number 26, while he plays with 25 on his back.

The man from Togo with his long, thin braids is an odd fish who takes some things more seriously than everyone else put together. When he's mucking around himself it's another story entirely. One morning he's put on my training kit and put his own in my place. When I discover this, he whispers to me with a shake of his head:

'Then you'll just have to use mine instead, Nicklas. It's too late to change now.'

'Nicklas', 'Nicklas', always with 'Nicklas'. He uses my name as if he were talking to a small child, and it triggers something in me.

Adebayor is only a couple of centimetres shorter, so his clothes fit easily – it's not a massive issue. But it seems completely illogical. I mean – why the hell is it so important for me to take off my boxfresh trainers as soon as I even look in the direction of the dressing room, while he's getting a free pass to do as he pleases?

Me, Dad and Jannick at the training centre at London Colney, autumn 2007. (Private photo)

Maybe it's a culture clash – the Africans mostly stick together. On the other hand, I get along pretty well with people like Eboué and Touré. It's only Adebayor I can't stand.

The feeling is apparently mutual. On the training pitch, we turn on each other. How do I know that? I know because our tackles are verging on reckless. They are preferably delivered so late that they would be awarded a yellow card if we were actually playing against each other. No one else gives me even half as many grazes and bruises out on the training pitch as Adebayor.

THE CLUB is in the midst of a transitional phase. The Invincibles are no more, and the backbone from the 2003–04 season has been split into rather a lot of pieces. Henry has gone to Barcelona, Pirès to Villarreal, Vieira to Inter, Campbell to Portsmouth and Ljungberg to West Ham. Bergkamp has retired, while Gilberto Silva is approaching his sell-by date.

As is Arsène Wenger's preference, the club has refrained from expensive marquee signings. No global superstars have been signed to be presented as replacements. That's not part of the philosophy. The Frenchman some refer to as 'the Professor' thinks long term and economically. He invests, develops and shapes.

It's not dissimilar to the boss's own back story. Eleven years after his appointment, he's considered one of the best managers in the world, but when he was introduced in 1996 – following a trajectory that included a sacking at Monaco – the fans protested loudly. Only British managers were good enough for the club steeped in tradition with ten championship trophies in its cabinet already. It didn't make matters any more palatable that Wenger came blustering in with all sorts of demands before he was even hired. He demanded control over all player sales and acquisitions, over contract negotiations, and over activities at the youth academy and new training centre that Arsenal established. It was hands-on, all over, and many took exception. But during his second season, when he secured the double by winning both the championship and the FA Cup – as the first foreign Premier League manager –

the haters fell silent.

In 2002, he took double number two, and in the following seasons the team reached its zenith. If you overlook the 2006 Champions League final, things have only gone downhill since then.

Nevertheless, no one seems dissatisfied – at least not seriously. The players' respect for the slightly ungainly and officious Frenchman has grown to lofty heights over the years. He goes in for being accommodating and humorous, and I can attest to both of those. He may well have banned us from drinking alcohol in the players' lounge, but if the team does well then we might be rewarded with a night off – which he doesn't interfere in at all. The boss is anything but unreasonable.

The time is approaching for people like Cesc Fàbregas, Robin van Persie and Emmanuel Adebayor to repay the huge levels of trust and confidence that have been shown to them. Cesc, our midfield creator, is the massive star and our best player by some distance, while van Persie has made remarkable progress in the time I was on loan at Birmingham. The Dutchman is now a first pick for the starting eleven, and Adebayor has taken on the role of clear number two. The Brazilian Eduardo, who has arrived from a Croatian club, also looks to be ahead of me in the queue. So I find myself in the position that van Persie and Adebayor were in two years ago – substitutes with the right to start in the Carling Cup and in Champions League group games.

But I'm also quite a bit younger than the others, so there should be time to change that. There's nothing to worry about on the training pitch. Out there, only van Persie and Adebayor are at the same level as me among the strikers. And it's not even because we're equally good at everything. We stand for something else that can be – depending on the opposition – difficult to contain.

MY FIRST three goals come in the Carling Cup against Newcastle United and in the Champions League against Slavia Prague and Steaua Bucharest. I've still not made it onto the scoreboard in the Premier League, but I've also not been spoiled with playing time. I've managed a total of 150 minutes over the course of ten substitute appearances, and by mid-December I'm still waiting for a chance to start. If you only have on average 15 minutes to score your goals, you really need to seize the moment. It's not as easy as I expected. I'm still getting used to the tempo while playing with the ball at my own feet. It's conspicuously higher in the Premier League.

I'm obviously pretty unhappy about the situation. When I visit Wenger in his office, he listens until I've finished speaking.

'Your time will come. Your eye for the game, your ability to set up others is something special for a striker as big as you are – so I believe in you. The important thing is that you are making progress,' he says.

It's derby day, 22 December. It's my first real encounter with Tottenham, and the visit of our north London rivals creates a stir at the new Emirates Stadium. The spectators sit further forward on their seats, and the stands are alive. The atmosphere at Highbury was sometimes compared to a library, but that will not be the case with Emirates.

From the bench, I see Tomáš Rosický find Fàbregas, who instinctively plays Adebayor on with his heel – 1-0 after 47 minutes. It's football according to the boss's manual of attack, and I think the ball barely leaves the grass in this example of perfect interplay.

Tottenham aren't exactly in the bag though. Berbatov equalizes after the break, and with 20 minutes to go Touré concedes a penalty. Robbie Keane steps up to take it, but Almunia – our Spanish goalie – reads his body language.

There's nothing like watching your worst rival make a balls-up, and the Gooners are gloating when Wenger calls me over. I can only just hear what our manager yells into my ear.

'Be the difference between us and them. They don't know you. Use your physique.'

When we get a corner, I get waved on. Fàbregas' dead balls have loads of air beneath them. This one arcs up steeply, and I recognize the spin from countless training sessions. I unleash a spurt of pace that my marker can't respond to. When I meet the ball it's so high up that no one else has tried to jump for it. My take-off is powerful, and I have to curl my upper body together to hit the ball with my forehead. Everyone else tracks me with their eyes. As if I was an alien. I head it down at an angle and it makes a loud noise as it hits the back of the net. I carry on my run, chased up the touchline by my teammates. The entire Emirates is on its feet. Joy surges through my body.

It's surreal – completely insane. From when the game restarted all it took was four seconds for the ball to cross the goal line. It's a new Premier League record for a substitute.

The newspapers describe me as 'the flying Dane' and many years later my contribution is nominated for the distinction of best header in the 133-year-history of Arsenal.

I'm only 19 and I've scored for my country, in the Champions League, in the Carling Cup, in the FA Cup and now in the Premier League. My friends back home increasingly get me and why I don't need heroes, but prefer to believe in myself.

'Nicklas,' they're always saying. 'When you find someone you idolize – and it can't be you – we would love to hear about it.'

A week later, in the middle of a tightly packed Christmas schedule, the boss's reward turns up. I land my first league start, against Everton. I can't be far behind Adebayor and van Persie, not even in Wenger's eyes. That's how I see it. Neither of them has been scoring all that prolifically when you take their playing time into account, and a class effort can pave the way for the breakthrough I feel I've earned.

It doesn't go entirely according to plan. The first time I draw attention to myself is when I provide an involuntary assist to Yakubu Aiyegbeni and Tim Cahill who work together to get the ball in the back of the net – our net. Five minutes later I pick up a booking for complaining, whereupon Eduardo – one of my direct competitors – pulls it back to 1-1 and then puts us 2-1 up. Things don't improve in the second half. I end up making a tackle far too late.

So late it looks like a stamp. That receives a second yellow card.

My first goal in the Premier League, also setting a new record for the fastest goal after coming on as a substitute, December 2007. (Photo: Clive Mason/Getty Images)

Sent off on my league debut.

I can't remember when I last saw a red card, but it must have been at some point during my time at KB. While I'm waiting for the others in the dressing room, Adebayor has come on as a sub and made it 3-1. It's far from ideal.

When I look back at that match, it's ludicrous how haywire everything went. Of course, I'm pleased that we win, but for me personally it throws away the momentum I've been searching for since the pre-season training camp in Austria. I've been gearing myself up so much that I overreact with frustration when things don't work out.

Throughout 2007, I've been listening to Nelly Furtado's latest album. In one of her best songs, the chorus goes: 'Why do all good things come to an end?' That's how I feel. I need to get better at keeping the good things going.

THAT'S MORE or less true off the pitch as well. Financially, things are going in the right direction – but no further as it's always possible to spend the money I'm earning. Every month my bank balance goes pretty much down to zero. That said, I do have three cars. The Audi has been sold on, but two Porsches have joined the fleet, a Cayenne Turbo S and a 911 Turbo S.

Wenger has handed me a five-year contract. It doubles my wages, so I'm now earning more than £100,000 every month. The deal has been negotiated by David Manasseh and my dad. I could have earned more at Manchester United and Bayern Munich, but now I've set my heart on becoming a first-team player for the Gunners, it's no use thinking about that. What's more, the contract can be renegotiated and by that time – in two years – Manasseh thinks I will have made myself absolutely indispensable.

My departure from Birmingham has been good for me. Fewer strip clubs with my teammates. No more shag pad. The fact that Amy and I have moved in together at Princess Park Manor – a luxury flat development in an old stately home where Fàbregas also lives – puts a natural dampener on my opportunities to party.

For the first time in my life, I'm living under the same roof as a girlfriend and I would say there's a lot I have to learn about the opposite sex. There are times I should shut my trap. There are times I should remember to show an interest. Events and invitations that I would do well to refuse if I want to maintain harmony at home.

Being away from London has only served to make me even fonder of the city. It feels like my own, even more so than Copenhagen has ever managed. The bustling people, the many opportunities, the restlessness, the joie de vivre that blossoms when it's time to knock off...We're a good match.

When I go out for a night on the town, I notice the glances. Being a first-team player at Arsenal is one of the most enviable jobs you can have around here. Pretty much every lad my age dreams of swapping places with me. And an awful lot of the girls want to exchange all sorts of other things with me, if you get my drift.

I've never had a hard time chatting up girls, but now it's almost too easy. And it happens that I'm tempted beyond my powers of resistance and cheat on Amy. Unfortunately – because she in no way deserves it.

I'm at my weakest when things aren't working on the pitch. If I've just scored or played outstandingly, then I can easily control myself. But if I'm not playing, or not playing enough, or playing badly...if we lose, or I get sent off...then I seek revenge in other stomping grounds.

Sometimes I hang out with some of the other players from the first team. Especially the ones who it's easy to speak English to. Johan, Ramsey, Wilshere and Fàbregas.

Cesc has developed in a completely insane way. I would go so far as to say he is the world's best or second-best player in his position. He can see the pass and he can make it. Technically, he is practically perfectly smooth and equally he has vast running abilities to throw into the pot. After he's sized me up, things click. The same happens when we go out together. To restaurants, nightclubs or the casino.

Most of my new friends, however, have nothing to do with football. Musicians, art collectors, poker players and party animals. I've fallen into conversation with them at restaurants or private gatherings. And I've also begun to take an interest in art. It's easy to get in touch with people for a private gallery viewing, because everyone has some curiosity and some interests in common.

The only thing I'm not collecting is Danes. I'm so famous in Denmark that it no longer feels safe. Danes might have all sorts of motives for wanting to be friends with me, and they can be seriously hard to avoid. London is packed with my fellow countrymen.

IN JANUARY 2008, we meet Tottenham once again. This time it's the semi-final of the Carling Cup. After drawing the first leg 1-1 at the Emirates, it couldn't be tighter. But in the return leg at their place we make a shit start. After two minutes we're behind, and when they get a free kick in our half of the pitch, I track back to join the wall. I climb high up, but not high enough. The ball hits the back of my head and lands in our own net. An own goal – clear as day.

Then when the score is 3-0, Tottenham's fans are gleeful like never before. I finally get a high ball in midfield, swing my right leg at head height and do a full volley so that it hits the underside of the crossbar and bounces back into play. Instead of it being 3-1 suddenly it's 4-0. It's late to pull it back, but Wenger still reacts. He sends Eduardo and Adebayor on. On the way past me, Adebayor shouts that it's my fault he has to come on and waste his energy.

'I'm here because you're playing like shit.'

It's not especially encouraging, and shortly after when we win a corner, we both seek out the back post. There's a lot of pushing and jostling, and suddenly we're fighting each other. We push back and forth while the Tottenham players watch in puzzlement. Afterwards, Adebayor claims I gave him the finger, but I don't remember that. What I do remember is him sticking his head forward. That's the thing with him. He behaves illogically. Completely unpredictably.

I don't know if it's totally deliberate, but it feels like a headbutt right on the bridge of my nose. The blood gushes out, and my nose swells up. As if it's not big enough already.

William Gallas rushes over and pulls us apart. But Adebayor isn't done with me. He has to be escorted away by Eduardo and

After clashing heads with Adebayor, January 2008. (Photo: Clive Mason/Getty Images)

Bacary Sagna, while the referee books him.

When the final whistle is blown, our arch-rivals have won 5-1. It's our biggest derby defeat in an eternity, and no one on the team can bear it. Of course, personally I blame Adebayor, which is probably overdoing it. But I really want to get hold of him for a quiet tête-à-tête, and I guess the feeling is mutual, because one of the coaching staff has to hold him back in the players' tunnel.

When we finally clash in the dressing room, we have a lot of shit to say to each other. Things I wouldn't be able to utter 12 years later. Neither of us is holding back, and it has consequences.

The boss fines us both two weeks' wages. It's my first fine – but far from my last.

WE MEET Liverpool in the Champions League quarter-final, and in the first leg I have one of my seriously unlucky days. I actually get laughed out of the stadium. It's not entirely fair, even if I do say so myself, but fine. In the television footage my dodge looks pretty clunky …Cesc not only catches Pepe Reina out of position in the Liverpool goal, but his finish also catches me by surprise and I end up wrong-footed. Quite simply I get in the way of the finish.

The clip is shown over and over, and each time the reporters 'forget' a crucial detail: the linesman had already flagged for offside. If I had avoided the ball, the goal would still have been disallowed. But obviously I understand full well that's not quite as fun as seeing clumsy clogs Bendtner letting himself down.

The following weekend, on 5 April 2008, I get another chance against Liverpool, this time in the Premier League. This is only my fourth start in the league. Agger is out with an injury, so in the air it's Martin Škrtel and their 6ft 7in attacker, Peter Crouch, I have to contend with. In the 54th minute I fool them both. I find my entrance and get to a corner first so that we level the Reds' lead. I need that goal. It definitely feels like a boost in a period where I'm fighting a headwind. The papers have carried on wading through all the stuff with Adebayor. They've been writing how the squad have frozen me out – that you can see it in my teammates. The lack of celebration in the wake of my goals. That Gallas, Cesc and a couple of the other leading players must still be angry with me.

If I'm really out in the cold, then I haven't noticed. Honestly. I think it's greatly exaggerated. I agree that Adebayor isn't celebrating, but right now I don't care about that kind of thing. I care about my own progress and the manager's backing. And neither of those parameters is up for discussion. Quite the opposite. I'm getting more and more starts. In the last three games Wenger backs me, and in two of them I reward his trust with goals.

In the end, I manage a haul of five Premier League goals. That might not sound like much, but those five goals give us seven extra points in the table. Without them, we might have finished fourth instead of third.

I notice a growing affection from the Gooners. Even though there have been some bumps in the road, the good things have been noticed more, and on YouTube and Twitter they've started to call me a goalgetter. They've also made up a song about me. An ode to the super sub.

'Super Nick, super-super Nick,' they bawl.

When I score the match winner against Everton, the boss has this to say about me on the Arsenal website:

'If you look at Bendtner on 1 August last year and Bendtner on 1 May this year, there's a huge difference. He's developed into a good player. He's always on the move, he meets the ball and he finishes well. I'm impressed by him.'

LESSONS IN PATRIOTISM

2007–2008

MY GOAL drought at Birmingham had also contaminated my appearances for Denmark. Across four matches in a row, I left the pitch without scoring – the last against Spain in a 2-1 defeat in Madrid in March 2007. When our next opponent turns out to be Germany – on top of being an away match – I daren't hope for a change in fortunes. It seems as if something really promising is transforming into something more mediocre.

But anyway…Morten Olsen has both played and coached in the Bundesliga, and he knows what he's up against.

It's a friendly, and the Germans have selected a team stuffed with reserves. We exploit this from the word go. Agger comes close with a header, and I have a shot saved on the line. At the end of the first half, I blow a chance that I'd have scored 19 times out of 20. Uncertainty is beginning to creep in. Even a guy with my self-confidence can be hit by invasive thoughts, and it doesn't take more than a split second of doubt or hesitation for you to misplace your kick. And that's what happens to me. The ball hits the outside of the post and ends up on the outside of the net.

Morten Olsen is experimenting with different players across several different positions, and to be honest I expect to be taken off at half-time. I feel like I haven't taken advantage of my opportunities at all and I'm really fed up with myself. But it doesn't happen. Our national coach keeps me on the pitch. I think he wants to teach me something about perseverance.

How do you do that? You do it by pushing me out there where there's nothing I can do except keep trying. I need to grasp that not everything happens with the same ease I've become accustomed to. I'm a long-term investment.

With ten minutes to go, Morten Olsen's trust pays dividends. In our own half, Jesper Grønkjær receives the ball and starts a rush up the field – one of those irresistible solo runs he used to do for Ajax. In the big leagues of England, Spain and Germany there has been less of it because there's not as much space, but in a friendly – and with fresh legs as a recently introduced substitute – Grønkjær cuts through anyone who so much as dares to approach him. After covering three-quarters of the pitch, he fires a cross into the centre. It catches the goalkeeper off guard and sets itself up perfectly in the gap between the two central defenders. I've seen it from a distance, and all I have to do is stretch out my right foot and tap the ball over the line.

It's not something I always remember to do, but on this occasion I hurry over to the mastermind of the goal to thank him for the set-up. A high-class counter-attack has been delivered by Grønkjær and it demonstrates Morten Olsen has the weapons to shake even the greatest of nations. That's something we'll need in due course.

IN THE DAYS following the match against Germany, the Danish press hail me as the man of the match. They write that I must be in contention to start against Sweden in June. The fateful match at Parken, as they refer to it.

I find it kind of funny. It would take very little for the mood to change and I wonder how happy they would have been if I had fluffed Grønkjær's build-up. Then my multitude of missed sitters would have been the big topic of conversation.

My mum and dad Skype me from Otto Liebes Allé. They read aloud from the *Ekstra Bladet* newspaper, which says representatives from the top three teams in Germany – Bayern Munich, Dortmund and Schalke 04 – were all at the match. Now they all want to buy me from Arsenal.

The next time I speak to David Manasseh, I ask him about the rumours. He says there's something in them. And that Bayern are of the most interest. Bayern have the most money and the best squad. The German champions have bid £10 million. Manchester United and Lyon in France are also said to be interested once my loan deal at Birmingham ends.

'Just relax. I've got it under control,' Manasseh says. 'If you want to move on, you'll move on. If you want to go back to Arsenal, you'll come back to Arsenal.'

My agent has a plan. He says I'm going to be the first player earning £200,000 in the Premier League. Per week. f

In 2007, a figure like that sounds absurd, but on the other hand the average wage in the Premier League has only gone one way. From £77,000 a year in 1992 to £960,000 a year 15 years later. You can do the maths. Major talents are a sought-after commodity, and all sorts of football agents are constantly trying to get in touch with me. Whenever that happens, I refer them to Manasseh. The whole idea of playing them off against each other and keeping track of what I've said to who is not my cup of tea. When I mess that up with girls, it's too exhausting by half.

Manasseh isn't taking any chances. He doesn't want to lose his golden goose, and he makes it attractive for me and my family to stick around. When I signed my contract with Stellar Group, part of the agreement was that my dad would take his FIFA licence so he could become an approved football agent and a member of the firm. Unfortunately, he tanks the final exam, which is the kind of thing you'd expect to frighten off Manasseh and his partner. But it doesn't. They still hire him.

Professional football is a tough business. The player is a commodity. And if that commodity doesn't generate revenue for the agency, then it is – in inverted commas – 'unfit for purpose'. Then the agent finds themselves a new best friend. A new golden goose. When I flew the coop, that became Gareth Bale.

IT'S MY FIRST encounter with the arch enemy. We play Sweden at Parken on 2 June 2007. The sun is high in the sky and people have been cooling off by knocking back the pints. It's going to be a scorcher.

After the loss against Spain, we have to beat the Swedes to have a real chance of making the Euros. Morten Olsen picked up a ban after a clash with the referee in Madrid, so Peter Bonde, our quiet assistant coach, is in charge for this game. We haven't set out to go all in from the starting whistle, which is why Jon Dahl is on his own up front.

A mere six minutes elapse before Michael Gravgaard messes up a back pass that Johan Elmander – a former Brøndby player – is easily able to put through the legs of Thomas Sørensen. And after 22 minutes, Zlatan Ibrahimović hands over his free kick to some white-haired lad I've never seen before in my life, Petter Hansson. He takes a long run-up and strikes the ball completely cleanly. But it's almost 30 metres out, so it shouldn't cause any serious problems. Yet it clips Lars Jacobsen on its way and Thomas Sørensen is sold down the river. 0-2.

A siege begins and when the Swedes get a chance to counter-attack, they strike. 3-0 down after 25 minutes. I'm sat on the bench staring into space in disbelief. Several of the others have buried their faces in their hands. This could be a complete disaster.

Peter Bonde pulls Jan Kristiansen off the pitch. Leon Andreasen comes on to play in defensive midfield. A lot of the crowd get up and head outside. The ones that come back have their hands full with pints of beer. They're going to drown their sorrows. I'm all too familiar with that feeling. The spectators who spend the longest queueing outside don't see Agger reduce the lead to 1-3.

During the break, Peter Bonde comes into his own. He pulls Rommedahl back into defence and instructs me to replace Kahlenberg. It doesn't get much more offensive than that. The duo in charge of coaching Denmark must really have faith in it. They must have seen something. Some gaps. Our local rivals must have shown some weaknesses. Now a surprise attack awaits them.

It all goes according to plan. We go all out from the very start of the second half. After 61 minutes, Sørensen launches a clearance. I win the duel in the air in the middle of the Swedish half and direct the ball on. It drops straight into Jon Dahl's path. Our striker has been absent thus far – completely invisible – but you have to give credit to his infamous inside foot that it can strike when it really counts. With his left boot, he lifts the ball over the goalie into the top of the net, and it's 2-3 with half an hour left to play.

The roar from the Danish fans is deafening. I've never heard so many voices cheering so loudly all at once. But here we go.

The Swedes are stressed out. You can hear them snapping at each other. We have all the possession, and in the 76th minute Leon Andreasen fires low through the forest of red and yellow jerseys and into the net. Parken goes crazy. We've still got 15 minutes left to finish the job. There's no doubt about it – we're going for the win. The Swedes are in disarray.

When they finally visit our half, it's with just two guys up front. There's five of us against them. And then…From my position on the centre line, I see Markus Rosenberg fall. He clutches his stomach. When the referee looks over to the linesman, he's raised his flag. There is a brief discussion between the two of them, and as the referee runs back towards Agger and Christian Poulsen, he pulls the red card out of his back pocket. It's shown to Poulsen. He also points to the 12-yard spot. A sending off and penalty kick with three minutes to go. And things get even worse. A second later, a stocky guy in black jeans and a Denmark shirt jumps the hoardings and makes straight for the referee. Just as he's about to land his first blow, Gravgaard gets in between them.

The referee turns his palms down and sweeps them to the side. The match is brought to a halt and we leave the pitch.

In the dressing room, there's a really weird atmosphere. We're waiting to see what's going to happen. Whether we're going back out to play the final minutes of the game.

The slow-motion replay shows it quite clearly. Christian punches Rosenberg twice with his fist. It looks violent, and of course Christian is in an absolute state. He's just spoiled an historic Danish comeback with a dirty trick that may be difficult to forget.

In a way, the pitch invader saves him. Without the hooligan, Christian would've been condemned. Scapegoats are handy in football.

Regardless, no one has an angry word to say to our midfield warrior – not in the dressing room. When it comes to attitude, Christian is the same kind of guy as Thomas Gravesen. They both want to win at any cost – and they both lead from the front. Always. Christian isn't malicious – he's a patriot – and something must have happened before those two punches were thrown. Something made him lose it – just like when Zidane lost it in the World Cup final against Italy the year before.

An UEFA official knocks on the dressing room door. It's over. The game has been awarded to Sweden as a 3-0 win. Christian goes around apologizing to everyone. One by one, his head bowed. We pat him on the back. There, there. The sport of football is full of mistakes. Some of them are bigger than others, but if you can't forgive, you'll never get anywhere. Then you end up a bitter old man at a very young age.

FOLLOWING THE DRAMA at Parken, I see the national team differently. I've always been happy to be involved, but now I've noticed it's completely different. Club football doesn't even come close to it.

Playing for your country, you're not some employee – you're playing for something and with someone. There's no sense of internal competition in the same way. One man's loss is not another man's gain. And it shouldn't be that way either. Everyone should stand together as a team, and that was exactly what we did when all hell broke loose.

I begin to reflect on what Morten Olsen has been trying to instil in me. How I should radiate that I actually want this. It's no use chewing my gum and looking totally vacant while the band strikes up and plays the national anthem. So the next time I start a game, I try singing along with 'There is a Lovely Country'.

Morten Olsen frequently comments on my body language. He's actually realized I'm not as lazy as I look – not always. He recognizes how my motor skills and posture are a little different – partly because I have longer limbs than most other players. For example, when I take ten paces, Romme has to take 12, which means that all his footwork looks hyper-energetic, while my own seems sluggish and like I'm trudging about. It's one of the disadvantages of being as tall as I am. It shouldn't be underplayed: if people think I'm a sloth, it might harm my career prospects.

'Look sharp and more alert,' my national coach says to me, and I try to keep my eyes open and lean forward a little more whenever I'm pursuing the ball during training.

The criticisms get served up one by one. Morten Olsen has probably noted them all long ago, but he crosses one bridge at a time. It says something about how clever he is. I'm not to be frightened off by too many demands being made all at once.

ALTHOUGH I AM making progress and feel accepted by most of the national squad, I'm far from done growing up. The home games against Spain and Latvia in October 2007 take on a whole different significance. The dream of making the Euros crumbled against the Swedes at Parken – which means the final two qualifiers are instead all about looking ahead to the 2010 World Cup.

I know full well not everyone in the squad is equally fond of me. If I'm ever in any doubt, I can go back to an article from the *Jyllands-Posten* newspaper. It quotes an anonymous Denmark player.

'He'll go far if he can be bothered,' my teammate says of me.

What use is that? Instead, I end up speculating like crazy: who would be such a snake and feed the press that kind of smear? I would have more understanding of it if I were some old tyrant who no one dared squabble with. But I'm anything but that. I'm 19 years old and happy-go-lucky.

It's a violation of the unwritten rules. No one should criticize anyone else by name without also standing up at the same time – not at our level.

We've been at the Hotel Marienlyst for a couple of hours when

Morten Olsen asks me to come with him to a conference room. Inside are the old boys and kings of the national team, waiting for us. We're talking about the real heroes – the ones who've been with him all the way. Thomas Helveg, Jon Dahl and Martin Jørgensen.

'Now you're going to hear it from the lads themselves,' Morten Olsen says.

They take the floor in turns, but they say more or less the same thing.

'You've got huge talent, and it may lead you to big things, but no one is bigger than the team.'

'You need to get better at fitting in.'

'You can't come strolling in after everyone else.'

'When we're training, don't rest up on the pitch. Everyone has to give it their all.'

The episode with Gravesen – those press-ups I refused to do – is brought up too.

I want to be on the national team more than ever – so I nod and agree and promise to mend my ways.

It's more or less the first time I've spoken to Martin Jørgensen and Thomas Helveg. The two of them always hang out together and they seem to share a lot of in-jokes. At least if you're new to the squad. Word is they consider each other as brothers of sorts. If that's true, Helveg must be the sympathetic big brother and Jørgensen the spirited little brother. In the media, Jørgensen has an image as a fun and charming joker, but I'm not convinced. He's far from offering me the warmest welcome, and he is very self-important. Something else is hiding just behind the joker facade. The need to feel doubly respected due to past performances.

I think several of the old guys wish I'd seemed more impressed with their football skills. Or at least even pretended to be impressed. Perhaps it's something that comes with age. When your best years are behind you.

Eventually, I give everybody less cause for complaint. When I put us 1-0 up against the Czech Republic in March 2008, I score for

Denmark for the fourth game in a row. According to the Danish papers, neither Michael Laudrup nor Preben Elkjær ever managed to pull that off.

The comparisons between me and Elkjær continue, and I've nothing against that. I've checked out the man who brought the first and only Italian championship to the provincial town of Verona and was voted third best player in Europe in 1984 and second best in 1985. That's also what I want to achieve one day.

Elkjær sought out many original solutions to get past his markers. I try to do the same thing. The hacks want to know whether I'm also inspired by his cheekier side. I'm able to answer quite honestly that I have absolutely no knowledge of that side of the man. It's only many years later that I gain some insider knowledge on that count. Like the time at Cologne when Elkjær had been out on the town the night before a game. The next day, the coach confronted him in front of the rest of the team. 'You were seen at the discotheque with a woman on your lap and a bottle of whisky in your hand. What do you have to say in your defence?'

Elkjær's reply is legendary:

'That's not accurate,' he's reported to have said. 'It was a bottle of vodka!'

Maybe it's just a tall tale, but his career in German football was extremely brief in any case.

My goal against the Czechs is blistering. I get the ball just before the halfway line, dodge two defenders and storm forward. Just outside the box, I one-two with FC Nordsjælland's Thomas Kristensen. That gets me past the last three, and when the goalkeeper swoops out I fire past him with a low shot. When you watch it on YouTube, you might well be flummoxed. Is it a PlayStation goal or what?

Afterwards, Jon Dahl tears over to embrace me. It's the first time he's done anything like that. Until now he's seemed demonstratively unimpressed whenever I've scored a goal. If everyone else has leaped off the bench, he's stayed sat down. Perhaps I've become a competitor in his eyes. But whatever – he's actually celebrating with me right now, and that must mean I'm behaving acceptably.

I must be doing as I'm told.

At the end of May we travel to Amsterdam to play the Netherlands. The Arsenal players who aren't going to the Euros have already been on holiday for two weeks by this point, and the same applies to me. My form is no longer what it should be. As it happens, I've been at NASA – a nightclub with the same kind of white leather furnishing as Pennant's old shag pad – so much that the staff have rechristened table 1 as 'Bendtner's table'. We end up there three or four nights in a row, week after week, drinking magnums. All on my tab.

Even though it's a friendly, I've got something to play for against Holland. All of Nike's European executives are coming. My performance will clearly determine whether I deserve a sponsorship contract with Nike on a global level, or whether I am to remain under Nike Denmark.

As a Nike World player, you can earn over £1 million a year for the next five years. Defeat against van Nistelrooy, van der Vaart, van Persie and all the other vans is not an option.

We end up playing out a 1-1 draw, and that's largely thanks to van der Sar. I get a whole bunch of great chances, but he saves them all. Fortunately, I also do some things just right. Like when I'm close to goal and control a floating cross with my chest before using Joris Mathijsen as a dribbling cone. I rotate one and a half times, and while he's still standing there swaying, I serve up the ball to Christian Poulsen. He can't avoid equalizing, and afterwards the people from Nike are so pleased I simply know I've got it in the bag. They're not the only ones who are happy with me. Morten Olsen describes my efforts as 'completely fantastic' and Jon Dahl continues to seem impressed.

'Bendtner played a blinder,' he says to the press. 'He's risen to the occasion. A year ago he wasn't ready. He is now. He's got some amazing skills and has the chance to become a class player.'

It looks to me like I'm well on the way to being accepted for the person I am. Including by those who have been used to calling all the shots.

Later that year my mum calls me to read something out to me.

Something Preben Elkjær said about me:

'Bendtner is one of the most interesting young attackers in Europe. He's the kind of player who can do it by himself and isn't dependent on the team playing spellbinding football.'

It feels like praise I can put to good use.

THE NIKE CONTRACT, the successful games for Denmark against a couple of footballing superpowers and a good end to the league season mean I can look back on my debut season as an Arsenal player and consider it passed with flying colours. And although I'd rather be at the European Championships in Austria and Switzerland, I've decided to enjoy the extra long summer holiday with a clear conscience.

Amy and I have invited our families to join us in Barbados where we're going to stay at Sandy Lane. The hotel has golf courses so superb that Tiger Woods had his wedding there.

Our parents hit it off. Amy's brother Alex is also along for the ride. Down on the beach we bump into Tottenham's Robbie Keane. He's Irish and turns out to be a pretty nice, easygoing guy. The animosity between our clubs is not something that ever comes up when we're talking. That's generally how it is with footballers. Hate is something we leave to the fans. For us, a club is as much an employer as it is an identity. Of course you play along in the press, but most of it is playing to the crowd. You can compare that element of football with wrestling, where everything is exaggerated in order to keep the entertainment machine going. In reality, most of us are unfussed when it comes to our opponents. It's all about winning and nothing else.

With Amy, however, the drama is real – and hardly a day goes by where she isn't pissed off about something or other I've said or done. It irritates her that I'm not prioritizing our alone time more. But to be perfectly honest, it's more fun to hang out with the other guys at the bar. Downing cocktails and chatting football.

One day she's so upset I go down to the hotel's jewellery store. She's been looking longingly at a tennis bracelet covered in diamonds. It's an expensive diversion, but it saves the mood. And if it can do that then it's worth every penny. Money really can be put to good use, after all.

LONE WOLF

2008–2009

WHEN IT COMES to music, I'm not all that picky. To describe my tastes as broad would be an understatement really. After all, it was me who flew a girlfriend to a classical concert in Italy. We sat there in some field watching Andrea Bocelli perform – side-by-side with married couples who were respectively double and triple our age.

Bocelli who? Bocelli as in the 'Time to Say Goodbye' ballad guy. The blind, smooth tenor who can see more with his heart than the rest of us can with our eyes. I like that kind of thing. It wasn't just romantic – it was also an expensive outing. We had to take a helicopter from the airport, but she was grateful afterwards.

On other occasions, I've sung myself hoarse along with the rest of the national team as we tackle the Danish singer Thomas Helmig's hits from the 80s. The same lines over and over: 'It's me standing out here knockin' on your door / Askin' you to try and understand / I only kissed her on the cheek / Say it's okay and let me in!'

It's pretty saccharine. In the song, a man is crawling back after a big night out on the town. And funnily enough, many footballers are able to give a nod of recognition to that.

But I mostly listen to hip hop. In London, I build up a love for what you might call the American loud-mouth rappers.

The king of them all – Jay-Z – is an Arsenal fan and he comes to watch us play every time he's in London.

Whenever the club holds charity auctions, the ex-dealer donates a fuckton of signed Nike trainers, and if they're the right size then I bid the most. Always. I'm totally fine with that since the money goes straight to the children's ward at one of the local hospitals.

Through Jay-Z I discover Kanye West. In those years, no one can match him. He's not just outstanding at creating catchy, epic beats – he also has some pretty cool and recognizable personality traits.

For one thing, Kanye is insanely outspoken. Of course, loads of rappers are, but he still stands out from the crowd. While others try to imitate each other, he forces himself to just sing. While others cross their fingers at awards ceremonies, he goes onto the stage and tells the jury they picked the wrong winner.

One of Kanye's coolest tracks is 'Can't Tell Me Nothing'. In it, he explains how he had to learn about life without finishing his education. And he straight up admits that he fucks up time and time again. And what does he do when he's in a bad place? He goes out spending money, while his mama tries in vain to talk some sense into him. It's as if those lines are taken straight from my own life.

And there's more. It can almost seem as if Kanye isn't bothered about thinking before he speaks. As if he willingly makes things difficult for himself. As if he desires contempt and opposition. He uses those slaps in the face for motivation. To step up another level. Kanye can't suss out the happy medium. It's got to hurt to get better, and once things are good again he gets mixed up in yet more trouble. That's more or less how my own life pans out. Like a roller coaster.

Then there's the colour pink. Pink in all its possible shades. When Kanye made his breakthrough, he insisted on wearing pink polo shirts, which drove the hip hop world totally crazy. They called him a 'homo' and all those kinds of things – obviously meant as an insult. Hip hop culture is extremely macho – a bit like the atmosphere in the dressing room and at the stadium can be. But Kanye didn't care. If he liked pink, he was going to wear pink. What others had to say didn't bother him one bit.

I'VE BEEN DREAMING of a pair of bright pink football boots for ages. The first time I mention it in a meeting with Nike, people smile as if I'm joking or something. But it slowly sinks in. That Bendtner guy actually means it.

It simply hasn't been on their radar – that men might play football wearing a so-called girl's colour. But I state my case and Nike get on board with the idea.

'Maybe you're right,' they say. 'Maybe the time is right.'

At first, they want to create the pink boots for me. But then Franck Ribéry at Bayern Munich hears about the project and says he wants in too. It doesn't really surprise me. Southern Europeans – especially the French – have always been quicker off the mark and braver when it comes to men's fashion and experimenting with colour.

Naturally, Nike don't want to turn down Ribéry – one of the best wingers in the world – on the contrary, it might help sales. We end up with a compromise of sorts. One player from each country will be allowed to wear the Mercurial Vapor SL Berry Pink – the name they give to the boot. And that player will get the flag of their country stitched into the side of the boot. Not that there's stars stepping on each other's toes to get to the front of the queue. Reportedly, there are several Premier League players who receive the offer, but when push comes to shove I'm the only one who dares go for it.

After Arsenal's promising opening of the season with five goals in a month, Arsène Wenger lets me start most of the games. Unfortunately, luck doesn't go my way – not like it did in the matches before – and my performances fluctuate quite a bit. When we lose 3-0 to Manchester City, I can't put a foot right.

A day later, Nike announce I'll be lining up against Dynamo Kiev in the Champions League wearing my pink football boots. That really wakes up the British press from its stupor. The *Daily Telegraph* calls them 'Barbie boots' and points out it will take something different if Arsenal are to deliver a real man's effort against the Ukrainian champions.

If we want to progress from the opening group stage, we have to win against Kiev. It has to be a success. An exit before the knockout stage would be a disaster for the club. Not just in sporting terms, but also financially – we have a brand-new stadium to pay off.

I watch the first 69 minutes from the bench, and when I come on I'm absolutely furious. Furious at the fans who take the liberty of whistling at me. Furious at myself for crashing out of the starting line-up. You can see it in the way I'm chewing my gum. My jaw is completely locked up – that's how obstinate I am.

With five minutes to go, it's still 0-0. Then Cesc gets a free kick which he takes quickly. I sprint from deep and control the ball with my chest without missing a beat. I tap it on with my right thigh and before the defender can reach me with his sliding tackle, I kick hard with my left instep. I barely need to follow it with my eyes, because the celebration from the stands is unmistakable. I tear off my shirt while the net is still rippling. Shouting in unison with the supporters who are beside themselves. One big hotchpotch of joy and frustration.

It's my most important goal as an Arsenal player to date, and a world-class goal on the counter-attack. Few can be in any doubt about that. The next morning, the newspapers land their catch.

The *Mirror*: 'Nicklas Bendtner was Arsenal's last-gasp hero – thanks to his dainty pink boots.'

The Times: 'Some may think that Arsenal lack character, but the man who scored the goal that puts them into the Champions League knockout stages, three minutes from time, did it wearing pink football boots and one has to say that takes courage of sorts, at least.'

Even after all these years, that's one of the things I miss most about England. People – even the biggest mugs – dare to admit when they have made a mistake.

Afterwards, I get ribbed by van Persie and a couple of the others. They say I'll wear anything so long as there's money in it. Even though it's said for a laugh, it leaves me a bit pissed off. That's the exact opposite of the truth. I would play in those boots without being paid. So I retaliate:

'But I don't think anyone at Arsenal is going to be able to

compete with me on that front,' I say into the sea of microphones. 'I have reached the top of the outstanding boots. The only way they can beat me now is to play in diamond-encrusted boots. And I don't think that's going to happen for a few years.'

Kanye West probably doesn't read newspapers. Definitely not from the UK. But if he did, he would have my back. I mean: first I get my critics to shut their mouths. And then everyone else dares to play in pink too. World stars like Cristiano Ronaldo, Eden Hazard, Arturo Vidal and many, many more. On one occasion I stumble across a photo taken in 2015 – seven years later. I've just settled the German Super Cup and my teammates are running towards me to celebrate the goal. There's five of us there, jumping around. Four of us are wearing pink Nike boots on our feet. *You can't tell me nothing!*

AT LONG LAST in the autumn of 2008, the apartment in Bushey in north-west London is finally ready. I bought it for me and Amy, but she doesn't move in with me. We're no good for each other any more, and I'm sick of hurting her as much as I do.

I'm going to miss her lovely family, but it's high time for us to go our separate ways. No doubt about it.

The apartment is in a complex featuring a fitness centre and indoor swimming pool, and had it not been for the sudden credit crunch there would have been an 18-hole golf course, helipad and a special hunting area in the pipeline.

The buildings look pretty extraordinary, and have previously been used for the Harry Potter and Indiana Jones movies. Before that, it was a boarding school for the sons of upper-class freemasons. To cut a long story short, a masonic lodge is a kind of business club that oozes secrecy. In the gigantic entrance hall there is an old motto inscribed into the tiled floor: *AUDI VIDE TACE.*

In Latin, that basically means keep your mouth shut about anything you see or hear. That you will be rewarded with eternal life if you can master the challenging art of discretion.

Personally, I thank my lucky stars that people don't end up

gossiping about all the things that go on in and around my new home. Otherwise they'd really have something to complain about. I'm not exactly living an exemplary life.

Take my circadian rhythm, for example. I'm probably the world's biggest night owl and I only get up when I can no longer drag it out any more. Breakfast has never been my thing, but I usually try and grab a bowl of yoghurt. At 10.30am, it's time for training at Bell Lane, and when that's done I've regained my appetite. By then it's 1pm and I eat like a starving dog. I shovel fish and rice, chicken and mash or spag bol down my throat.

Afterwards I drive home, throw myself on the couch and have a kip. When I wake up again, it's 4 or 5pm, and I hurry to drive into London to shop and hang out with some mates.

Around 6pm, we eat a snack and at 10pm it's time for dinner. I might be in a larger group, or maybe with a girl I've asked out on a date. If I've got training the next day, then I'm back in bed by 1 or 2am.

I'm rarely alone in the new apartment. I'm no longer interested in being left alone to my own devices. The silence makes me uneasy. Until I was 16 and moved to London, I was the exact opposite. Then I really enjoyed being sent outside or dribbling around on my own on the training pitch. Peace and quiet, as well as space, were important factors back then. Now I constantly seek out other people.

I think it's about the high life. I've got a taste for it. Once you've tried it, it becomes addictive. There's always something fun to do, and your money and your status open doors that are closed to others.

I know that full well. I have some slightly different problems. There are a lot of things about a completely normal life that I simply don't get.

Everything has come at me so fast that I haven't learned what other people my age have had to learn.

I mean, 11 years later – at the age of 31 – I've tried cooking food 20 times – maybe 30 tops – in my whole life. And I've never opened a bill addressed to me. There were people for that at

Arsenal. If I got a parking ticket, I would give it to one of the fixers and it was basically sorted. I've paid my way through boredom and practical issues, and I've probably paid a lot for it. But when that kind of thing doesn't interest you – like not one bit – and when your advisor tells you that you never have to do that kind of thing yourself…Well. You choose to believe them. I did in any case.

LONDON HAS the highest number of good football teams in any one city you'll find in the world. The majority of men are obsessed with a crazy leather ball, and even if you don't support a team yourself, you can be pretty damn sure one of your mates has got you covered. Just like the wages, it's only going in one direction. The bigger the money and wider the media coverage of the sport, the more the footballers dominate the consciousness of the average Londoner.

I notice that pretty quickly. When I go out, the paps start taking up positions in front of the restaurant or by my car. And when we go to a nightclub, the girls know right away that I'm from Arsenal – not just that I'm a footballer, not from West Ham, Chelsea, Tottenham, Crystal Palace, Wimbledon, Millwall, Charlton or Fulham, but from Arsenal.

England is known for its gold-digger culture. In Denmark, you might occasionally bump into a girl who wants to get with a footballer just because he's a footballer. In England, those kinds of girls are all over the place. And they don't hide the fact that's what they're after. Somehow, they imagine there is something superhuman in us – that we have some kind of superpower – just because we're famous. It's sort of taboo to say it aloud – but that's how it is. They elevate us to something unreal. Something we can't live up to, but which still goes to our heads.

It doesn't matter who I take home. Whether or not she's famous isn't something I need to shout about.

But for some girls it's exactly the opposite. For that kind of girl, I'm a trophy. They want to brag about having pulled me and they're under no illusions that we'll be getting married or anything like that. That's just as well, because a girl is never potential girlfriend material unless I have to fight for her first. Anything else goes against my competitive genes. A fling isn't some shortcut to a long-term relationship, and the way I see it we're both fine with that – the girl and me. We're taking advantage of each other. And we know it.

But there are exceptions – of course there are exceptions. Sometimes a girl feels cheated or tricked. A lot of crazy things happen in Bushey. Especially in the months after Amy is out of the picture. One of the girls I've been with comes back and claims I've got her pregnant. That there's a price if she's going to do something about it.

'And what does that mean?' I ask.

'It means you've got to pay for a pair of new boobs for me. I want my titties fixed,' she says.

I've no way of knowing if it's true, so at first I try to refuse. But when she threatens to go to the *Sun* it's too difficult to overlook. So I end up paying for her trip to the cosmetic surgeon.

Another night, a girl chucks a cobblestone through the back window of one of my Porsches. I'm up in the apartment, and I can hear her shouting and screaming, but I don't go outside. There's nothing to talk about. She's pissed off because I don't want to keep seeing her.

On a third night, a girl checks my phone while I'm asleep. I guess she finds out I've got a few others on the go besides her. The next morning she's gone. So are my clothes. They've been thrown out of the window and are lying on the footpath.

DURING THE WINTER, Andrey Arshavin arrives from Zenit St Petersburg. The Russian club won the UEFA Cup in May 2008, but during the Champions League group stage in the autumn, the team go out to Real Madrid and Juventus, and Arshavin is allowed to leave.

He doesn't make much of an impact, but one day after training he comes over and asks some questions in broken English. I get enough to find out that he's a few years older than me and that his family are still in Russia. The others on the team have recommended me as a tour guide if he wants to experience London nightlife.

'Can you take me out one night?' he asks.

We can certainly arrange that! We start by eating at Nobu, then we head on to Boujis, which isn't your typical footballer nightclub. The whole place is a little more edgy and high maintenance. Membership is £500 and the members include hotshot artists and aristocrats – members of the ancient British upper classes.

Prince Harry, who is an Arsenal fan, is often there. And when he is, he comes over for a chat. Although Harry may have had a really tough upbringing, he's not like the tabloids make out. He's always really nice with everyone. Always friendly, always down to earth.

I'm not saying Arshavin drinks like there's no tomorrow. Things are going a little slowly and when we get our table in the VIP section, I misunderstand and order vodka for us both. Although he's a Russian, he's not having any of it.

'What about whisky?' he asks.

When the waitress brings over a whisky bottle and a mixer, he waves his hand dismissively.

'Just whisky,' he says.

The alcohol softens him up, and we pretty quickly end up talking about loving your club. Arshavin has played for Zenit since he was seven years old.

'Zenit is in my heart,' he says, asking whether I have a club that is the same for me back in Denmark.

I don't. I'm definitely seriously fond of FC Copenhagen, and I would watch matches from the Lower C stand back in the day. But it's not the same. If I had been given permission to train with the FC Copenhagen first team back in 2004, it would be in my heart. But to have feelings that strong, I need to try out the product first. So I have to play for the team and wear the strip. Now I can't get any closer to that than Arsenal. And that's probably how it'll stay. That was why I didn't leave last summer. And that's why I don't want to go to Spartak Moscow, even though Michael Laudrup is now the manager and the money on offer is temptingly big.

I like my Russian teammate. He has a dry sense of humour

and the most outlandish laugh. It sounds like a grunting donkey, and he just can't stop if he happens to say something he finds the slightest bit funny.

On one occasion, we have a European away fixture in Russia. Afterwards, we hit the town. Now it's Arshavin's turn to show me around. And believe me when I tell you that he's on home turf. Every door is open, everyone is buying. He reigns supreme like a king – even though he barely measures up to my ribcage. Arshavin's fellow countrymen regard him as a kind of demigod. They're completely subservient. I think to myself how he must be as big a deal here as Beckham is in England.

On that subject, I see a TV report on YouTube many years later. In the clip, Arshavin comes swaying out of a nightclub in Moscow. He gets onto a horse and rides off. Just like that. He's kind of crazy and unpredictable. Even though he's a faithful club man, he's curious about everything he hasn't tried before. That's certainly one way of putting it. He's a man after my own heart.

WE QUICKLY become friends and when we play West Bromwich Albion away in March 2009, we both start up front. Van Persie is on the bench, and Adebayor hasn't even made the matchday squad, so it's basically up to the two of us to deliver. So we do. I put us 1-0 up and score again to make it 3-1 just before the break. During the second half I hit the woodwork. It's awful to think about. Just a centimetre separates me from my first hat-trick for the club.

I stay in the flow. Twice I play Arshavin into space in front of goal, and even though he misses them both it's obvious there's a chemistry between us on the pitch as well as off it.

Afterwards, Wenger is very satisfied. He tells the BBC I've visibly become more dangerous every three months.

'That is the right way to mature. I liked his presence. I liked his determined attitude and the way he took people on. That shows he has improved.'

I've scored eight goals during spring 2009 in the league alone, and the Gooners sing my song pretty frequently. Even when I'm not scoring.

'Super Nick, super-super Nick!'

I love it. Especially since I no longer have to put up with being a supersub. I'm part of the squad rotation. It's only in the really big matches that the boss prefers the experienced attack forces.

The English championship is well out of sight. Manchester United are running away with it, and it just happens to be Alex Ferguson's team that we meet in the semi-final of the Champions League. During the first leg, we're beaten 1-0 at Old Trafford. I have to settle for playing the last 19 minutes, so when I get less than half an hour in the return leg I'm not at all happy. By then, United are 3-0 up and it feels like a waste of time and effort. We are obviously not going to create five goals against one of Europe's best defences.

After the match, my teammates hurry home. They keep their heads down, grumble and set their alarm clocks so they can make it to the debrief and light training session the next morning. Everyone except me.

It all begins pretty innocently. A friend comes out with me to eat, and after a couple of drinks my mood has improved a couple of notches. Like on so many other occasions before, the alcohol soothes my disappointment and we agree to carry on to Boujis. I message a Danish girl that I'm kinda on-and-off dating. I've flown her in earlier that day and we agree to meet in the members' only section.

The next thing I remember is my bathtub in Bushey. My teeth are chattering and the water is ice cold. I'm still wearing clothes, and I've pulled my leather jacket over my head. My trousers are around my knees. Everything is soaked – my shirt, tie, jeans and Converse – but somehow my mobile is still working. There are a number of missed calls. An immense number.

When I get online, I see myself everywhere. In a photo that turns up everywhere, I'm being escorted to a cab with the jacket pulled over my head. My trousers are in exactly the same place in the photo as they are in the bathtub. It looks insane. Insanely scary, because I remember absolutely nothing.

I get hold of my friend who tells me what he knows. After hanging out in the bar area, one of the totally aggressive gold-diggers came over. I suddenly began chatting at random and from then it didn't take many seconds before we disappear off towards the toilets. Here we must apparently have done the deed. Or at least we tried to. Then I passed out, and no one – not my mate or my Danish girl – can get hold of me.

When Boujis closes an hour passes while they try to get through to me. I stagger as I'm escorted out to my taxi. The driver has pulled right up to the main entrance, but that's not enough to save me. At shit o'clock at night there's no one there but a bunch of paparazzi standing by, waiting. Someone inside has tipped them off – no doubt about it. They flash away as if their lives depended on it.

There is absolutely nothing that dawns on me. But I remember a night a couple of years earlier at NASA in Copenhagen, during the summer of 2007. On that occasion, a mate took my drinks, which is when it all went wrong for him. He ended up in Copenhagen University Hospital and the doctors thought he'd been doing drugs. But it was my drinks that had been messed with.

Someone or other had put something in my glass, and the same must have happened at Boujis. They call it 'spiking'. That has to be the explanation. I mean, I wouldn't vanish off to the loos with some random girl while I was waiting for a date. I'm not that crazy. And I wouldn't pass out from drinking booze either. To be honest, I'm not that out of practice.

The media make a big deal out of it. Wenger isn't happy, and for the second season in a row he fines me two weeks' wages.

I don't regret when I squared off against Adebayor. But I would have preferred to do without this. It's an act of utter stupidity. The kind of act of stupidity only stupid lads commit. And unfortunately it's a public act of stupidity that will only be the first of many.

IMMORTAL

2009

MY FINAL MATCH of the season is with Denmark. It's June 2009 and we're playing Sweden away. The 1-0 win is absolutely perfect for us. It means we are masters of our own World Cup fate, while we also get payback for last time. The scandal at Parken cost us a trip to the Euros – now we're costing them the World Cup. It's a bearable trade-off.

In the opening stages of the match, it all looks shit. Simon Kjær, making his debut, manages to concede a debatable penalty, and we're pressed so hard I have to go back to break up the Swedes' play. My pressing game has never been my strong suit, but I do my bit and climb the highest to reach one of Fredrik Ljungberg's venomous crosses.

Fortunately, Thomas Sørensen is himself. Our ever-friendly last man standing holds the fort and pulls off one class save after another. In fact, I don't think he's ever stepped out of Peter Schmeichel's shadow as much as in this match.

Afterwards, we're sentenced to our summer holidays, but I don't plan to relax – not yet. First, I'm going to get smashed. I've moved out to the Hilton by Copenhagen Airport because the Hotel d'Angleterre in the city centre is under refurbishment. It's a good bargain. The presidential suite is big enough for me to have 20 Amager lads round.

We get started early. Room service makes sure we can have lunch while we play cards and dice. When we've really started getting the beers in, my phone rings. A girl's voice introduces herself as Caroline.

'Thanks for yesterday,' she says. 'It was SO lovely to meet you.'

'I don't think we've met,' I reply.

'Yes, yes! At MASH with all your friends. You came upstairs and fetched me – you asked whether I wanted to have a drink with you.'

'You'll have to forgive me, but that wasn't actually me. I didn't go out to any restaurant yesterday.'

'Hmm, okay,' says the voice on the line. And then along it comes, of course. Because everyone always wants something:

'But now that I've got you anyway…'

'Yes?'

'Well, we're making this TV show where I move in with people. Today it's with two fantastic kids up here in Gilleleje – and do you know what? They're your two biggest fans in the whole world! They're dying to meet you!'

Long story short, she wants me to run out the door and drive to the north coast of Zealand to be in some shoot for something I've never even heard of. I explain that there's no chance. I've had a beer and have my own show on the go. But she just won't take no for an answer. Eventually, I promise to get back to her. I just need to call home.

It turns out my mum knows all about the pushy lady.

'It's her from Kanal 5!' she exclaims. 'Caroline Fleming. She's a baroness.'

Mum urges me to do it. After the shitshow at Boujis, it would look good if I took the time to surprise a couple of kids as part of a TV show.

'It's about helping families in need. That's a good thing. And you have been talking about starting a charity,' she adds.

Granted, my mum is right about that. I have been talking about it. I hang up and go back to my friends. They're also familiar with the baroness.

'She's shit hot, totally loaded after a divorce,' says one of them. It's not long before all my friends are shouting along in unison:

'Do it, do it, do it!'

I get picked up by a runner and driven up to Gilleleje. Once I'm there, I stand around waiting behind a hedge while the baroness – wearing sunnies, a silk suit and high heels – plays football with the two lads on the long grass.

'I could do with a little help. I could do with a little help,' she says.

That's my cue – and I make my entrance as the big surprise. Before I can say hi to the boys, the baroness throws herself around my neck. She acts totally like we're best friends.

'Hey Niiiiiiicklas!' she shrieks. 'It's so great you could come!'

Everyone is happy. Obviously things go the way they're meant to and they actually end up keeping their word. I'm there for less than half an hour before I can bugger off again.

A couple of days later the baroness writes to me. She says she lives in London too and would love to buy me dinner when I'm back in town. By way of thanks for helping out.

I'VE INVITED my mum, dad and little brother to California for a fortnight – but before that I have to head home to Bushey to pack my holiday things. I've got three days and I make use of my stopover to see a couple of proper women.

The first night I go out for dinner with a friend who is 16 years my senior. Despite the age difference, I've been kinda into her and I know by now that it's reciprocated. But neither of us has dared go for it.

Nadia. She's just different. She says what she thinks, but she never judges me. Lately, people have been way too busy judging me. As if they know me inside out. As if there can't be two sides to the same coin.

It's been going on for eight months, ever since she came by Bell Lane and gave yoga instruction to the first team squad. Afterwards, I hired her for a few one-on-one sessions. One thing led to another and we began going for walks together, eating together, hanging out together. But nothing more than that. Still nothing more.

We've not had a workout between the sheets, and in a way she's become my longest project. Ever.

Now it's happening. We end up in her tiny flat and go all the way. It's an amazing experience. It really does mean something to wait so long for someone.

The next night I'm meeting Caroline, who's actually an ex-baroness. I put on my suit, buy a bunch of roses and meet her at Draycott Avenue in Chelsea. It's probably the most expensive, fancy neighbourhood in the city. Her chauffeur drives us to Nobu, and it turns into a fun night. We drink the bar dry. Forty-two Passion Fruit Martinis – that's how many we manage to drink before we move on.

On the third day I see Nadia again. I don't say what I've done, but when it's time to go she gets really upset – she's totally crushed.

I've never got away from that. That my whole life, my whole career could have looked totally different if it had been her that I spent my last night in London with.

But instead, I'm ringing Caroline's doorbell just an hour later. This time I'm not wearing a shirt and jacket. I'm wearing a cap and tracksuit. Like the Amager lad I can be. When she opens the door I get the funniest look. As if she's thinking: Is that really the guy I was with last night?

IT'S MY THIRD start in the Arsenal first team. And it's now. Now is the time. If I'm going to fulfil my ambitions, this has to be the season in which I become a fixture in the starting eleven and score loads of goals at the highest level. Otherwise I'll lose my patience. That ever-present threat. I notice it as a constant jitter – something that boils over into irritation or slightly crazy actions when not enough is happening.

Judging by the Emirates Cup, Arsenal's pre-season tournament, it looks a reasonable assumption. If the squad remains the same, I'll be starting up front with Arshavin and van Persie.

Over the summer, Arsène Wenger has recast our match formation. We've gone from 4-4-2 to 4-5-1. Arshavin plays out on the left, van Persie leads the attack and I head onto the right wing. It's not my favourite position, but it's a step in the right direction towards solid match time. That's not the only thing that's happened. The boss is also in the process of disbanding 'the African clique'. It's actually pretty normal to form groups with the people you get along best with. Sometimes it's about something as low-key as being able to talk to each other effortlessly. Footballers aren't all language geniuses – including me – so the French talk to the French, the Spanish talk to the Spanish. And I stick with the lads from England and Wales. Jack Wilshere, Aaron Ramsey, Kieran Gibbs and so on. Not that that means I *only* hang out with them. It's not that divided.

'The African clique' is a term invented by someone in the media. And while I've got nothing against Touré, Song, Gallas or Eboué (who is also rumoured to be leaving), it's good news for me. You see, Adebayor has just been sold to Manchester City, and I won't miss him. Some hacks have written that Wenger had to choose between us. To be honest, I hope they're right.

EVEN THOUGH I start in the Premier League, play well and provide some assists, the goals don't happen for me. We win most of our matches, but the goals come from the second and third lines. It's our midfield and back line who secure our victories. People like Denílson, Vermaelen and Gallas. And, of course, Cesc.

I don't panic. Wenger knows what I stand for. It'll come. In fact, I'm so confident about it that I've clubbed together with Arshavin for a VIP box for our guests at the Emirates. We take the biggest one available. With the player discount, the cost for the rest of the season is almost £50,000 each. But then again, there's room for 15 people, a private bathroom and a waiter included in the price.

I'm good at using the box, and I always have friends and family visiting. One day a guy phones up – it turns out he's a big-shot banker back home in Denmark. He introduces himself as Lars Seier and wants to know whether I can help him out with a couple of tickets for the next Arsenal home game. I like his style – really direct – so I invite him to the box. It marks the beginning of a friendship that continues to this day. We have some bad-boy traits in common. And we aren't intimidated by the picture painted of us by the media.

There's something else I like about Lars. I like that he's a little older. That's come to me over time. The more stuff that happens to me, the better I feel around people who have got a few years under their belts. That way our baggage matches, if you get my drift.

Perhaps it's the same with women. After all, Caroline isn't many years younger than Nadia. There's a 13-year age gap between us, and somehow that turns me on. How she must have her own shit together. How it's not all up to me.

MY DAD says there's a prospect of an improved contract at Arsenal. This is seriously good news because I'm saving nothing. Still. My latest purchase is an Aston Martin DBS. Aston Martin is the original James Bond sports car – and it blows everything else I've tried out of the water. It feels legit. Like it's filled with the past even though it's come straight from the factory.

Nadia has been sidelined, while I'm seeing more and more of Caroline. Our chemistry feels insanely powerful. It's hard to explain – it's just there. When she smiles, I smile. And the other way around.

However, nothing is official. We haven't agreed to be boyfriend and girlfriend or anything, so I'm still seeing other girls and they sometimes come home with me to Bushey or to the hotel room I have on standby.

Maybe I'm scared of giving Caroline a real chance. Even though there's something appealing about older women, it's also a bit of a handful. After all, she has two kids from her broken marriage. This is something my mum keeps bringing up. But she's only sceptical half the time. The rest of the time, she seems impressed. My grandma is the same. She reads all the gossip mags – she always has. In her world, the royal family and nobility are basically demigods. It's clearly a bigger deal to date a former baroness than it is to play for Arsenal. Even my dad seems curious. He doesn't normally take any interest in my girlfriends.

Personally, I don't care. I mean – it was fun to meet Prince Harry and his big brother on the London nightlife scene, but it wasn't anything more than that. Other people are other people – and if you imagine otherwise you end up being disappointed.

But I do have some use for it. You see, the Amager lads have started to call me baronen – meaning the baron, or the lord. An Amager boy who became a baron and got a baroness…It has a ring to it. It sounds like an adventure.

IN SEPTEMBER 2009, Morten Olsen does something unusual. He speaks out in the press: says that I am the whole package, but that I'm not scoring enough. That something needs to happen on that front.

'Score more goals,' he says.

I know he's right. I need to be more cynical – more selfish. I should go for the goal instead of sticking to the Arsenal way and providing nothing but assists.

We play Portugal at Parken. It's the third time I'm playing against the Portuguese since my national debut. In the first two matches, I scored. And I'd prefer to continue that way. We need to secure a point from the match if we want to go to the World Cup in South Africa, and towards the end of the first half it's still 0-0. I've lost two balls that have been played on to me, and Martin Jørgensen – who is out on the wing – has lost patience.

'Nick,' he shouts. 'You need to fucking get on it!'

We're not exactly mates off the pitch. But on the pitch that doesn't really matter. He's a teammate and we have to achieve something together. So I listen to him and try to get in gear.

Michael Silberbauer gets the ball on the left-hand side of the Portuguese box. There's plenty of people in it, and I'm immediately picked out despite the heavy defence. The cross sails in towards the penalty spot. It's arcing in a way that means I just know it has to be controlled with my chest.

On the training pitch in Elsinore with Jon Dahl, Søren Larsen and Morten Olsen,
September 2009. (Photo: Keld Navntoft/Ritzau Scanpix)

Just before I set off, my marker turns around to look for the ball. He ought to be keeping his eyes on me, and a half second of inattention is all it takes. I give him a shove and take his place. My chest reaches the ball high up, and the bounce is so small that no one can reach it to stop it. Not even Pepe, even though he tries. A lot of people call Pepe a sick bastard, and on TV we've all seen him lose his temper. But to me he's always behaved fairly. He doesn't do anything heavy handed when the referee looks away, and he says thank you after the match.

I let the ball hit the pitch and use the energy from the bounce to give my shot some extra force – almost like when goalies use their goal kick to start a counter-attack. My left instep hits the ball sweetly and it shoots off like a rocket into the top of the net. Completely unstoppable.

The sequence – from control to goal – takes less than two seconds and feels like one gliding movement. I'm at one with the game and don't have to make any decisions. The decisions make themselves and my body just follows orders.

When I see the ball go in, I don't really think it's anything special. To me, it's an okay goal – but also it's going to be one of many. I'm going to carry on the way Morten Olsen wants me to. I'm going to pull my finger out and score a few more. But the lads are celebrating like it's totally outstanding. Martin Jørgensen comes over and pats me on the cheek.

'What the hell are you playing at?' he says. 'I didn't bloody tell you to put it in the roof of the net, did I?' Maybe he's all right when it comes down to it. I really don't know.

Four days later, I also score our goal against Albania in Tirana. And three days after that I'm in the Arsenal squad heading to Manchester. We're playing City, who've been bought by a bunch of oil sheikhs. It's more than just a match at the top of the league – it's the match in which we're facing Adebayor for the first time.

It's clear to everybody that he's totally sulky and pissed off. In the *Daily Telegraph* he talks about leaving Arsenal and calls me spoiled. He's quoted as saying, 'I was not born with a golden spoon in my mouth' – unlike me. That kind of thing.

I've no idea where he's got his information from, because we weren't exactly swimming in expensive cutlery while I was growing up. It's weird to read. It goes from being a football squabble to something much more personal. As if he somehow has more of a right to behave badly because I had an easier time as a kid.

However, it's impossible for me to be Adebayor's biggest enemy. That honour goes to the Gooners. When he scores during the second half, he runs three quarters of the pitch – all the way to the away section – and does a five-metre slide on his knees while cupping his hands around his ears. Did you say something? Pure provocation.

I've never seen our supporters that angry before. People are spitting, whistling, throwing all sorts. To me it seems ungrateful. It seems contemptible – really contemptible actually, the more I think about it. Wenger brought Adebayor to Arsenal, and gave him the chance to have a big career over several seasons. He ought to show some gratitude instead of this. Who was using the word spoiled again?

MY DAD has gone solo as a football agent. Even though he's still not passed his FIFA exam, that hasn't stopped him. Quite the opposite. We've split from David Manasseh and the rest of Stellar Group. And not without drama. They were so livid. There was also a dispute over my Nike contract that we had to sort out. Fortunately, they didn't get anything, and that makes my dad so smug and self-confident he reminds me of me on my worst days. Or perhaps it's me who is like him.

I have no clue about the new contract. How good it is, or anything like that. But Dad reassures me. He says it's twice as good as the old one. That it will secure my future for the next five years.

While he wants to celebrate his triumph, I have a hard time rejoicing with him. Our relationship has become less about family and more professional.

At least my money is good enough for them. Both my parents have quit their jobs. They say they want to slog on behalf of my career. In return, I make sure they never want for anything.

They have more and more ideas. Like when my mum suggests I look up one of her friends in Tårnby. Her friend is a professional fortune-teller. Or a clairvoyant, as she calls herself.

I don't know whether I believe in the power of thought, but the sessions provide me with some okay exercises. I have to close my eyes and see the things I want to do – goals and actions and so on. Then when I'm in that situation in reality, it won't feel like it's the first time. These thoughts will equip me with a sense of routine so that I spend less time having to think. It actually makes sense.

It's also Mum's friend's idea to change squad number. She thinks 26 is a shit number for me, because 2 + 6 = 8, which is my so-called 'bad number'. She's found this out…somehow. According to the friend, 7 is my lucky number, my strength number. Unfortunately, 7 is already taken. And 25 – 2 + 5 = 7 – was Adebayor's, which means it's all tied up with bad karma.

It might all sound totally superstitious to you. But believe me, I've seen worse. There are people who have to put on their left boot first. People who have to cross themselves. People who have to kiss their necklace. And so on.

We settle for 52 in the end. When it's made official, everyone thinks it's a hint about my new wages. That I must get £52,000 a week. That wouldn't be a very smart move for the fans, but my dad sorts it out. He says he has a plan that will change people's minds. I'm going to be promoted as B52. The B52 is an old US military bomber plane, and I'm the human bomber.

Things go so far that they make a film of me on the wing of a military plane. There I am, juggling a ball, and inside the aircraft I'm interviewed about all sorts of stuff. The whole thing gets posted on a website being run by my parents and a PR company in my name: www.nicklas-bendtner.com.

I feel kinda sick when I think about what that internet project must have cost me over the years. The expenses quickly add up. For instance, anyone who has bought my shirt from the Arsenal shop can get it changed for a shirt with the new number – and the bill gets sent to me.

STILL, I feel pretty okay about everything. Both in life and with my mum's fortune-telling friend. Things are going my way. I mean, the English press have started to praise me, my club is crawling towards the top of the table, I'm earning tonnes of money and I've got rid of my biggest enemy in the dressing room.

And on top of everything else, I've fallen in love. There's no doubt about it – not any longer. For the first time in my life I'm floating around on cloud nine.

It's awesome, and I get the idea into my head that it's something you can only experience once in your life. Once you've tried tempestuous infatuation – the kind of infatuation that's beyond teenage puppy love – things can never be the same again. You may well feel something even deeper later on in life, but that insane feeling is one you can't get back. Not ever.

On 26 September 2009, after we have beaten Fulham 1-0 away, and I've once again played a full match up front with Arshavin and van Persie, we're approaching the top three in the Premier League. A new team of invincibles is under construction, and I'm part of it. It's almost perfect. If I were leading the attack and it was van Persie on the right, then I would have nothing to complain about.

I head straight over to Caroline's in Kensington. It's the night I get to meet her two kids, Josephine and Alexander. They're cute – it's a really great experience. Like getting a whole new family. Once they're asleep, we agree to make it official. Including all the commitment that goes with it.

The next morning, I get into my Aston Martin and head for training at Bell Lane. I'm in the best mood ever. I feel like I did when I chugged a bottle of Fisherman the night before my first training camp with Denmark. Although not like that either. That feeling times a thousand. I'm happy, invincible, immortal. That's how I feel. Nothing can touch me, and when I hit the motorway I put my foot down and turn up Andrea Bocelli.

ACCIDENT

2009–2010

THERE'S A MEMBRANE covering London – a blanket of rain and exhaust fumes. It lingers in the streets whether it's windy or not. I've always thought it's the price you pay for living in the world's coolest city. There has to be a downside that keeps us Londoners grounded. The grey weather is all for the common good. So there's space for us. If the sky were cloudless, no one would ever bother living anywhere else in the world.

Today, Sunday 27 September 2009, is an exception. The sun is shining and the birds are singing in the bushes behind the petrol station on the A1. I've stopped to fill up, but I'm really on my way to a combined training and debrief session following the away match at Fulham on Saturday. I was the only striker that got all 90 minutes and Arsène Wenger's trust in me seems greater than ever. It warms the cockles of my heart to think about it. There's a lot warming me at the moment.

When I get back behind the wheel, the stereo Bluetooth is bugging me. For once I can hear the insistent beep-beep-beep reminding me that I've forgotten to put my seat belt on. I feel like I'm flying and unbeatable, but I still buckle up. Otherwise the beeping just keeps going on and on and on.

Andrea Bocelli and Frank Sinatra are crooning in shifts in harmony with the roaring cylinders, and I slowly push the accelerator towards the floor. I love driving hard. It's one of the things that can give me a rush when I can't get it on the football pitch. But right now it's not something I really need. I'm getting enough of a rush on the pitch. And between the sheets.

Maybe I'm doing 70mph as I approach the exit for London Colney. It's just me and another car ahead of me – but suddenly there's one car too many. Without indicating, he cuts across the painted lines and into my lane. It's impossible for me to brake to get out of the situation – I have to dodge him and turn the wheel sharply to the left. I just manage to think to myself that it might be good enough – but then I spot the kerb. As my two left wheels slam across it, the tyres blow right away. My entire upper body is heading out of the windscreen but the seatbelt holds me in place while the car rises in slow motion. I'm floating. Past the crash barrier and onto the bank. The real rough ride begins as the car makes its landing. The car turns over and over and I spin with it. I'm being torn at from all sides – down, down, down. There's so much happening right before my eyes there isn't space for my life to flash before me. And then bang! Suddenly everything goes white. Three airbags manage to envelope me before the car smashes into something big. Everything is clanking and creaking – and then… silence. I must still be alive.

The inside of the car has been transformed into a one-man kayak. Thighs, knees and feet are tangled up with each other. One more rotation and I could have kissed goodbye to my abdomen.

I pull my legs free and crawl out on my stomach. I get to my feet. I'm standing in a field at the foot of a steep bank covered in small trees that have been ripped to shreds by my former Aston Martin. Feeling slowly returns to my right leg. The blows to my hip must have paralysed it.

Now comes the adrenaline rush. The car is a crumpled mess. One wing mirror is dangling and I tear it off completely. I undress until I'm standing naked in that field. I use the mirror to check my body's blind spots. Whether it's all still there – or if there's something out of place. The seat belt has left a glowing red burn mark, and I've got splinters of glass in my cheeks, neck and arms. Otherwise there's nothing to see. Nothing serious.

Up by the motorway a man appears. It's only when he gets all the way down to me that I realize it's not the driver of the other car. That bastard must just have driven on.

The man suggests I put my clothes back on. Says it'll look weird when the ambulance arrives. I do as he says. Afterwards, I call the club.

'There's been an accident. I'm going to be a bit late for training,' I say.

'You must be in shock,' the man says when I've ended the call.

No one really gets how lucky I was. Not even me. It's only many years later when I show the photos in the newspaper to F1 driver Kevin Magnussen that it sinks in.

'You should be dead. You're only alive because you were driving a really expensive sports car. That's the only reason,' he says.

The *Sun* published an article with the cheeky headline: 'Nicklas Bent-car'.

I know full well that I ask for some of the crap I get. But making fun of a car crash that could have ended in deep tragedy? Come on.

After training, I head to Caroline's. She sends everyone else out of the house and takes care of me like my mum would have done. It feels like being little again. That's how much I get spoiled.

At the club, it's more or less business as usual. On the Monday – the day after the accident that wrote off my car after it rolled over for several hundred metres – I train on my own on the fitness bike and they note I've avoided a concussion. Wenger decides quite rightly to rest me for the Champions League game on the Wednesday, but the next Sunday when we hammer Blackburn 6-2, I get to seal the goal fest. It's a gem, lashed in from over 20 yards out while running at full pelt, and it goes in off the inside of the post.

A little after the match, I notice a tear in my right knee. I must be mistaken, I think to myself, ignoring it. But the pain comes back. In the bath, I examine it and glimpse a shard of glass. It's gone halfway through my kneecap. I pull it out, put a plaster on and say nothing about it to anyone. If I did, they'd examine me from my head to my arse, and the second they thought there was something seriously up with me I'd be straight to the back of the queue.

During the course of October, I fight back and score an easy goal against Liverpool. I take the ball with my heel, dribble away from Martin Škrtel with lightning-fast footwork and lift it up just below the crossbar with my left foot. It's a class goal, and if it hadn't been in the Carling Cup then it would have won a bunch of awards.

When we play Spurs at home, I'm back in the Premier League starting line-up. That lasts until the 37th minute. Then I'm tackled by two opponents, and although they don't actually do anything against the rules, they manage to hit me so hard something snaps. The pain emanates from somewhere deep in the pit of my stomach, tingling in my bowels. I cry out and have to be carried off the pitch. The next day the doctors are clear in their verdict: my groin is in pieces. I'm out for four months. At least.

IT'S MOSTLY Caroline who wants to leave for Venice. But I go along with it. We visit the floating city two or three times during autumn 2009. We book a suite at the most expensive hotel – it's gotta be swanky. We also rent a speedboat to take us around the place. And, as usual, it's me who picks up the tab.

I don't know how it gets out, but some Danes must have recognized us. At any rate, we're now gossip fodder. In all the mags you find at any hairdresser's in Denmark. It's my mum who calls to tell me.

I can hear in her voice she's excited about Caroline. But she's naturally also worried.

'Does your coach definitely know you're in Venice?' she wants to know.

The boss doesn't know. But he soon will. Because thanks to the ruckus at Boujis, the Aston Martin crash, my pink football boots and my massive ego, I've also become Hot Stuff in the English tabloids.

They're about to discover Caroline. Until she met me she's managed to fly under the radar. That's another great thing about London. It's so crowded that people lose track. If you really want to live in hiding, it's more than possible.

But now it's a different story. I mean, a former Danish baroness is with a 21-year-old Arsenal player, and she's been married to one of the richest men in England. A relative of James Bond author Ian Fleming – to cap it all. Of course, it makes riveting reading.

When a few of the lads from the team head out to a restaurant or nightclub, it's no longer the biggest stars – Cesc and van Persie – who attract the most attention. The photographers are after me in particular. So much so that the others take the piss.

'You go first, Nicklas. Out you go so the rest of us can be left in peace,' says Cesc when we're about to leave somewhere.

It's pretty funny, but I know it comes with a flipside. It's an interest stemming from nothing genuine. If you step up and bask in it, there's no way out. Then they won't take no for an answer. They'll still be standing there when it's pissing it down in your life.

I decide to try going out less. Instead I become a wine collector. Thomas Sørensen gives me mini tutorials while we're sat on the back row of the Denmark team bus. He buys his bottles through a store called Bordeaux Index. He's really into it and the idea appeals to me too. The best wine is wine that improves with age. One that doesn't push itself forward or mature too soon. Only in the perfect conditions can it develop and deliver the optimum result.

Caroline knows a fair bit about that world. Her father – the baron – had his castle's wine cellars filled with expensive vintages. And of course she knows someone who can help. The husband of one of her friends owns Corney & Barrow – one of Bordeaux Index's competitors – and we invite one of the salesmen over.

The salesman is called Tom Bird and it turns out he's a pretty nice guy around Caroline's age. He's good at his job, because after a couple of hours I've bought £150,000 worth of Bordeaux.

We're only interested in the best. The stuff Caroline likes and I think I may like. Bottles from Petrus, Lafite, Ausone and Margaux.

Eventually, Tom Bird says stop.

'Isn't that enough for now?' he asks.

It occurs to me that maybe he doesn't want to squeeze my pips so hard that afterwards I feel like I've been cheated. I'm doubtless an interesting client to work with – long term, in fact. Young,

Arsenal player, and a big spender. What's not to like?

The next time I hear from him I'm invited to France. To the Bourgogne region and a winery called Romanée-Conti. There's a small party of us. A handful of wealthy men in their 50s and 60s. And me. Corney & Barrow's most important clients. All the others treat the tiny samples like they were drinking liquid diamonds. And to be perfectly honest, I can believe they know a thing or two – but my own taste buds are simply not up to anything that exclusive. It's like casting pearls before swine.

Looking back now, I'm almost ashamed. After all, I've been drinking stuff that true wine buffs idolize. That's what I'm like during those years. I try tonnes of things others can only dream of and I don't really appreciate it for what it is.

Perhaps Tom already saw through me when I was shopping at random during our first encounter, but after a couple of lunches in London he's absolutely sure of himself: I don't know shit about wine.

So we start over. We slowly work out what I'm actually into. And it isn't Bordeaux. Whether it's red or white, I'm way more into Bourgogne. The region where Romanée-Conti is king. Wish I'd figured that out before…

There are lots of upsides to Bourgogne. The pinot noir grape from around there causes less of a headache, and I can easily drink a bottle without any trouble. Bordeaux gives me a dry throat after just a glass or two.

Corney & Barrow can't take back what I've already bought. But the firm can store the bottles for as long as is necessary. And if I want to sell them on, they'll sort that out for me too. The more I think about it, the more I become aware of my spending, the more it appeals to me. Seeing wine as more than just an expensive hobby. Seeing it as a form of investment.

In autumn 2009, I haven't got that far. What I'm trying to do is buy myself – and all sorts of other people – a slice of happiness. Back home in Amager, my little brother gets a brand new Audi for his 18th birthday, and friends and family members get cash for jewellery, holidays and deposits on new homes. Whatever they want, if they come and ask me for it. And they do.

I surprise Jannick with the car when I'm in Copenhagen anyway to attend the Danish Football Awards 2009. It's held in the Circus Building in central Copenhagen and it's a weird show. A little tame to be honest – even if Alex Ferguson is there to hand a special award to Peter Schmeichel. A year earlier, he tried to sign me for Manchester United and now we give each other a friendly hello. And that's it. It's a cold business. And the only one I know.

My instep goal against Portugal is named goal of the year, and at the end of the evening I'm awarded Danish Football Player of the Year. It's handed over by the winner from the year before, Martin Laursen, who I've been pretty cruel to in the Premier League. I like him. He's a class guy who has no need to impress anyone. Laursen is well-balanced. He prefers to praise rather than pressure young players. That's what I want to be like when my career is finally heading towards its end.

It's great to be player of the year – especially at the age of 21. But I'm not all that surprised. Up front on the pitch I've been our highest profile player.

Which is why I'm honest when I get asked about my ambitions afterwards by the newspaper *Ekstra Bladet*.

'I want to be top scorer in the Premier League, and my dream is to win the golden boot at the World Cup – even if that can be hard when you play for a small country. And within the next five years I want to be one of the world's best strikers,' I say.

EVERY TIME someone manages to snap photos of us – at a restaurant or out walking – it all gets whipped up as some big revelation. As if it's a sensation that we're even seeing each other. The fact of the matter is, I already moved in with Caroline and the kids in October.

It's a new world – a very overwhelming one – becoming a de facto stepdad overnight. And I'm starting from scratch. 100 per cent.

Caroline is raising her kids in a completely different way to the upbringing I got. She runs a tight ship with a bunch of rules on how to behave. During mealtimes and all sorts of other times. So I try to listen and do things her way.

It's hard. In my family, we've always sworn and reacted to stuff. I'm from Amager, so it comes naturally. But whenever I say 'fuck' or 'bloody hell' or 'wanker' in the house at Draycott Avenue, the kids demand I put a bank ote in their swear jar. I don't think there's even a Danish word for a swear jar!

One day I can't get into the house. The door is stuck because a children's scooter has got jammed on the other side. Eventually, I kick it down. It just seems the natural thing to do. Nine out of ten people in Amager would do the same. But not here, nor in the castle where Caroline grew up. Once again, she gives me the look. The same look as four months ago. As if I've arrived from outer space.

Although I really like Jose and Alex, it quickly gets tough having a daily existence where you have to get up with the kids and then give it your all before heading to training where you're expected to give even more. I don't know if it makes sense, but I maybe feel like it's extra hard because they're not my own kids that I'm herding around and taking to school and stuff.

When Caroline isn't making TV shows in Denmark – which she doesn't do all that frequently – she has loads of time. She's waiting for me when I get back from London Colney, and she prefers to eat out for lunch. Later, while the nanny stays at home with the kids, we go to dinner parties where we drink wine until the end of the night.

Her friends come from England, Denmark and France. It varies a lot and there aren't many repeat faces from month to month. Compared with my own core group from Amager – and, to be honest, the new gang in London – the churn rate is enormous. It seems like people hook up because they can help each other out in one way or another. What they share in common is wealth. They're almost all loaded, and if they happen to have access to something you'd like to get a finger on then it's easy as anything for them to become your new best friends.

I mostly hang out with the men. It's not difficult, even though they're twice my age. We're all into cigars and wine and that kinda stuff. And I do something for a living they definitely want to hear more about. When they get onto business chat or share prices, it's easy enough to get back in the game. All I have to say is 'Arsenal' or 'Premier League' and I have their attention.

I don't talk to the women much. They don't have much to say to me either. It's as if a lot of the men have picked their partner based on how good looking she is. And nothing else. The woman is a trophy wife to be parked up on the sidelines while he runs his own show. That's why she constantly needs gifts. Otherwise she'll get bored and unhappy.

Caroline's friendship circle is exactly what Adebayor accused me of: they've been born with a shiny spoon in their mouths. They come from old money, as they like to say. On the other hand, I'm nouveau riche and I don't want to feel left out. So I insist on buying dinner. No one can be allowed to think that I'm tight. Or can't afford it. I won't have anyone think that about me.

Caroline is the last person in the world who would stop me. She really loves gifts, and when we're out shopping there's an unspoken rule that I'll be buying her a gift or two. A £20,000 bag or a £5,000 suit. We're talking those kinds of prices. It never comes up that she might be richer than I am. That's how we divide our roles and what suits me best.

ONE NIGHT in December, I borrow Caroline's computer to send an email. It's obviously connected to her phone, because a notification pops up from Messenger. The notification is from a name I recognize. The actor Jonathan Rhys Meyers. The name appears on a DVD boxset on the shelf. A show called *The Tudors*.

I click on the message – I just can't help myself. And I can see they met for a coffee date earlier in the day. He's writing to thank her. It was good to see her at The Connaught – one of the poshest hotels in town.

It seems a bit fishy. People will probably say I'm mistrustful because I've been unfaithful to some girls myself. Thieves think every man steals and all that. But since Caroline and I took the plunge and made it official, I've stuck by her. And it was really my plan to stay that way.

I finish my email, send it off and sit down next to Caroline in the living room. Then I ask her, straight up, whether she knows anyone called Jonathan Rhys Meyers.

'No,' she says. 'Not at all. Why?'

'He's just written to you on Messenger,' I say.

She continues to deny it, and when I wake up the next morning it's really bothering me. When you keep something like that hidden, you have a reason. I know all about that. I call my mum.

'You've got two options,' she says. 'Either you forget all about it, or you confront her.'

I feel like I need to know the truth. I need to know where I stand. So that night I confront Caroline.

'I know that you've met. It was on your computer.'

She has a total breakdown. Even though they only had coffee, and it 'meant nothing', there's tears and everything. But she'd lied to me about not knowing him.

For Christmas, she gets me some hunting gear. Something or other tweedish – the stuff the old money wear. Now I can go out shooting with her friends' husbands. I get my game licence without having to take a test or anything. I just sit down in front of some duke or whatever and tell him I was practically born with a rifle over my shoulder. It's total bullshit, but because of what I do and the circles I've begun to mix in, it all goes without a hitch.

In many ways we carry on as if nothing happened – me and Caroline. And there are good nights at times. But below the surface everything has changed. My infatuation has gone. The spark is missing. She's lied too deeply for me to just forget about it.

The feeling of happiness is gone. I'm still injured, I've lost my regular starting spot and I feel trapped in a house filled with rules. With a woman I can't trust and two kids that can never fully be mine.

I MANAGE to sit out three months. Three months is a long time and in the interim, van Persie has gone the same way I did. Now he is long-term injured, but that isn't really any great help. I'm a long way from the starting eleven. Both Eduardo and Walcott are ahead of me, and against Aston Villa, Manchester United and Chelsea, I only come on as a sub in the dying minutes. Those three matches generate just one point – and that's a problem. Something drastic has to happen, otherwise the championship is beyond our reach. Against Liverpool, it's my turn to start and we win 1-0. From then on, the berth is more or less mine.

Trust works wonders. I'm back where I left off and I score against both Sunderland and Stoke City. When our visitors are Burnley, I get at least three solid-gold chances. I hit the post, put a header a foot wide and end up kicking the last one into a teammate. It's comical, because I'm literally exactly where I should be. After 74 minutes, the boss has had enough. On the way off, I notice the odd atmosphere in the stadium. No boos, but quite a lot of laughter as they clap me off the pitch. I think it's probably meant mockingly. Like they were saying 'finally he was saved from his own misery'. In the video footage, you can see that I can't help but smile as I high five Eduardo who is coming on. That's how absurd it is.

The next day the press nail me. I simply can't bear to read what the *Sun* has to say about me, but when the usually objective BBC call my efforts 'embarrassing', it makes for uncomfortable reading.

Wenger is immune to that kind of thing. He sees more than chance in my performance, he tells me.

When the *London Evening Standard* demands that I'm dropped from the Champions League game against Porto, he steps in to defend me:

'I believe he is on the way up in his game and in terms of his contribution,' says our manager.

We left Portugal with a 2-1 deficit from the first match, so we need to win the return leg at home if we're to advance to the quarter-finals. But we've still not lost a European game at the Emirates, which is clearly something in the back of the Portuguese minds.

Arshavin is playing like greased lightning, and after just a few minutes he gets to a header that their goalkeeper manages to reflex save. Just after, the Russian once again causes havoc but at the last moment he's tackled by the goalie and a defender. The loose ball escapes from them and I step past an opponent and get the tip of my boot to it. There aren't many tall strikers who can react quickly enough to such a sudden chance. And none of them come from Togo. 1-0.

We push harder and halfway through the first half Arshavin dribbles past his marker. The Porto players are struggling to rein him in, and when he smacks the ball hard between the back line and the goalkeeper, all I have to do is put my foot to it. That's two easy goals – but I've been in the right place without being offside. That's the art.

During the second half, Arshavin continues his massacre with yet another couple of deadly assists. When we hit stoppage time it's 4-0 and the quarter-finals are well and truly in the bag. But then Eboué is brought down and the referee points to the spot. I'm in no doubt. The penalty kick is mine and no one protests. I can't imagine blowing it.

I put my shot comfortably in off the left post and then the stands are alive. Everyone is singing along. 'Super-Nick, super-super Nick!'

We've beaten Porto 5-0 and when the whistle is blown I take the ball with me to the dressing room. My first hat-trick ball. Everyone signs it. 'You got lucky!' and that kind of thing.

'Typical you,' says one of them. 'Every time you're left in the lurch, you get up and do something crazy.'

At the press conference, Wenger backs me:

'One of Bendtner's strengths is that he doesn't struggle with self-confidence despite the criticism often levelled at him.'

He's right about that. My family have been over to watch the match, and afterwards I talk to my mum about it.

'Why is that?' I ask.

'Listen to me, Nicklas,' she says. 'You've spent your whole life hitting your head just to get up again. It's always been like that.'

'I'm with you on that,' I say. 'But why? Why the hell can't I just progress normally? Like everyone else?'

'I don't think that's your way,' she says. 'It'll always be like that for you. You'll never get a big wave of good things. There will always be lows in between. And then you'll get back up again.'

The next day the English papers are apologizing for giving up on me after the Burnley match.

The *Guardian*: 'Fortunately, Nicklas Bendtner's prodigious twin took the field, and gave a performance that was as composed and authoritative in front of goal as he was hurried and flustered three days ago.'

In Denmark, it turns out I'm the first Dane to score a hat-trick in the world's finest club tournament in 24 years. It hasn't happened since Michael Laudrup put three past Valur from Reykjavik in 1986. Of course he's a massive player to equal. But to be perfectly honest, I'm totally okay with having scored my hat-trick against the Portuguese champions.

I HAD thought things would turn around. That I'd be less frustrated once I was rid of my injury and that it would rub off on my relationship with Caroline. That we would find our rhythm and pull through. But that's not how it goes. It's as if she can't understand that it takes something extra to be successful as a sportsman. I can no longer be the person I was while I was out injured.

Things were different in that regard with Amy. She had grown up with a dad and big brother who thought about nothing but football. She understood how some consideration had to be applied.

For example: I've been used to taking a nap after training and lunch, and that requirement has only increased since I've started getting up early to help with the kids. But Caroline isn't a fan of my afternoon routine. And she simply doesn't get that I'm a young man – 22 years old – who can't be bothered to spend all his evenings at dinner parties and family dinners. That nights out on the town with the lads sometimes appeal to me.

She talks a lot about us becoming a 'power couple'. How we have a shared brand that needs to be built up. Her dream is for us to become the Elizabeth Taylor and Richard Burton of our era. But she also likes Victoria Beckham. The Beckhams are clearly a source of inspiration too.

Personally, I know David Beckham a little. He spent a month training with Arsenal in 2009, and even though he'd bleached his hair and cut it so short that he seriously stood out, he was a pleasant guy and totally calm and steady. An out-and-out good guy who was in no rush to dominate in the dressing room.

A few years earlier he had been taken to the cleaners by the English press. It's possible he really did have an affair with his personal assistant – there were definitely a lot of things that seemed pretty difficult to explain. But so what? No one on the outside can know how it went down and the way he was treated was decidedly inhumane. Imagine being exposed to the whole world like that just because you're a well-known face. For something so commonplace. It wasn't like he was running around the streets fucking prostitutes or underage kids.

I personally often have a hard time always doing the right thing. At the dinner parties, some of which we're still attending, I zone out of the conversations and drink myself into a stupor on expensive red wine. And I start sneaking out to nightclubs and to hit the casino. Our relationship is doomed – it has been for a long time – and in the spring I move my things out of Draycott Avenue. We're no longer a couple.

WE COME close to beating Barcelona in the first leg of the Champions League quarter-final, but we have to settle for a 2-2 draw at home. Ahead of the return leg, some English hacks find my quotes from the Danish Football Awards. But they don't bother including my caveat about Denmark being a small country that barely ever makes it to the World Cup and I'm unlikely to ever get the chance of being the top scorer of the tournament. Nevertheless, I don't get their angle. What hungry footballer wouldn't dream of developing into one of the very best in their position? And why is that so unrealistic? Over the course of two injury-free months, I've scored seven goals for a team that is – year-after-year – one of the final eight in the strongest club tournament in the world. There aren't many 22-year-olds who can match that. Not right now. There's really only one. His name is Lionel Messi.

When we meet the red and blue team at the Camp Nou, it's actually me who gets off to the best start. Alone with two defenders and Victor Valdés, I reach the ball first on two occasions. Eventually I manage to toe-poke it over the line. The 1-0 lead is enough for us to go through, and with five goals I overtake the little Argentine as the top scorer in the Champions League for the season. But my satisfaction is short-lived, because after that he scores four phenomenal goals. A left-footer into the right corner. A right-foot chip into the left corner. A lob over Almunia. And finally a rock-solid nutmeg straight through the legs of the poor goalie. I've never seen anything like it.

It's a thing of beauty, but it's a mixed blessing to see it first-hand. Because I've been playing well. In addition to my goal, I've delivered two huge free kicks and a header that's hit the inside of the post. Still, I pale in comparison. And for the first time I realize that all my talk of becoming the best of the best is going to remain just that – talk. We can all forget about it. Everyone except Messi. No one in my generation will ever even come close to him. On his best days he has serious superpowers.

But maybe being not quite as good as Messi is okay. Back in London, I'm genuinely chuffed when the Gooners name me player of the month for March. Right ahead of Cesc. The fans who started the month by laughing at me have capitulated.

I keep riding my wave. I score again against Tottenham. At the end of the match, van Persie comes on. It's his first time on the pitch in five months, but he does well and after a mere two games he's back in the starting eleven. At my expense.

For the first time in my Arsenal career, I've been at the front of the queue and in no time at all I've scored nine goals in the Premier League and Champions League. I've stretched myself hard to come out of the cold and hold my own. I've sorted out my personal life so I can dedicate myself to football. Pushed myself hard in training, even when my body has complained and told me to stop. In spite of that – even though I'm sacrificing myself like never before – van Persie only has to get back on form before I have to give up my spot. I see it as a sign from the boss. Van Persie is his number one. No matter what. It hurts.

But I've got other things to worry about. Other pains. You see, my groin is still a problem. With two weeks until the squad is announced for the World Cup, it's getting worse and worse. The more I think about it, the more pessimistic I get. Maybe I didn't make it out of that car crash scot-free. Maybe the rollercoaster ride was so brutal that my body is no longer holding together. Not like it used to.

GAMBLER

2010–2011

IT CUTS up through from my groin. Up through my abdomen and flowing into the pit of my stomach. It's a shooting sensation and I have to grit my teeth in a pure reflex response.

The pain. It's there as soon as I move my left leg. If I stay still as a mouse, I don't notice it. At bedtime, I build a pillow fort around me so my legs are fixed in the position I've chosen for the night. Either on my side or on my back.

If the pillows are too loosely arranged, I wake up constantly and that's no good. Bad sleep is a no go for me. It slows down the healing process.

I'm 22 years old and if I'm going to be able to play football – whether at training or in a match – I need to dose myself up with Voltaren. Not the 50 milligram tablets from the Denmark team doctor. The ones from the English doctor. They're four times as strong. In England, they prescribe that kind of thing without asking any difficult questions.

Voltaren – the anti-inflammatory painkiller also used by people with arthritis – is effective, but they recommend against taking it in larger doses over a longer period of time. It harms your internal organs, increases the risk of heart failure, and some people reckon it can darken your mood.

And believe me, my mood is seriously affected in the summer of 2010. Arsène Wenger didn't want me to go to the World Cup in South Africa, and late on in the season I had to play down how bad things were. It was uncomfortable going against his wishes, and now that I'm here there's no doubt about it: I'm still not over that fucking car crash. The one that shook me up like a milkshake and crushed my Aston Martin beyond recognition.

I've been so obsessed with seizing the opportunity once it was finally on offer that I've ignored all warning signs. Including the ones that had hurt like hell. Or rather, the ones that are hurting. Because it still fucking hurts, and if I've given it my all in training or a match, I can't get out of bed the next morning. That's how bad it is.

Even though it must have been obvious to the club's fitness team, no one has actually told me to stop. Not that I know of. No one has encouraged me to take a break. No one except Wenger, and he only said it once van Persie was back to fitness and I was heading to the World Cup with Denmark.

'Stay at home – get ready for next season.'

Now I'm gambling with my health again. I've guaranteed to Morten Olsen that I'm 100 per cent ready. That my injury is recovering and won't get worse if I play in the three group games. On the one hand, I think he can see right through me. He knows full well that things aren't okay. On the other hand, he knows they can't do without me. We both know it.

'If things go the wrong way, Nicklas, then we'll have to send you home again. You're too young to destroy yourself,' he said right until the final squad was announced.

Today I can see that those finals are going to do more harm than good. Because the honest truth is that my groin isn't recovering. It's only getting worse, but I'm keeping that to myself. I'm not going home until we're knocked out. And several of us feel the same. Our key players are so injured that we should be laid up. Me, Simon Kjær, Daniel Agger and Jon Dahl Tomasson.

When the press ask whether things are going forward or backward, we all answer with empty words. We make every possible proviso and say pretty much nothing. And even then, we avoid saying anything they can pin onto us. It's what Jon Dahl calls the 'Vedbæk record'. He's the master of saying absolutely nothing and has no problem wasting the journalists' time. When they wrote shit about the national team in 2008, it was him who led our media boycott. Of course it was.

MY FAMILY have come with us to South Africa, and the older generation have become best buds with Agger's and Kjær's parents. During the spring, my dad and Agger's dad ran into each other in a furniture store, and now they hang out as if things were never any different.

Later on my mum tells me that it's on that trip some home truths dawn on her. By spending time with the other players' parents, she suddenly realizes that our family does things totally differently. The Kjærs and Aggers don't play at being agents, press spokespeople, website managers or advisers. They are in no way dependent on their sons. Agger's dad has his own business, and his mum does some cleaning job out at the airport. Just like she has always done. There's no money at stake. They're proud mothers and fathers – and that's as far as it goes.

Everyone at Arsenal has talked about how incredible the atmosphere is at the World Cup finals, but we barely notice. After a training camp in the mountains, we head straight into a hotel with guards outside Cape Town. We're staying in a bunch of small houses – three players in each one – and running down the clock before the first match. In the mountains we could see giraffes wandering around in the distance, but personally I've got more in common with the animals at Copenhagen Zoo. I suppose this is how they must feel. I feel trapped. There's no room for anything – especially no pranks. Obviously booze is banned, as is leaving the hotel or having visitors in your room. The rules are easier to bend back in Denmark – at the Marienlyst in Helsingør and before that at the Marina in Vedbæk. When Morten Olsen bans us from hitting the town after a match, we hold our own little room party instead.

It's pretty easy, and I'm often the ringleader. The others call me 'Bamm-Bamm' – like the kid in *The Flintstones*. It's a good fit.

Because when we're together, I keep a high profile at nightclubs and drink the hotel bar dry. The Denmark team rooms are at one end of the Marienlyst, and we get a few girls who are up for it to bring supplies and book rooms at the other end.

Once Morten Olsen and the other coaches have gone to bed, we can sneak over. It's a long-held tradition – and it existed well before I arrived on the scene. Actually, it would surprise me if the DBU were completely in the dark about the whole thing. Either that or they turn a blind eye to plenty of stuff so long as it doesn't get out of hand.

Partying with the national squad is almost like playing for the team itself. While everyone sticks to a small clique at their clubs, it's all for one and one for all when you're with your countrymen. The vast majority of people can put up with room sharing, and if anyone happens to get a little intimate with our special guests then there's space for that too.

In football, we talk about never throwing anyone under the bus. That means no grassing people up. Not about some stuff. Stuff done in confidence. You're not a witness to anything that you'd then use to out the guy you've been hanging out with. It's unsportsmanlike and out of the question.

But no one will be hurt by a couple of lightly camouflaged anecdotes about our national team. For example, there was the time we played a strong opposition team at Parken. Even though the match was an important one with a lot at stake, there were no unhappy faces.

A couple of hours after the final whistle, the two nations were at a pub, privately booked out for the night. Thirty footballers and the same number of women that I'd been involved in selecting and inviting. Totally hot ones. If our room parties could end up on the wild side, this one was completely mindless. Pure rock 'n' roll – except without the hard drugs.

At one point I was standing looking out of the windows near the top of the walls in this basement bar – straight out at one of the opposition team's players, who was up on the street and in the middle of satisfying a Danish reality TV star. Later on, he and a couple of teammates took three of the women back to the hotel and got an orgy going. You'd probably call that hospitality done the Copenhagen way.

MORTEN OLSEN is grumbling. He is anything other than happy about the injury situation. But that doesn't change anything. He is gradually becoming the only man – or at least one of the very few – that I respect completely without any reservations. I mean, he's always telling me off, but it's almost always a fair cop. Like last autumn in Helsingør, where Søren Belling and his little boy came to watch the Denmark squad train. Afterwards, I invited them back to the hotel for a bottle of pop. I had completely forgotten that we are supposed to register visitors like that in advance. When Morten Olsen found out, he totally lost his shit. Right there in the middle of the hotel bar in front of the other guests.

'What makes you think the rules don't apply to you? How many times do I have to tell you?'

I had nothing to say in my defence.

There's no malice when I forget that kind of thing. I was just trying to cheer up Søren's son and didn't fully consider the consequences. It just happens. Less frequently than it used to – but it still happens.

If the old guard still have a grudge against me, they're hiding it well. I feel accepted. We've partied together our fair share – here and there – and we've covered for each other. They're a practised bunch. Most of them have been around since the beginning of Olsen's reign ten years ago, but I'm no longer the baby. Far from it. That honour goes to Christian Eriksen of Ajax Amsterdam. I'm unaware of quite how good Christian is going to get. He's just 18 years old and along for the ride to learn. It can go in any direction at that age, but I know that we're two of the best technical players in the squad.

Beyond that we have little in common. Christian is quiet, and he often stays behind to practise free kicks and penalties when the rest of us go back to the dressing room. I don't. Free kicks are never going to become my forte, and penalties aren't something you can train for. Penalty kicks are a matter of holding your nerve.

The Danish press corps – fifty or so sweaty men in dodgy shorts and sandals – expend a lot of effort on Jon Dahl and his long-term goal crisis. For two years he's been one strike away from equalling the record of 52 goals for Denmark.

Now there's talk of how the World Cup is the end of the line for our striker. It's also a hot topic among the squad. There's no doubt that the record matters to Jon Dahl, and that he would rather score a goal in South Africa – or two, because strictly speaking his goal from our abandoned 2007 match against Sweden shouldn't really count. It's been removed from the international statistics.

When we joke about Jon Dahl's goal drought, he's stopped laughing with us. He doesn't think it's funny any more. To be honest, I get it. If he gets that record then he'll go down in history. He's made more of his talent than anyone would ever have predicted. If he fluffs it, he'll find it hard to put it behind him.

EXPECTATIONS FOR Denmark are minimal. The star of the finals – Lionel Messi – hasn't completely written us off. In an interview, he shows me something akin to respect.

'With his height he is very difficult to mark, but it is thankfully not my headache,' is one of the things the Argentinean says.

We play the Netherlands in the first game. On paper, they're the toughest opponents in the group. I'm barely able to join training the day before, so I'm expecting to be rested. A few hours before kick-off, Jon Dahl's thigh injury gets worse. My groin is sore – far too sore – but I still end up declaring myself fit. I don't actually feel like I have any choice. Better I do that than betray Morten Olsen.

Okay, so that's only half the truth. Because I'm also raring to go. I've still not been able to train with the rest of the team – all I've done is recovery work with Jens Bangsbo, the Denmark fitness coach, so that my body stops screaming with pain. It wants action.

It goes badly. Truly badly. We don't even come close to threatening the Dutch and lose 2-0. After that we need a point against Cameroon. We meet the Africans head on. It starts out as a horror show. They push us deeper, and Thomas Sørensen plays the ball low to Christian Poulsen. Under pressure Poulsen loses the ball to his right, where Eyong Enoh shambles in. He has time to say thanks for the gift and pick his nose before looking up and finding Samuel Eto'o, who scores the easiest goal of his career.

Fortunately, our opponents can only move in one direction – forwards. Cameroon push on as if they're in a hurry and then we get our chances at the other end of the pitch. That's something Morten Olsen specializes in. Rapid changes. All of a sudden, Romme is running free towards the goal line. He's not got any slower with age – not yet. The cross is aligned so that I have to stretch with every fibre of my body. I do, and it's an extremely uncomfortable position to be in. Especially when you're injured. But I reach it with the tip of my pink boot and I'm able to direct the ball into the goal. I know it at once. It's Romme's goal. He deserves the credit for the set-up, and I go so far as to kiss him on the head.

But that's enough of the love-in. Cameroon are closer to making it 2-1 than we are. They get several chances in front of goal, several corners and they have more possession. But Thomas Sørensen is having one of those days at the office he sometimes has.

During the second half, we make a series of rapid changes and with half an hour to go I find Romme who slaloms past the opposition defence. It must be his best goal for Denmark.

Now it's up to us and with five minutes to go Jon Dahl receives the ball while running. He's one-on-one with the goalie and all options are open to him. But he's out of luck. He puts the ball into their goalie's gloves. Where previously his inside foot was seemingly gilded, it now seems to be more or less cursed.

Nevertheless, we run out winners. It's a fortunate victory, and we're lucky to be able to shape our own destiny. Against Japan, as it happens – who on paper are an easily beatable country. I'm also personally satisfied because I've fulfilled one of my ambitions. One I've been trying to keep to myself. Our long injury list means it's unrealistic for me to become the World Cup top scorer – I've grasped that much. But now I've scored. At my first finals. I'm keeping up with Zlatan Ibrahimović. Over the past couple of years, it's him I've been compared to most – and I'm beginning to understand why more and more. He's a bit of a troublemaker too, we're both from Scandinavia, and we're more or less the same in stature.

When Zlatan was 22, he had scored six goals for his country, including two at the European championships. I've scored 12 times – twice as many. If I score just once against the Japanese, I'll be ahead in the total figures. Totally indisputably. That would be a good thing to take home. If you're on par with Zlatan, maybe even slightly ahead, there's no cause for concern.

During the deciding match, Thomas Sørensen plays as badly as he played well against Cameroon. The small, hard-working Japanese players catch our defenders napping, and after half an hour they've managed to win free kicks twice just outside our box. Neither of the shots is perfectly placed, but they make it around the wall and completely throw Sørensen. I've no idea what's happening inside that poor guy's head – because after the break he makes his third costly mistake. Yet another free kick sails towards the box in a soft arc, and at the top it's caught by the wind which guides it into the corner. He's way too far out, but just manages to touch the ball, which instead hits the corner of the goal frame.

We're tired – exhausted after a long season and an ambitious training camp. By the end of the match we're more than that. We're desperate and throw everything we've got up front. But then Agger dominates in a heading duel and gets pushed in the back. A penalty is awarded and it's a bit of a gift – but of course we don't complain.

Jon Dahl is going to take it. Finally he can equal the stupid record. But it's not that easy. It's a soft kick and the Japanese goalkeeper is able to block it, after which the ball bounces straight back into play. Our striker just about manages to hit the rebound over the line, his last act in a Denmark shirt.

To cap it all, he tears a muscle in the process and since we've used up all our subs, he has to hobble around uselessly for the rest of the match. One goal down, things are far from optimal and the Japanese – who have proven themselves to be intelligent opponents – take advantage of their superior numbers. We go out of the World Cup in a 3-1 defeat.

LONDON FEELS EMPTY. When you've been around so many teammates for so many days, even a huge city can seem completely silent. That lasts until Caroline calls. We've barely kept in touch since I moved out. But now she wants to talk. About serious stuff.

She says she's pregnant. That she's already quite far along. When I hang up, I'm verging on collapse. My brain is on fire. I can't cope. I'm 22 years old, single and quite simply not ready to be a dad yet. My lifestyle isn't suited to it, nor is my career. It could be, if I were in a stable relationship. We're not even in a relationship.

I'm on holiday with some mates when Caroline messages me with her final decision. She wants to keep the baby. On the phone from Florida, I get hold of my parents to let them know Caroline's final decision. Later that day the news is on my website. It's surreal to read it – it seems as if everything is all sunshine and roses. The truth is quite different. It feels as if my plans for the future are crumbling.

I move back to Draycott Avenue. I mean, I really try to do the right thing. My groin needs absolute peace if the pain is ever going to go away, and the start of the season is still a long way off. I explain my situation to the boss. He doesn't really say anything, but he does give me some extra holiday. I spend it with Caroline – I invite her to the Maldives. Without Alexander and Josephine. I hope we can use the week to get together and become a real couple once again. If it feels right, I want to go the whole hog – so I pack a ring in my hand luggage.

The next day we're wandering around in our swimming costumes on a white sandy coral beach. You can almost see her bump already, and I'm slowly getting used to it all. It feels a little sexy to be walking around with a pregnant woman by my side. The romantic side of things develops – just like I had dreamed it might back home – and I decide to go through with my secret plan. On the final night there, I get them to close off part of the beach so we can eat alone and I can propose to her undisturbed. There's enough food to feed 15, but I can't manage even a bite. Not because I'm nervous. But because it just feels wrong. We're not meant for each other – and we never will be.

I give up on my plan, but when the alcohol wears off later and I'm lying there restlessly staring at the ceiling, I can't see any other way out. I can't have a kid out of wedlock. I've always pictured myself having a family, pictured myself prioritizing it – just like my parents did. Back home, it was some kind of horror story – being the child of a divorce. And that's where I'm at in August 2010. Apart from sharks, my greatest fear is becoming a divorced dad.

Finally, I take a deep breath and shake Caroline to wake her up. She blinks and rubs her eyes while I say something that shouldn't feel so wrong to say:

'Will you marry me?'

BACK IN LONDON, I keep on making an effort. And in the meantime, Caroline has ambitions for us both. Once again, we're going to be Denmark's leading power couple. She's been talking to the people at *Elle* – a women's fashion magazine. They want to put us on the front cover together and tell us it's never happened before. I'm gonna be the first man on the cover of *Elle*. Not just in Denmark – but in the world. To be perfectly honest, that's part of what persuades me. I was the first guy to wear pink football boots, the shoe designer Christian Louboutin gave me his first man's shoe, and I was allowed to buy Chanel's very first leather jacket for men. I love being an early adopter.

If you look at the photos, Caroline is rocking it while I'm staring into the camera in terror. And the article is no better. It's insane how dishonest it is. We're described as soulmates and come across as if our lives are nothing less than perfect. It says things like:

'They gaze happily and adoringly at each other as they talk' and 'They're so in love it goes straight to the heart.'

If that's true then maybe I should become an actor. Because at home we quarrel like we did when we drifted apart the first time around.

At one point in the article, I'm asked about our ability to radiate success. I give an answer along the lines of: 'I think it all comes down to happiness. When you're in love and also have a career that's going well, you can't do anything else.'

For one thing, it's off the mark in terms of my private life. But in sporting terms too, it's all an illusion. My career isn't going well. My participation in the World Cup has resulted – just as Arsène Wenger predicted – in my groin continuing to cause problems, and when I'm finally ready, I'm back right where I started. Even though I give an interview where I predict to score 20 goals over the course of the season – but that kind of thing requires playing time – and our manager has spent his summer buying a Moroccan from a French club. His name is Marouane Chamakh, and although I obviously consider myself the better footballer, he, van Persie and Arshavin end up ahead of me in the pecking order. And just behind them is Theo Walcott.

It's kind of the same theme on the Denmark team. Morten Olsen hasn't closed the door, but he gives me the rest of the year off. Even though I beg and plead to be included.

'You need to be injury-free, Nicklas. Completely injury-free. I want to see that you can play without pain before you come back,' he says.

I've got absolutely nothing to fall back on. Not even my parents, who have practically taken Caroline's side. They don't believe me when I say that we're bad for each other. It's as if they have more confidence in her than me – no matter what she comes up with.

I FLEE. Back to the nightclubs where I drink to forget and score to put the other lads in their place. Nab her – the one everyone wants to get their hands on. That's my only victory. But it's also too easy – because I've been there before. It's not enough. So I head to the casino. I've had a taste of that world – including with Cesc – but now it has an extra pull. I take out memberships at the serious venues – they cost something like £5,000 each. They're not for just any Tom, Dick and Harry, and it's enough to keep the snitches away.

London's oldest, finest casino is Les Ambassadeurs Club in Mayfair. That's where I feel alive again. One night I'm at the poker table, and even though the others have deep pockets and buy more chips, they eventually run out and can't shut me down. I survive their counter-attack and end up winning £220,000! It feels like scoring against Spurs in front of 60,000 crazy Gooners.

When I wander across the street to my hotel, I've got a backpack stuffed with £50 notes (vacuum-packed!) and I'm so high on adrenaline that I can't sleep. Instead, I send pics of my winnings to my boys in Copenhagen.

'It was a piece of piss,' I write.

My worries evaporate and I can barely think about anything else. So I keep going to the casino – over and over. I end up gambling on Sundays, Tuesdays and Thursdays – every week – from six o'clock in the evening until four in the morning. Les Ambassadeurs is the epicentre of private poker, and the real big boys are sitting at my table. Various wealthy men and some professional poker players, including Phil Ivey, who is the absolute world-leading player at the time.

Many of the others have such deep pockets they can keep playing no matter how big their losses. Obviously I shouldn't be there. But I can't help myself. Instead of getting back to the hotel on a high, I start crawling into bed knowing I'm down twenty grand, or fifty, or two hundred. Money that's been lost in just a few hours.

After a while, Caroline smells a rat and blabs to my mum. I deny everything and control myself for a week – but that's all I can manage. Then I'm back. I have to go back. To the poker table, to the baccarat table, to the blackjack table. And roulette.

I BECOME a dad to Nicholas. The name is a compromise. Caroline wanted to call him Nicklas Junior, and that's just too weird. But he's a cute little boy and I love him from the very first moment

I cast eyes on him. I feel love like I've never felt before. But it's only for him. Me and Carolinee can barely stand to be in the same room together. Everything turns into a fight and that can't be healthy. Not for the baby and not for the woman who has just given birth to him.

We break up while she's still on the postnatal ward. She just wants me out of the door, so I head for Liverpool where Agger is throwing his Christmas party.

We both know it's over, which is why it's so unreal to keep reading about my happy little family on www.nicklas-bendtner. com.

'On 16 December, my fiancée gave birth to a beautiful baby boy. I can't describe all the emotions that ran through me, but I've had the most amazing Christmas you can imagine. I had my family and grandma to visit, and we enjoyed a traditional Danish dinner on Christmas Eve. It was my son's first Christmas, and he spent most of it sleeping and eating. Wishing you all a happy new year.'

I mark the beginning of 2011 with some playing time – but not up front. I only get to play on the right wing. And as Morten Olsen says in an interview, it's a stupid way of using me. I'm best up front, and if I were on the left wing then I could pull into the field and finish. Now it's just about crosses. I'm servicing van Persie with plenty of top balls, but I'm no winger. I'm too big for it.

The backing from my national coach means something to me, because there's not much inspiration to draw on from my club. The fans are bitching about me, and they're writing some grim stuff online. Things I've not seen before. Not from the Arsenal fans, anyway. It's almost as if they can tell how bad things are off the pitch. How something is fundamentally wrong.

Someone or other at the club leaks an internal self-confidence test that we've taken. We've assessed our own abilities in terms of headers, mental strength, breakthrough power, confidence on the ball and much more. The papers say that I scored 10 on a scale of 1 to 9. But that's total bullshit. I've not given myself full marks in even one category – so it sounds pretty bloody unlikely.

It's annoying because they're helping to dig my hole even deeper.

And it also sets me on my guard. Someone at the club has got it in for me. The most negative Arsenal fans see the leaked test results as proof of my lack of grounding. They're also holding a grudge about an interview I gave to the *B.T.* newspaper in Denmark. The article has made it into the British media where it's been interpreted as me issuing some kind of ultimatum to the club. That's not really true – but okay, I do say that I want to move on if I remain number three or four or five in the pecking order. Who wouldn't say that?

My manager is the one who seems least offended, and at a press conference in January he leaves the door ajar:

'I've been very satisfied with his spirit and attitude. Now he has to carry on with the hard work, and when he's match-ready he'll get to play.'

On 27 February, we play Birmingham City in the Carling Cup final. As we've progressed through this minor cup competition, I've contributed three goals and been a regular starter. But four hours ahead of kick-off when we have our players' meeting at the Four Seasons Canary Wharf – Arsenal's hotel ahead of games in and around London – I'm not picked. Wenger goes through our starting eleven, and he's put van Persie up front. He's only just returned from injury and hasn't played much in the league cup. I can't believe it. Finally I'm in a final – finally I have a chance to win something. And someone else is going to get to finish the job. To top it all, against my old club where I was on loan – who we ought to beat nine times out of ten. After all, we're 13 places above them in the league and 26 points up.

Once the others have trudged back to their rooms, I ask the boss for an explanation.

'That's just how it is, Nicklas. You'll have to make your contribution from off the bench – you'll do your bit to make sure we win. There's nothing else to say about the matter,' he says dismissively.

I replace van Persie with 20 minutes to go. It's 1-1 and we're more or less in control. At one point, I break loose and kick the ball towards the far corner, but miss. When we reach stoppage time, it looks like we're heading for extra time and maybe even penalties.

Birmingham have just one weapon, and that's long balls up into our box. It looks hopeless. Everyone does the same thing. Even their goalkeeper. His goal kick lands in front of our reserve goalie – Wojciech Szczęsny from Poland – who unlike me has been given the chance to start the game. Somehow, one of our defenders gets in his way. The ball hits Szczęsny in the chest and it falls to the feet of Obafemi Martins, who gets his boot to it.

There was no danger – absolutely no danger. I crack completely. The disappointment is suffocating. We're an absolute fucking fiasco if we end up losing. I'm not usually like this, but right now I just want to blame someone. And the best candidate is our goalkeeper, because we're not exactly best mates anyway. While we share the same cliques in the dressing room, and both hang out with Wilshere and Ramsey, the Pole's mouth is too fucking big for my liking. Not that he means anything bad by it, but he sticks his nose in too much stuff that's really not his business.

However, in the end I don't blame Szczęsny for our collapse. Everyone makes mistakes. It's the boss who ought to get my grief. Normally, Wenger is a fair man – but not in this case. It feels like he's denied me the chance to secure Arsenal their first trophy in years. Even if it's 'just' the Carling Cup, a place in the starting eleven would have been a big deal for me. And I would have been sharp and psyched like no one else – no doubt about it.

I pull the silver medal off as soon as I leave the stadium. I think my mum might have picked it up, but I never see it again.

This time I've lost my patience. My motivation is gone. If I'm staying at Arsenal, I know all I've got in my future is 20 minutes here and 20 minutes there. And that's no longer enough. It doesn't matter whether I've been injured and made bad decisions in my life, or whether I've done things right. If I played every time, I wouldn't make half as many bad decisions off the pitch. I would enjoy it and build on it. Football is what makes me happy. I can't sit by and watch others doing what I love above all else. I'm not made for the bench.

Three days later we play Leyton Orient in the fifth round of the FA Cup. I wasn't selected in the original tie at their place but they

With Nicholas, June 2011. (Photo: Jeppe Michael Jensen/Ritzau Scanpix)

held us to a draw after nicking a late goal. In the replay I'm totally fucking indifferent and do as I please. I play a stubborn game. When the match is over, I've scored the second hat-trick of my career. It's against a third-tier club and right after each goal I look like an angry man. I put my hand to my ear to mime that I can't hear the Gooners. It's not thought through. They obviously can't stand that kind of thing.

Just ask Adebayor. But then it begins.

'Super Nick, super-super Nick.'

They're singing my song. And it warms my heart, because our fans are the most important thing to me – they always will be. But I'm done being a supersub. When I'm playing we're less predictable, more reckless and more dangerous. And if that hasn't sunk in in the right places, it probably never will.

I ONLY SEE Nicholas when his mum or the nanny is there. Caroline doesn't want to leave me alone with him. There's not much for me to do. A nap on my chest is a total no go. He's to sleep in his cot and only there. The numerous rules put a dampener on my joy. One day I need to be close to my son. I can't think about anything else, so I turn up at Draycott Avenue unannounced. Caroline isn't home, but the nanny is. And so is Nicholas. After a bit of persuasion, I trundle off with the buggy. My phone rings while we're sitting on a bench in Hyde Park.

'Bring him back right away!' Caroline shouts.

From then on, Caroline and I basically don't speak to each other. Most of it goes through lawyers.

One weekend I have my little brother to visit. I overhear him calling our mum back home. Jannick says what a bummer I am to hang out with. That he can't be bothered to stay when I'm in such a bad mood. That he doesn't recognize me.

My life is a massive zone of frustration. Nothing is going my way. That's how I feel, anyway. Me, who has always been so happy and carefree.

Instead of building a family and getting established on the

pitch, I find myself a new place to go for a night out on the town. The Box Soho is an invite-only cabaret club where strippers and sword swallowers are up on the podiums. It's extreme, and there's always a sexual overtone or undertone. Men screwing men. Women spanking or fistfucking each other. Totally hot women who turn out to be extremely well-endowed men. I'm the only footballer to be invited to the opening, and I spend the next few months hanging out with the London A-list. Jude Law, Kate Moss and all sorts of pop stars. If Alexander McQueen hadn't killed himself, he would have been a shoo-in. And I think we would have bonded.

But alas. Not even the best party is enough. Occasionally, the freak show bores me – and when it does I move on to the casino. Before I would arrive at Les Ambassadeurs somewhat sober – but that's no longer the case. Now I arrive wrecked, late in the evening. It's pure hazard.

There are nights when Craig – one of the hosts at the casino – asks me to leave. He's scared I'll be ruined if I take a seat at one of the poker tables.

'Not tonight, Nicklas. The others have got really deep pockets,' he whispers.

It's a discreet setting, but I can feel the rumours running riot. Maybe Wenger already knows. At any rate, Steve Bruce, my ex-manager and ex-girlfriend's dad already does. Late that spring he calls me.

'Stay away from all that shit, lad,' he counsels me. 'It ruins people – no one is spared.'

I promise him I'll take a breather, but I also know it'll be hard to make it stick. Especially with the summer holidays just around the corner and my trip to Las Vegas with five of my boys from back home. That alone causes trouble in the Danish press, because it's at the same time as the U21 Euros, which are being hosted by Denmark. The DBU have named me as one of their reinforcements in the squad – they're allowed to pick three older players. But I'm not interested in that. I take it as a minor insult. Me playing in the U21 Euros again? Five years after I last did?

Over the course of a week, we – well, I – burn through £400,000 on gambling, parties, girls and bodyguards. The bodyguards thing is something I've picked up at Arsenal. Every time the team goes out, we're escorted by some burly blokes who get between us and people who aren't into the Gunners. It saves us a lot of hassle and potential clashes. And it looks cool. It makes us look really important.

Money and power. It's a combination the opposite sex are attracted to. So I copy the trick and hire four burly Hawaiians who follow me and my boys around through thick and thin. While they've got my back, I'm rolling in women. A lot of them every day. I might see one for lunch, hang out by the pool with another, and hook up with the third after darkness falls on Sin City. Most of them we find through a dating site for rich and famous Americans, while the rest of them are attracted by the attention we're drawing.

When I head back to London and a futile beginning to the season, I've lost grasp of my own situation. While the rest of the squad is in Asia to play in an exhibition match and the papers are writing about a potential loan deal with Everton, I head out on my own.

One night I leave The Box for Les Ambassadeurs. I arrive around three o'clock and I'm way too drunk to sit at a table. That much I get. But roulette is a different matter – I'm still able to handle that. Red, black, red, black. How hard can it be?

After ninety minutes I've lost £400,000. Money I don't have. My bank account is overdrawn and I'm bankrupt if my luck doesn't turn. Even the flat in Bushey is mortgaged.

I stagger into the loos and splash water on my face. Then I find a cashier and get another £50,000 of chips.

This is before they introduced a limit per night, so of course they say okay. They know me. They think I'm good for the money.

I win a little, bet the house, and win a little more. By five o'clock, my losses are down to £20,000. All things considered, it's a cheap escape – and I let my credit card take the strain. My heart is pounding. This was too much. Too risky. Even for me.

OFF COURSE

2011–2012

IT ENDS up being Sunderland. On 31 August 2011 at 11.50pm – just ten minutes before the transfer window slams shut – the papers are faxed back and forth with signatures on them. I'm at the Hotel Marienlyst with my dad. Thomas Brookes, who is kind of below the radar, is my new agent and he's on the phone with us. It was Neil Banfield, the Arsenal reserves coach, who recommended Tom.

My dad is mostly there for appearance's sake. I've known for a long time that he wouldn't be my agent for ever. He has neither the contacts nor the know-how to help me progress. So now he's being installed in the jewellery company I'm planning to launch. Everyone is happy. Dad doesn't feel like a decrepit old wreck and gets paid a fantastic wage, and I no longer have to listen to him and his promises that never pan out into anything concrete. This way I can get on with my career.

Tom seems to know his stuff. There are several options, but we end up with a loan deal to Sunderland. The northern club will pay me the same wage as Arsenal, and that's fine by me. I'm not just in it for the money. I'm doing it for the club's manager. Because of Steve Bruce.

I don't feel like celebrating. I'm gonna miss Arsenal. My club. Over the past seven seasons, I've perceived Arsenal as a part of me. However, something about it feels right. There's a relief of sorts. Being hard-nosed about it, I know that I'll no longer be disappointed once or twice a week.

Suddenly my body doesn't hurt as much when I get up in the morning, and a week later when we play Norway in the Euro qualifiers I'm able to play the full ninety minutes. My superpowers are back. The first goal is insanely good. I get the ball in the centre, move it quickly on to Christian Eriksen who finds Romme in space. Romme looks up and sees I've stopped my run. He sends the ball back at an angle and all I have to do is lift it beyond the goalie's reach. I put my hands together and bellow a deep 'yes!' I've no idea where the sound comes from, but it's from somewhere deep inside my chest.

For the goal to put us 2-0 up, I play a one-two with Eriksen and strike while I'm still on the run. The ball streaks away across the wet grass, completely unstoppable. I'm not sure how many times I've put them away from 25 metres out, but I must be able to count them on one hand. They're my first goals for Denmark since the World Cup, and the sensation is like having an orgasm. Even though I've lost the Emirates, I still have Parken and 40,000 of my countrymen shouting my name and yelling stuff like: 'About fucking time, Nicklas!'

The victory puts us back in serious contention for an automatic qualifying spot for the Euros the following summer. And the Danish media go bananas about my performance and call me King Nicklas of Norway. There's also speculation about me and Arsène Wenger. How dumb it was to let me leave. That I've just sent him a postcard. That kind of thing. But to be perfectly honest, it's not even crossed my mind. Things are the way they are, and I just want to get some solid playing time and kick-start my development again. I want to be good enough to play for a club at Champions League level – whether that's for Arsenal or in another country.

THE NEXT DAY I'm due at training with Sunderland. I arrive in a blazer and must look like I've come to the wrong place. I'm totally overdressed. After the fitness test Steve Bruce takes me to one side. We've not spoken about this since his call back in the spring, but that alone was enough to remind me of the man's big heart.

And now he repeats his concerns.

I'm able to reassure him with a fairly clear conscience. I'm gambling less now. It had spiralled, and I don't even dare do the sums to figure how much cash I must have flushed down the toilet. In future, I'm going to set a ceiling on my stakes. I'm allowed to spend £5,000 in one night – not a penny more.

Steve Bruce and I are standing in the middle of the canteen, and everyone's looking at us, but it doesn't bother him one bit. He begins his famous pep talk:

'Now – right now – you're gonna get going. Now, Nicklas! You need to live up to your potential. I want to see your boots talk! Pull yourself together – you need to give it your all! Get started! I know you've got it in you, son!'

It's nice to be seen like that. It's also a shade too familiar. He's singing the same tune as he was five years ago.

Just when I think he's done, he starts back up again. There's more I need to be warned about. A teammate.

'We've got a lad – a really good lad. He's our captain.'

'Lee Cattermole?'

'Yes…You and Lee…It's not gonna work. You need to stay away from each other. Do you promise me you will?'

I look Steve Bruce in the eye. I've no idea what he's on about. Why is Cattermole a problem? But I can see that he means it.

'Okay,' I say. 'It's a promise.'

When I get to the dressing room, my clothes are hanging from the ceiling – so high up I can barely get them back down again.

A few days later the joke escalates since I haven't managed to properly fit in yet. This time I've turned up for training in a Tom Ford suit and when I get back from the training pitches, my suit no longer looks quite how it did. It's still on the bench where I left it. But someone has cut it up into hundreds of pieces.

'You know it was from Tom Ford, right? It cost me four grand.'

No one answers, the laughter rings out from the baths. And to be honest I get it. I might very well have pulled a stunt like it myself. It's just coarse lad humour. It's not about being unwelcome or anything like that.

Another couple of weeks pass. Then someone grasses. It doesn't matter who – because you don't grass. Especially not on the grass himself. But that's how it always goes in the dressing room. Eventually, there will be someone who can't keep a secret.

I find out Lee Cattermole is responsible for it all. Naturally, I need to give him a taste of his own medicine. He comes in to find his rags all cut up. Unfortunately, the lad has awful taste in clothes, so it's not all that expensive for him. And he doesn't get pissed off either. Quite the opposite. He laughs and asks whether we should go out for a few beers. But I come up with some excuse, remembering my promise to Steve Bruce.

I MAKE MY debut in the candy-striped Sunderland jersey when we play Chelsea at home at the Stadium of Light. We lose 2-1. It's not a surprise. Roman Abramovich's playthings are in contention for the title while we'll be happy if we stay up. It's my new reality and I know full well that it'll take some getting used to. Even though I reject the idea when the hacks ask me. I give them the Vedbæk record.

'I'm looking forward to playing more regularly, and we'll see what happens,' I say.

Jon Dahl would have been proud.

Afterwards, I take my 911 up to Newcastle Airport. At the airport there's a private jet waiting to take me to London. The plan is for me and Alex, my old classmate, to pack up a few things. Then we need to get our heads down. We're going to spend the whole Sunday driving the 250 miles back north in one of my other cars.

Obviously, we end up out on the town for a bit, but nothing that stops us from getting up pretty early. I'm going to stay in a hotel until I find a house, and when we get to the Hilton in Newcastle it's still only the afternoon.

We park up and get something to eat before heading to, supposedly, the best nightclub in the area. But if I'm honest, it's not a positive experience. The food is crap and the dance floor is like falling asleep in Cannes only to wake up at a shithole in the back end of nowhere. Alex agrees. We bring a few girls back to the hotel room for a small after-party. Before we left the club I caught sight of Mario Balotelli, Manchester City's new striker. He was surrounded by his Italian friends. They must have come to Newcastle so they can party in peace. A few of us use that trick when we don't want to put up with all the shit from local fans.

Back in the room, we chug a few bottles of white wine and after a while Alex pops out to fetch some more ice. When he gets back he looks ready to burst into tears and his eyes are completely red. It turns out that Balotelli and his mates are staying down the corridor and are throwing their own little room party.

They've been shoving Alex and flinging ice cubes at him. I react like it's the school playground, grab an empty wine bottle and storm down to their room where I hammer on the door. When it opens I hurl abuse at them. Once again I catch a glimpse of Balotelli, but he seems to be trying to stay out of it.

The next night we hit the hotel bar. There's a wedding on and the guests seem nicely pissed. A small group of four girls and two guys have come out of the ballroom and are sitting on a couple of sofas a few metres away chatting. After a couple of minutes the first girl totters over. The other three quickly follow, leaving the guys on their own on the sofas.

One of them must be Scottish. At any rate, he's got bright red hair and he's wearing a kilt. He yells at us to stop nicking his women, suddenly turning aggressive out of the blue. I get up from my bar stool and say we're not up to anything. That he can keep his girlfriends.

'We're not looking for any trouble, buddy.'

But he doesn't buy it.

'It's too fucking late, and I'm not your buddy,' he says, headbutting me.

It's not like with Adebayor. This isn't up for discussion. This is 100 per cent intentional. I notice my eyes go blurry, but I stay up on my feet. Then I take a step back and throw a punch with my right fist. There's a dull sound. Blood sprays out of his nose. He falls back onto the carpet, his kilt riding up around his stomach.

He's a true Scotsman – no doubt about it. Has a pierced dick and everything. A real Prince Albert.

His friend is just staring at him. The mouth is gaping open, but nothing comes out. The girls run off shrieking. Alex and I decide to head over to reception. We want to try and explain the situation, but we don't get far. The Scot is right on our heels. He's shouting how he wants to kill me and starts chasing us around the fountain. Round and round – right there in the lobby. It carries on for an eternity until hotel security manage to calm him down.

Alex and I retire to our room to wait for the police. When the officers arrive, they get the whole story. We're convinced it must be possible to see it in the CCTV footage. How it was the Scottish guy who attacked me. Not the other way around.

'That's quite possible. But we won't be able to check until tomorrow, so you need to come with us right now. For now, you're under arrest for a breach of the peace.'

We're both handcuffed and put in the slammer. The next morning they release Alex. He has a flight to catch and they can easily see he had nothing to do with it. He's pretty relieved. Things ended up a little more dramatic than he was expecting on his trip away.

A couple of hours later I'm told I'm free to go. The videotape shows everything we said during questioning.

'If you want, you can report him for assault,' says one of the officers. 'He headbutted you.'

I decline. If I'm lucky, no one need ever know all this happened in my first week at my new club.

But it's as if my innocence is already gone. All that stuff about starting over rings hollow now. And things don't get any better when I move out of the Hilton to a house on the most expensive street in Newcastle – Runnymede Road. That's where the best paid lads in the Sunderland squad live. As soon as the estate agent is gone, my mobile rings.

'Try going upstairs,' says a voice that seems vaguely familiar.

'Why?'

'Just do it now.'

'Okay.'

'Go into the big bedroom – the one looking over the street and open the window.'

When I look outside I can see someone waving at me from the house diagonally across the road. It's...no way...it's Lee Cattermole. Here comes trouble!

IN REALITY, I don't feel great. Here at least I thought I had figured things out. That I could move away from the things that hurt most. That I would think less about Nicholas, who I only get to see for an hour at a time – and always with the nanny there.

The exact opposite has happened. I think about him more and more. Miss him when I'm sober. My lawyer is pushing, but in legal terms I've got no chance. If I want shared custody in the long-term, it's important I can see Nicholas whenever Caroline suggests a date. Every time. But unfortunately pretty often the times when Nicholas is available, don't work alongside my playing commitments. And with that, I'm quickly judged as unworthy – utterly no chance.

Every now and then I have some contact time together to look forward to. Then I fly down from Newcastle and wait in a suite at The Westbury – my favourite hotel in London. But it doesn't always work out. Sometimes Nicholas and the nanny don't make it. Each time I react by breaking down.

I hate it when people ask after Nicholas. How he's doing and that kind of thing. Because what am I supposed to say? When he learns to walk I only find out weeks afterwards. When he gets glasses, it's left up to me to find out – and a month or two can pass by before I see him. To me, his life is a distant country.

A WEEK after my arrival at Sunderland, my only real competition up front leaves. A club in UAE want to take Asamoah Gyan on loan for such a huge sum of money that he insists on going. In autumn 2011, I still don't get that kind of thing. Straight to the Middle

East after one acceptable season in the Premier League? Surely it's impossible for money to be that important? Or is it? If you come from a seriously rough background in Ghana, then perhaps it's pretty damn important.

The lack of competition up front makes me think about my time at Birmingham. The clubs beneath the top six or seven in the Premier League have less competition for a spot in the starting eleven. There's a hierarchy, a clearer ranking order and a smaller squad. For the manager to make a radical change requires some massive let-down by the established players – or a massive effort by the newcomers.

At Birmingham, we had so much fun – us lads – that the sporting stuff pretty much slipped into the background. And the same thing happens at Sunderland, because I'm still drawn to the daredevils. Sebastian Larsson – the talented Swede from Arsenal and Birmingham – is at Sunderland too. He's one of the people who recommended I make the move, but we don't have much to do with each other here either. Today I wish I could go back and change that. Seb would have been good for me.

I make a serious effort to ensure Jannick doesn't get bored with me when he comes to visit. I've bought a self-playing piano for myself, and I buy him a Gibson guitar so that he can practise on it while I'm at training. And who knows, maybe we'll start a band one day. It sounds pretty unlikely, but it's also a really fun idea to imagine. The Gallagher brothers would finally meet their match.

My new best friend is, of course, Lee Cattermole. On the pitch he leads from the front like the badass he is, but off the pitch I find him a really decent lad. We hang out every single day and when my family comes to visit they borrow his box at the stadium. Our mums sit there playing best friends while our dads pretend to know what's going on down on the pitch.

If one of us has friends visiting, we take them over to the other's house to hang out. Other times we meet when the local pub opens. If we've played on Saturday, we're on standby for opening time at noon on Sunday. Lee was once involved in some fight that got him a three-year ban from every pub in Stockton. From December

2008 to December 2011. But even though Stockton isn't far away, it's not a strictly enforced ban.

We throw dice and play drinking games, sing football songs and knock the beers back, and then we do it all again on Monday. While it's happening, it's just really nice – but of course it's not all that grand.

Results start to let us down too, and when we hit November we're almost in the relegation zone. A club with lofty ambitions and a brand-new stadium can't live with that, so they sack Steve Bruce. We're only 13 matches into a long season. I'm both sad and angry. He was the whole reason why I chose to go to Sunderland. And obviously I ask myself whether I've done enough. Whether I'm responsible. Two goals in the league isn't exactly brilliant – so I must be. My head has been all sorts of places other than where it should be. On the pitch.

I CLING ON to the Denmark team. It has gradually become the most successful and stable factor in my life, and when we play Portugal in October 2011 in the Group H match that will decide who tops the group, I score the winner. It's my fourth goal against the Portuguese, and once again it comes from an assist by Romme. He's got better and better at reading my runs – a quality I could do with a bit more of at club level.

A month later the national team gathers once again. Just like so many times before, I have a couple of my mates from Amager in my room for a visit. It's all a bit under the radar, so we're just chatting. The discussion turns to how I'm not really happy over in England. That I'm lonely, I'm not doing well and that partying is making me feel even worse. Especially the day after. We agree I must need some lovin'.

We come up with an amusing scheme. We each write down five names of famous girls and fold up the pieces of paper and put them in a hat. The name I pull out is the one I need to contact.

The name on the piece of paper is Julie Zangenberg, and to be honest it doesn't mean anything to me. But Alex explains she's the chick from *Catch That Girl* – a Danish movie that came out in our early teens.

The night after she happens to be a guest on the late-night Danish talk show *Natholdet* hosted by Anders Breinholt. I watch it with Agger and mention I'm planning to make her my girlfriend. He reckons it's a good idea.

'She seems like a bit of alright,' he says.

A girl's mobile number is never more than one or two text messages away, so it's pretty easy to get hold of it. Then the charm offensive begins. At first she seems dismissive, but that doesn't bother me. It only makes her more interesting. I try really hard. I write longer messages than I usually do, and even though my spelling's atrocious it seems to make an impression. We manage to agree to a date.

Julie invites me back to hers somewhere around Fisketorvet in Copenhagen. There are framed pictures and platinum records on the walls that all say Medina. At last, Julie admits that the apartment actually belongs to the pop singer Medina, and she's borrowed it for the night. It's more discreet to bring me here than it would be in the city centre.

I need to be back by 11pm, but the date lasts for so long that I have to sneak into Marienlyst after midnight. It's been fun. She's sweet and exciting and gets what it's like to have a face people recognize. I also imagine that she's not too easily impressed. Not like most of the others. She must meet loads of extraordinary people as an actress. Or maybe she's just pretending she's not easily impressed. Whichever it is, it works. I may not be head over heels in love, but I'm definitely curious.

We close our account for the year with Denmark by winning a friendly against Finland, and I score my fifth goal in as many games for my country that autumn. But we've already qualified for the European championships in the game before against Portugal, so Morten Olsen gives us permission to have a bevvy or two.

So we do. A lot of us, in fact. We dominate the hotel bar, but there's also a couple of sweethearts there holding hands. I recognize one of the girls – she was in the year above me at school and

I snogged one of her friends. The two guys are a bit bikery, but seem alright when we chat across the table.

It turns into a seriously boozy night and there's a scuffle because my school-friend's boyfriend has threatened to beat her up and somehow opened a door right into the face or back of one of the other squad members. After that he left along with her. I haven't seen the incident, and really shouldn't interfere. But I do. Nicolai Jørgensen, Christian Eriksen and I head down to the Amager girl's room. Eriksen decides to wait round the corner while Nicolai comes with me to the door.

'Are you okay?' I ask when she opens up.

'Yeah, yeah – everything's fine,' she says.

And we never get any further than that before the boyfriend comes out yelling at us and clouts her. I've no idea what he's been drinking, but it's stronger than beer. He ends up lashing out at me. I do the same as I did back in the hotel in Newcastle. I hit him once – it's enough to put his lights out. Afterwards, I pull him back into his room by his legs while the girl apologizes and says he was asking for it. It's so crazy, like something out of a silent movie.

When he comes to his senses he goes totally nuts and runs around hammering on all the doors of the Denmark team. He yells that he wants to batter me and that kind of thing.

The next day he's standing in front of the media with his arm in a cast. He was so pissed that he smashed his own knuckles to pieces without even noticing. In the articles that follow, it goes without saying that they suggest I have something to do with his smashed-up hand. I definitely don't.

The police show up as well, and I'm taken down to the police station in Helsingør for questioning. They're in no rush to charge me. On the contrary, they've checked the guy out.

'Might he have got his injuries from being shoved into a door by you?' says one of the officers.

'That's very possible,' I say.

Back at the hotel, we hold a peace meeting of sorts. The guy claims to remember nothing.

'My girlfriend says I was playing up.'

It all ends with me giving him my shirt from the Sweden match, putting my autograph on it and leaving it at that. Neither of us wants to take the matter any further.

THINGS ARE going to get even worse. One Monday night in December, Lee and I chow down at a restaurant in Chinatown in Newcastle. We decide to head on to the only casino in the city. We've been drinking all day and the day before that too. Ever since our 2-1 defeat against Wolves, we're in pieces. We're so drunk that we no longer have any idea what we're doing.

On the way to the casino I kick a wing mirror or two – just like I did in the good old days when I was on the streets of Kastrup and Tårnby. When I've had enough, Lee keeps going. He jumps on some cars and that kind of thing. Neither of us is thinking about the consequences of our actions. How it's really fucking annoying for the owners. In our eyes, it's just fun and games.

When we get inside, Lee begins to brag.

'Oh, hey, you were there too,' he says, pointing at me.

'Definitely not,' I say in that ironic tone us Danes are the masters of.

Ten days later the police show up at Sunderland's training ground. They pick up Lee in the clubhouse and me out on the training pitches. We were followed via CCTV. In England, cameras are everywhere. The five cars aren't exactly write-offs. The total repair bill for the lot is something like £5,000, and we're willing to pay on the spot. But we don't get off that easy. We're both charged with vandalism.

Lee ends up being cautioned while the charges against me are dropped. I'm not doing anything wrong in the CCTV footage, and in the casino recording I flat out deny it.

It's not an episode that makes us popular at the club. Most of the fans are working class and consider us overpaid and over-pampered, all while we underperform far too often. To be honest, I get it. In one single season I earn what the typical fan might earn in a lifetime. The figures are mental – and they're only getting crazier and crazier. Naturally, the fans expect more.

YOU'D THINK I was lying, but the condemnation from Denmark is way harsher than it is in England. In Denmark, the vandalism case is the straw that breaks the camel's back. Suddenly everyone is pointing their fingers at me. Politicians, coaches in the Superliga and sports journos. It all ends with my press adviser – hired by my parents – writing an open letter to the people of Denmark and signing my name at the bottom. It's one big belly flop and it includes things like:

'I'm really sorry. I deeply regret being involved in these episodes that have been so violently interpreted. I accept full responsibility for not putting a stop to things before they got completely out of hand. It's my fault and I'm so incredibly sorry to have let down so many people. I'm basically just a normal guy with an abnormal job. Sometimes I forget that, but I know full well that's the case, which is why there is no excuse for me getting mixed up in these events.'

To be honest, I've not dictated even one single full stop in that letter. You see, at the time I don't really have a heavy conscience. Sure, I kicked a wing mirror, and yes, I punched a couple of pissed hotel guests, and yes, I drove too fast on the way to the airport, and fine, I asked some other drunken morons to lend me cash for a couple of pizzas on Gothersgade. But no harm has come to any innocent parties.

If it were up to me, I would have written something very different in that press release.

'Just imagine you're not allowed to see your son. Imagine strangers are constantly telling you how to live your life and do your job. Does that sound like it's easy?'

That's what I feel like writing, if I could. Because I still prefer to put the blame on others whenever I can. But I can't write. And I'm not supposed to write that kind of thing, either. It would totally piss off Caroline and destroy my chances of seeing any more of Nicholas. I'm not that stupid.

THE NEW manager at the club is Martin O'Neill, and so far he's seemed fairly competent. He's not trying to perform magic or anything. He's carrying on where Steve Bruce left off. We're talking about the kind of British manager who expects 100 per cent in every training session and appreciates fighting spirit and big tackles. On the flip side, you get loads of time off and there aren't many rules.

It's the right thing to do. Our squad doesn't have the depth to change its style of play. Definitely not up front. It says in the papers that O'Neill wants to recall Gyan from his loan, but the Ghanaian is apparently not up for it. In other words, Sunderland will have to rely on me if the team are going to survive with the best of them.

When we reach late February, things haven't been going well for me, although we have hauled ourselves up to mid-table. I've been out several times with groin pain, but despite that I've started 16 of my 18 appearances. Nevertheless, I've only managed three goals in the Premier League. Everyone is unhappy with me when I have to go to the magistrates' court as a result of a speeding ticket I picked up just before Christmas – just before the vandalism case exploded. This time I'm out of luck, because I've been caught driving way too fast on the motorway from Sunderland to Newcastle. I was heading for the airport so I could make it to Copenhagen for a joint birthday party for Julie and Medina. The penalty for doing 103mph when the limit is 70 is pretty harsh, and I'm banned from driving for 56 days.

At the very same time, Chrille loses his job back in Denmark. I immediately offer to hire my childhood friend as my driver, and it might sound weird but I still look back today on that decision as being a good investment. I go from having wandered restlessly around my house that's too big for me to feeling comfortable. We play PlayStation, watch DVDs and eat out. For the first time in my spell at Sunderland, I'm actually happy, and it shows in my performances in the Premier League. I score four times in March and the mood around me changes once again. Both at the Stadium of Light and in the press. After all, I'm a real goal poacher, I'm also our biggest hope for the Euros, and I've actually got older and wiser too.

I'm not so sure about that last one, but I've at least had a major fright. Fabrice Muamba, who plays for Bolton Wanderers in the Championship, has collapsed – cardiac arrest. In the middle of a match. Muamba, who was my best mate at the academy. The one I drifted apart from when we arrived at Birmingham and life in the fast lane took over. Muamba, who never partied but just took care of himself. Muamba, who stayed at Birmingham when I went back to Arsenal. He survives, but he's played his last match. Football can be a cruel sport.

One Wednesday night we're out celebrating Chrille's birthday at a restaurant in Newcastle. We had really planned for a quiet night, but then David Meyler – who plays in midfield for Sunderland – and one of his mates turn up. They're well up for it. Switching it up a gear.

'Let's hit a nightclub,' he says.

'But there's nowhere any good,' I say.

'Everywhere's good if your name is Nicklas Bendtner,' he jokes.

No further persuasion is necessary. Once we've found a table, David and his buddy come over balancing a tray each. On the trays there are 30 identical shot glasses. Full.

'Meet the Flying Hirsch,' they say with a laugh.

I've heard of the drink. The Flying Hirsch is a shot mix of Jägermeister and Red Bull, and it really gets you going. We drink up and head home. We're pretty tipsy. Chrille has already hit the floor when I log on to Twitter. It's not all that smart, but I share some photos of us and write a quick post in Danish.

'7 Flying Hirsch in a row. Now sleeping soundly.'

Back home in Denmark, the newspaper *Ekstra Bladet* picks up on it. If I've been on a wild night out three days before an important match, that's pure fodder for all the readers who love shaking their heads at that guy Nicklas Bendtner.

The press adviser gets deployed yet again. He denies everything. It was only my good friend, the birthday boy, who was drinking – and anyway, the picture is a month old. Not one word about David.

If it weren't for the fact that my adviser was being paid so much,

I'd feel a bit sorry for him. He begins to look like a clown standing there and denying the obvious. And so do I. Seeing as three months earlier, I promised the people of Denmark I would turn over a new leaf and party less, it doesn't look all that good. But I can't think about it like that. Not at the time. It wasn't me who wrote that apology. It was written by someone who preferred to have me apologize rather than understand why it had happened in the first place. Why I had gone off course.

Ekstra Bladet try to find someone in England who will say something. But no one is bothered. In England, it's not that mad to drink three days before a game. English footballers have always drunk like fish. Until the 1990s, it was generally the rule rather than the exception. That's what I'm told all the time.

Saturday arrives and I play my best game of the season. We're up against Manchester City and manage a 3-3 draw against the champions-to-be. With the score at 1-1, I win a battle in the air against three of the Sky Blues. As I head the ball back in the direction it came from, Joe Hart is in a desperate situation on his line.

Shortly after, I run past the back line and deliver a cross straight to Seb's feet. The very same *Ekstra Bladet* who have been on my back all week surrender and describe the assist as a 'sugar ball'. Suddenly it's 3-1 and although Balotelli and Kolarov secure a point for City, we not only prove that we can play football, but that we can also never go down with such a good squad. With Steve Bruce as manager or not. We just had to get started.

I finish the season as the club's top scorer. When you play for a mid-ranking team and get injured three times in one season, eight goals and five assists doesn't sound too bad. But when I look back, I see it could have been double that. The playing time and trust were there – but the bucketloads of motivation I had at Arsenal were missing. I've had my head in all sorts of other places. I've partied – of course I have. I've tried to forget my son. For a brief moment, I've considered becoming an actor. And I've launched a jewellery company. I've lost focus in a way I never did at Arsenal. Not even when I was injured and more or less lived at the casino.

Martin O'Neill gets all that. Without difficulty. He's already made it clear that new forces need to be brought in. Still, I would have preferred a better end to things than I get.

The final game of the season is at the Stadium of Light. We're playing Manchester United, and while I'm having a nap at the players' hotel the coach sends everyone a text message. It says we need to be on the bus at 2pm instead of 2.30pm. I only see that text message when my alarm goes off at 2.15pm. I run outside in my pants but the door closes in my face. O'Neill gets it opened, but only to tell me to make my own way to the stadium. At the team talk, he just looks at me.

'Nicklas, you're out of the squad today.'

Apparently I'm to be punished in front of everyone else. To be honest, it seems like an overreaction. It's as if I'm not given the benefit of the doubt. And my apologies no longer seem to hold water. It's not always been like that. In the past, I would speak out a lot.

After the match O'Neill thanks the players who have been on loan at Sunderland. Everyone except me. It's not a nice start to the summer holidays. Well, they're not exactly summer holidays. First there's a training camp to survive and then the European championships to play.

FAMIGLIA

2012–2013

I CAN HEAR my mum shaking her head. She's got her head in her hands. I just know it – I've seen it so many times before. It's Tuesday 12 June 2012 and right now she's in the cabin up in North Zealand. The one I bought together with my parents with my first real Arsenal wage. She's all alone. Jannick is on holiday and my dad is off at some jewellery fair.

When we bought the summer house in 2006, I thought I would make so much money I would never be able to spend it all. That's not quite how it worked out. The money got plenty big, but then so did my spending.

'Don't you dare! No more underpants, no more scandals!' my mum begs me on the phone.

I'm in a hotel somewhere in Ukraine. Tomorrow we play Portugal – my favourite opponents – in our second group game. Thirty seconds earlier, I shared a secret with my mum. It all began a couple of weeks ago. An acquaintance from the London casino scene sent me a text message asking:

'Do you want to make some crazy money?'

So I was curious. An Irish betting company wanted to pay me for flashing their name. But only if I scored at the Euros. I was meant to pull up my shirt so that the waistband of my pants was visible while celebrating. That was it.

'What do I get for that?' I asked.

'Two hundred thousand.'

It's not the first time I've been in this kind of situation. A few years earlier, back in 2009 or 2010, a guy came up to me while I was on a night out. We'd talked before, and I knew full well that he was bad news. You know the sort – standing around flashing thick wedges of cash for no fucking reason at all. Later on, I heard he'd worked his way into the football industry and was in deep with some younger players. It's just sickening to think about.

'If you get two yellows or a red in the next match, I've got 250 big ones for you,' he said.

We could keep talking if I gave him my number. I asked for his instead. But I didn't use it. Getting sent off on purpose is the same as fucking over your teammates. I would never be able to do that to the team. But flashing a logo in front of all the world and his wife…That's another matter entirely. And I could definitely use the money. So this time I said I was up for it, if the opportunity arose. Before long, a package showed up for me at the Marienlyst Hotel. It contained ten pairs of pants. Different sizes and styles.

Tomorrow I'll be putting one of the pairs on. They're green and white, and the bookie's name is written in large letters on the front. My mum isn't wild about the project, but it's an offer I don't really feel like I can refuse. And it might be fun. Give me a kick. I'm been bored at the training camp and bored at the hotel. Something needs to happen.

I've decided not to do it if I only equalize or pull one back. I'll only do it if we go ahead and our qualification is as good as guaranteed. With our victory against Holland in the first game, one point might be enough. But there needs to be something to celebrate. I've promised myself that, and I've also promised Agger, who is in on my plans. He always tries to get me to give things a second thought. Sometimes he succeeds, sometimes he doesn't.

We quickly fall behind. 0-1 then 0-2. For once, we don't have the advantage when playing Portugal. Man for man, the Portuguese are so good that us Danes pale into insignificance beside them. Still, we've crushed them several times before. Most recently during the qualifiers for the tournament. Why? Primarily thanks to Morten Olsen. When his plans succeed, he gets us to over-perform.

Equalizing to make it 2-2 against Portugal in the final round of Group B at Euro 2012 in Poland and Ukraine, June 2012. (Photo: Laurence Griffiths/Getty Images)

He makes us a better team than Portugal.

Today we get into a scrape. The Portuguese have learned from their mistakes, but we are slowly eating away at them. And then, all of a sudden, the ball falls to little Michael Krohn-Dehli, who does something I've never seen before. He uses his head. A perfect nudge that sails over the goalkeeper. I run and reach it just before it slides across the back line. I guide it in with my own forehead. 1-2. Right now, I'm not thinking about those pants. I'm thinking about scoring again. The opportunity presents itself when Lars Jacobsen storms up the right wing and fires in a cross. It's almost impossible for my old mate Pepe to reach, but somehow I manage to angle my header so that the finish clips the inside of the post and goes in. It's too good to be true. 2-2. It's not the winner, but it feels like it and we've got one foot in the quarter-finals. I pull down my shorts and lift my shirt.

After the match the press go completely nuts. First, the reporters want to know about my stunt. What was it all about? Then the anger turns towards UEFA. The Union of European Football Associations hands me a 100,000 Euro fine, while clubs with racist fans in their stadiums get off much more lightly. The two host nations, Poland and Ukraine, are well known for their xenophobic hooligans. And not long before, FC Porto got off with a 20,000 Euro fine for their supporters making monkey noises at a black player. That's a fifth of my fine, and it just doesn't make sense. But that's how it is. It's all about money. No one is allowed to advertise unless they've put money into the deep pockets of the football bosses. Cheating UEFA or FIFA out of their income is five times worse than encouraging hate. That's what they teach us to think.

My casino mate passes on a message from the Paddy Power people. They'll take care of the fine. Bets went through the roof thanks to my stunt, so they're not exactly short of the cash. Still, I'm not entirely sure whether that's good enough. Whether the risk was worth it. What if my mum is right? That it'll diminish my value as a player? I'm left with that concern. Paddy Power got what Paddy Power wanted. And the football bosses have sent their signal. A signal that can hardly be misunderstood.

WE'RE ON a knife edge ahead of the final group match. We may end up paying handsomely for conceding a goal against Portugal in the dying minutes which saw us lose 3-2. If we still want to proceed to the quarter-finals, we need a draw against Germany. Not exactly a great starting point.

The Germans get off the mark quickly, but in the middle of the first half, I climb highest to reach a corner and head hard for goal. It's a practised moved, and just as agreed Krohn-Dehli pops up in the six-yard box to direct the ball over the line.

After the break, I beat my marker and provide Jakob Poulsen with a sitter. His low finish whistles past the near post. Just after, Agger dispatches me on a run. His perfect pass flies three-quarters of the length of the pitch and just as I'm about to take it and finish, I'm pulled down. It's a penalty – clear as day – but the referee waves to us to play on. Instead, the Germans do what the Germans do best. They seal the game with a few minutes to go, and we're out of the Euros where Spain eventually beat Italy in the final.

It's a bloody pity, because I've not felt my groin once and our opponents have had real problems dealing with me in all three games. Hopefully, it's enough to secure my future – pants or no pants.

The top scorer honour is shared by several players, including Balotelli, Torres and Ronaldo. If I had scored one more goal, I would have been up there with them. Top scorer at one of the great football finals. It would have been a pretty cheap win, but nonetheless I'm only one goal away from achieving what I've been ridiculed for daring to dream of over and over and over again.

Now I need to find a new club. I've completely given up on Arsenal and don't want to go back after the summer break. I don't think I'm ever going to get the time and patience that I need to make to first pick for striker.

That's how I have to look at it. Otherwise I'll lose face. Not in front of others, because that doesn't really matter to me. But to myself. And it's not good enough. I need my self-confidence.

Tom Brookes has begun to look at other leagues. Especially Serie A in Italy, where Inter were previously interested. Now the other big club in Milan, AC Milan, are making inquiries about me and it doesn't sound bad at all. Milan is an epic football city with an incredible stadium. And it's the mecca of men's fashion.

When the rumours first start spreading, several clubs make offers for me. But to be honest, I barely keep up. You see, a few weeks ago while I was back in Denmark for a summer visit, my mum got some bad news. She's been diagnosed with breast cancer, and she's having surgery in August. At the main hospital in Copenhagen. She's scared – we all are. My dad and I doze in the car down in the car park and when she wakes up a nurse is sent down to fetch us.

A couple of days later Tom calls. There's three Italian clubs on the table. Siena, Genoa and Fiorentina.

I'm most keen on Fiorentina, who've made a pretty good contract offer. We agree to fly down there and negotiate the final details in person before the close of the transfer window. We're due in Florence on the 30th, but make a stop off in Milan on the 29th and check in at the Four Seasons.

We've just landed when Tom gets a call from Beppe Marotta, the Juventus Sporting Director. He clearly knows we're in Italy.

'We would love to sign Nicklas. Can we meet?' he asks.

There are pros and cons. At Fiorentina, I'd basically be guaranteed playing time. On the other hand, Juventus is…well. Juventus. The club with the most silverware in Italy. The club with the most Ballon d'Or winners. A genuine superclub. A club where I can win trophies. I seriously need that.

When Tom informs Fiorentina, the club up their bid.

'Don't pick Juve,' they say. 'Juve have loads of strikers. People they're invested in. They just want to annoy the rest of us. Nicklas will never make it onto the team.'

I'm not so sure – I think it all depends. So we call Juventus back and two hours later Marotta and another guy from the club are in Tom's room. Negotiations are under way. The owner, Andrea Agnelli himself, is on FaceTime.

'What do you think of this figure?' the Italians want to know.

'We think it's a little on the low side. What about this?' Tom replies.

They put their heads together for a bit, then make a new proposal. No one needs to go outside the door or anything – all the cards on the table. And it takes less than half an hour.

According to the reporters, I'm a last resort. If that's true, the Juventus people are impressively up on my strengths and weaknesses. They have my stats and must have been tracking me for a while. For example, they know I am – if you count the number of minutes played – one of the most dangerous strikers in the Premier League, and I have one of the highest assist rates. And they know I deliver in big matches against technically strong opponents and have scored against countries like Germany and Brazil. My six goals in five games against Portugal also get mentioned. They also pass on a greeting from Antonio Conte, the coach.

'When you're ready, you'll get a fair chance,' Marotta says.

I'm no longer in any doubt. I don't want to go to Juventus just for a season. I want to do so well that Juventus exercise the option to buy me. I want Juventus to last. And Fiorentina can forget about me.

THE MEDICAL is the most thorough I've ever undergone. I'm not injured, so it's good news. Then they go on and on, testing my fitness. Once Conte has looked over the figures, he's completely honest. My fitness isn't good enough to train with the rest of the squad. Instead, I'm assigned an assistant. I train twice a day. In the morning and the afternoon. After a couple of weeks I join the others but only in the morning. In the afternoon, I'm left to sweat it out on my own.

Julie and I are put up at a hotel. We've arrived in what is a really beautiful city, around the same size as Copenhagen. The Po flows through it and some castle ruins remain in the surrounding region.

I don't have to worry about the frenetic Italian traffic – not yet, because for the first fortnight we are driven around by a private chauffeur. That only stops when I get a Jeep. Everyone in the team has one, because Jeep is the main sponsor and is also featured on the black and white shirt.

When I signed, I went on Twitter and celebrated the deal: 'I'm fulfilling a dream. I'm very humbled,' I wrote.

Half an hour later I was contacted by the press office.

'We handle all communications,' they said. So then I deleted it.

It doesn't bother me. If that's how it is for everyone then that's fine by me. But it takes me slightly by surprise. You see, I'd heard the Italians were majorly disorganized, but nothing could be further from the truth. At Juventus it's the exact opposite. There's a procedure for everything – everything happens according to a neat schedule and they take care of you, they're sweet and helpful, and they know their role and function.

You would hardly know that Juventus have just fought their way back from an historic crisis. In 2006, it was revealed that a number of Serie A clubs had bribed referees and Juventus' then-Director of Sports – Marotta's predecessor – was the ringleader. As punishment, Juventus were stripped of two league titles. However, the worst bit was immediate relegation to Serie B. This famous club that has been around so long it's known as the Old Lady, that has won twice as many championships as its closest rivals, was forced into Serie B and made to start on minus nine points. A proud club brought low. But now Juventus are once again reigning supreme. It's gone unbelievably well, especially thanks to a couple of the biggest stars eating humble pie and pulling their weight to get the club back where it belonged. People like Pavel Nedvěd and the 2006 World Cup winners Gianluigi Buffon and Alessandro Del Piero. Major legends.

In May, Juventus were able to hold aloft the league trophy for the first time in nine years – and we're favourites again this season.

Our coach also has a past. After a great playing career at Lecce and Juventus, Antonio Conte took over as coach at Siena – and that period is haunting him now. It's not something I give too much thought to, but he clearly kept his trap shut about match fixing three years earlier. Basically, Conte got mixed up in a scandal after the whole thing exploded in 2006. That means he's in the middle of serving a ban. From 1 August until 1 November, he's not allowed on the bench when his team is playing.

You might think that Juventus and Conte would make an unhappy couple. That the club would distance themselves from him, just to wash their hands of it all a little more. But that's not how it is. No one is throwing dirty looks at Conte – everyone respects him.

And I like that. People aren't stuck in the past. They seem less moralizing. No one is in a rush to point fingers. Not even at me. Naturally, they ask about my pants at the Euros, but only out of curiosity. And when I explain what it was all about, they all grin. It doesn't go any further than that.

Even though I'm still some way off getting match time, I feel like I'm in good shape. Both on the training pitches and in the clubhouse. Our dietician has introduced me to the coffee machine, which is running nonstop.

'Do you drink espresso?' he wants to know.

'Yeah, I guess,' I reply.

'How many espressos a day? 10, 15 or 20?'

'Er, I probably drink two or three.'

'Then you're not drinking enough,' he says.

We also have to take some blood tests. Juventus is lightyears ahead of the English teams when it comes to the body and what it needs. Everything is customized. We get individual dietary supplements and pills, and it's all signed off and certified by the club doctor. That's their department.

I've obviously heard the rumours about doping in Italian football. In the 90s there was talk about EPO at Juventus and when Zlatan arrived in Turin in 2004, he supposedly put on 20 kilos. Everyone is speculating that he got ripped thanks to taking muscle-building supplements. He's adamant he didn't. I can only say that I'm making progress. I'm clearly getting stronger. And it's not just thanks to the pills. We train differently. Some days we stay in the fitness section and work on nothing but power. Maximum load and explosion, over and over. That makes you grow. We plough through and suddenly I've put on 10 kilos. I weigh 98 kilos, but I don't feel at all slow. I feel like I'm heading for the best shape I've ever been in.

If there's anything illegal going on, then it's happening without my knowledge. That's the honest truth. Sometimes the anti-doping people come by, but they never find anything. Because there's nothing to find. That's how I choose to see it.

Juventus is hard work, but it's also great fun. The club chef's pasta – just a basic dish with tomato sauce – tastes absolutely incredible. It's so delicious that everyone looks forward to lunch.

My first day at the club – just after breakfast – I stroll into the dressing room. I can smell the cigarette smoke right away.

'Where's that coming from?' I ask.

'Oh, it's just the lads,' Paul Pogba says, nodding to the loos.

I stick my head round the corner. Right there – by an open window – are ten of our players, puffing away. Several of them have brought espresso cups with them. I can hardly believe my own eyes. In England, smoking is looked upon poorly, but here half the team are at it. And that includes the big names: Pirlo, Buffon, Vidal, Marchisio, Storari and so on.

'Come here, Nicklas. Have a cigarette,' says Pirlo. Yet another offer it's hard to say no to.

Everyone tries to make it easy for me to settle in. Pogba only lives a couple of streets over from me, so we drive to training together. And Matri and Storari are great at taking me out to eat whenever I don't have plans with Julie.

It occurs to me that for the first time in my life I'm somewhere where football is more than a job. Juventus is owned by a big family. The Agnellis. They also own Fiat and Ferrari. In a way, the club is in their blood. It even feels like a family. And just like in a real family, there are some people you get along with better than others. There are good times and bad times. And there are duties and struggles. But on the outside, you try to stick together and show your best possible face. You share something. You look after each other. I think I love this place.

WE FIND an apartment on Via Pompa. It's by a square with a garden right in the city centre, and there's a great restaurant that does lunch on the ground floor. *Molto bene.* I buy some furniture and also get some stuff from the flat in Bushey sent over. It ends up being a bit of a mishmash, but something needs to be done. Otherwise the apartment just seems way too empty. It's so huge you completely forget that there's also a butler living here. But there is. And if it felt like I had the easy life before, that's nothing compared with now. He deals with everything. He irons shirts, puts out food, buys flowers for the tables, sorts out cleaning and does the shopping.

Julie likes it too. She's shuttling between Turin and her tiny place in central Copenhagen. Two weeks here, two weeks there. It suits me down to the ground and gives me freedom without feeling lonely. It works in the same way it did with Amy back in Birmingham.

In October when my little brother has reading week at Copenhagen Business School, my own family come to visit. They've driven my Porsche 911 down from Denmark. I've been missing it.

My mum is in the middle of her chemotherapy and it quickly becomes a topic of conversation. Her hair has started to fall out overnight and it's freaking her out. She ends up going home, while dad stays along with Jannick. I think she feels let down by her family, but I can't think too hard about it. Not if I'm to maintain my focus. And I need to.

MY FITNESS is almost at a decent level. Back in September after three weeks at the club, I got my first chance. The last ten minutes against Chievo in the league. It was clear I lacked sharpness and pace, but now I've also got 180 minutes under my belt from two games for Denmark.

None of our strikers have seriously got off their backsides and, once again, I'm overlooked by Conte. He prefers Giovinco, Vučinić, Matri and Quagliarella, which leaves me hanging my head for a couple of training sessions. When I do that it's blatant from a mile off. I act out on the pitch, which is fine on the odd occasion. Anyone can have a bad day. But you can't have two or three bad days.

Gianluigi Buffon knows a thing or two about that. Juventus's legendary goalkeeper, at the age of 34, is in such good form that I've never seen anything like it. If you don't hit the ball as hard and close to the edge as possible during training, he'll save it. Other goalkeepers don't do that – not every time.

In some of the breaks, you can see Gigi – which is what most people call him – enjoying an espresso and an unfiltered ciggie between the posts. It might sound far, far too relaxed, but don't be fooled: as soon as it's time for business, it's time for business. As soon as we hit the grass first thing in the morning, he's focused like no one else. Not unpleasant – just focused.

One day in October, Gigi comes over and puts an arm around me. He's charming as hell.

'You have to carry on, Nicklas. You can't stop now. Your chance is coming, you'll see,' he said.

Amazingly, that's all I need to hear. The very fact that a person that great – the world's best goalie in 2003, 2004, 2006 and 2007 – takes the trouble to say that to an underling ten years his junior… it means something. I can't speak positively enough about Buffon. Whether he's on the pitch or off. Always smiling, always helpful.

It's masters like him and Pirlo that give me a new take on life as a footballer. You can combine the good life with big ambitions. One doesn't rule out the other. And ironically enough, it's because of them I take up smoking. I don't smoke many cigarettes – maybe only four or five a day. I have them with my 15 espressos, which I've managed to get up to. It's simply too nice not to. And when you're having that nice a time of it, you don't need to party as much. So I party a lot less. Occasionally, Pogba and I drive to Milan to hit a nightclub, but he doesn't drink at all – he dances like crazy instead – and that tempers my own drinking. It's good to be in sensible company, because I really don't want to be unable to resist temptation and slip up. I've come to stay.

When we reach the end of October, Conte proves he's a man of his word. After coming on as a late sub in the Champions League game against FC Nordsjælland, I get two full games against Catania and Bologna in Serie A. Three matches in eight days is good enough. I seem to be a fully fledged member of the stable of attackers on rotation.

By early December, I'm still to score my first goal, but it must only be a matter of minutes away. I've scored in two of my last three games for Denmark, and I've been extremely close in Serie A. The club must have the same impression, because one night I get a call from Tom Brookes.

'Juventus want to use the buy-out clause. They also want to boost your wages. Next season you're going to be one of their focus players.'

This turns out to be true. After training, Marotta taps me on the shoulder. We're to have a more thorough chat once we reach the Christmas break.

'But now you know, Nicklas.'

He grips me with his hands and pats me on the cheek. Total mafioso style. And I'm over the moon. And then some. It's the happiest I've felt in ages. Probably since Nicholas was born.

THERE ARE two kinds of serious groin injury. Both require surgery and lots of rest. But if you get lucky when misfortune strikes, the muscle doesn't disconnect from the femur, meaning that you can be match-fit again in around four months. If the muscle comes away from the bone, then you're looking at six months or more. I know what I'm talking about, because I've been there a few times.

Our last home game of 2012 is a cup match against Cagliari. I'm in the starting eleven and playing well. On one occasion, I almost come close to my debut goal, but I'm over the bar. With the clock ticking down to half-time, I'm cursing myself. It would have been pretty good to open my bloody goalscoring account.

Conte is known for changing his strikers at the break, but perhaps I can still make it. A high ball comes in towards me, and I have to stretch my left leg to reach it. Just as I make contact, I get shoved in the back. There are a few tiny things that add up to make the load so extreme. I can feel the tear right away and put my hand to my crotch. My groin is simply not there any longer.

It's let go. It's completely gone.

In the dressing room, all the guys come over.

'Are you okay?' they ask. I don't have to answer. They can see how crushed I am.

Even though Vidal picks up an injury in the same match, it's not him that Conte is worried about.

'I'm especially sorry for Bendtner – I would have liked to see him spend longer on the pitch,' says Conte to the Juventus website.

He knows it, and I know it: I'm nowhere near being okay. Because I'm still an Arsenal player, I have to be treated by an English specialist. The guy who previously sorted out Steven Gerrard when he had the same issue. He has it under control, but it all goes to shit anyway. The three anchors that are supposed to bind the muscle to the thigh get infected, so we have to start all over again. Suddenly, I'm struggling to maintain the optimism that – looking back many years later – had made me complacent. I always thought my talent would make me invincible. But now doubt is creeping in: will I ever get as good as I should be? Can I ever regain what's been lost?

The press don't know that Juventus were ready to offer a three-year contract. Instead they write stories saying I'm already done at the club. How Juventus are ashamed of their bet on me and want to get rid of me as quickly as possible. Danish journalists base their own stories on those by their Italian colleagues, who know absolutely nothing about it.

It was the same when I got here. Several papers wrote about my wages being halved. They cited 'sources close to negotiations'. But my wages haven't been halved. It's not what it looks like. There are very few players who would willingly give up half their income. Especially not if they like spending money.

Sometimes, it must be an easy job to write articles: find someone who wants to be famous and ask them about something they don't have to prove they know anything about. Voilà! You have your news story.

As if that weren't bad enough, the Danish tabloid *B. T.* is raising the dust around Viktor Fischer, some 18-year-old lad at Ajax Amsterdam. The kid is a good talker. He's only been on the pitch for one international – against Turkey in November – where it was me who scored our only goal. Now he's saying he wants to take advantage of the situation and take over my spot.

I'm only out for six months. Is he for real? If that's how I made my entrance to the Denmark team almost seven years ago, I'm beginning to better understand all the angry faces. But at least I scored before I mouthed off like that.

MY REHAB is going well. It's taking place at Arsenal, where no one is in any rush to keep a tight rein on me. When my mum finishes her treatment, I'm given permission to go home and celebrate with the rest of my family.

On 28 February 2013, I start the party early when I meet a friend at Fugu – a cocktail bar in central Copenhagen. When we're three or four drinks deep, we agree to head to Ruby and meet up with Julie before my parents join us. Ruby is 150 metres down the street. Seriously, it's just 150 metres. Even so, I get in the car to move it – it's a Mercedes I leased the day before. I just manage to get in before there's a knock on the window. It's a police officer. First he wants to see my licence. But the only one I've got on me from the UK has expired. Then he wants me to take a breathalyzer test. I figure it can't be that bad. But it is. In Denmark the limit is 0.5 milligrams per millilitre. I'm 1.75.

'You need to come down to the station,' he says.

That's when I begin to panic. I explain to him that I've not even turned on the engine. Then I remember the envelope in my inside pocket. There's 100,000 kroner inside it – £10,000. It's a gift for my parents.

'You can have this if you let me go,' I say.

'Shut your mouth right now,' says the officer.

Sober, it's not hard to see how this is one of those totally idiotic situations. It's at least as stupid as wanting to move your car 150 metres from one bar to the next. Fortunately, the officer takes pity on me. I'm not charged with attempted bribery. That would have looked pretty shit.

The story about my drink-driving attempt hits the media right away. And this time I don't get off lightly. They're going to make an example of me. In addition to a fine of almost a million kroner – heading for £100,000 – and a three-year driving ban, the DBU decide to hand me a six-month ban. Granted, they call it a 'pause for reflection', but I can't tell the difference. When Morten Olsen calls to break the news to me, it sounds like it's a decision taken at board level. It hurts to be excluded from the national team, but I'm reluctant to face the seriousness of the situation. So I console myself with the fact that I'm only missing a couple of unimportant matches.

My PR person draws up yet another public apology. I read it out in front of the Copenhagen City Court. My dad handles the rest of the talking. There's no loyalty or nuance. It's almost as if he's trying to shout louder than everyone else.

'There's absolutely no excuse for Nicklas and his drink-driving,' he says.

My dad offers no support, and it would probably be easier for me to accept if he wasn't also living the good life as a result of me being his son. At the very least, he ought to show some care behind the scenes. But he doesn't. In fact, it's the opposite. My little brother tells me our dad has been going around Otto Liebes Allé calling me 'the idiot'.

IN THE PAPERS it says I'm going back to Italy to be taken to task. There's nothing in it. I'm going back to Turin because that's where I'm continuing my rehab. Of course I get fined, but otherwise they mostly laugh the situation off. There's nothing unusual about driving a little drunk in Italy. Especially not 150 metres. And the fact of the matter is that I hadn't even managed to turn the engine on.

No – the club want me back on the pitch. The Juventus people want to see whether I've still got it in me. And in the middle of April it finally happens. I score. Twice, to boot. Unfortunately, it's for the reserves so it doesn't really count.

On 6 May 2013 we become champions of Italy. It's the club's 29th Scudetto, and the whole city is celebrating us. Everything changes. Discipline drops and we do nothing but attend receptions at the Agnellis, the city hall and god knows where else. We drink Peroni by the bucketload and even though it feels kind of weird to celebrate something I've barely contributed to, it's still pretty class to finally win something.

In the final league match of the season away against Sampdoria, I get 16 minutes on the pitch. It might not sound like much, but it means a lot. It proves everyone wrong who claimed that Juventus wanted nothing to do with me. That I was a *persona non grata*.

Not long after, they make a new contract offer to me. Even though the club is being linked with Carlos Tevez, and Fernando Llorente is already reportedly on his way, I'm welcome to stay by all means. Just for a much lower wage than I was offered back in December.

This time you really can talk about halving my financial terms, and I'm not sure I can afford it. I've learned that money is important. And I've got used to it.

Looking back on it six years later, it's a decision that will come to haunt me.

FATHERS

2013–2014

I'VE STRUNG it out for as long as possible. The closer we get to 11.59pm on Monday 2 September 2013, the higher the clubs will bid. The most desperate ones will, anyway. And if I'm leaving a top club for one that's just been promoted, then I want them to show they want me with more than just words. There needs to be some serious cash on the table.

I've settled on Crystal Palace. Another long-standing London club – without any of Arsenal's silverware or titles in recent years but with a proud heritage and loyal fans.

When the transfer window slams shut in just a few hours' time, it'll finally happen. At 00.00 on 3 September, I'll no longer be an Arsenal player. All that's missing now is a signature from Arsène Wenger.

The details are in place. Two years at Selhurst Park. The same basic wage I got at Arsenal and some crappy bonuses – unless we happen to wildly overperform. I'll be a starter up front alongside Chamakh, my competitor from back in the 2010–11 season.

It's a sensible solution in a lot of ways. It means I can keep living close to Nicholas and if things between Caroline and me get better, then I can see him far more often than I have for the first three years of his life. The way things are right now, I have to make do with a glimpse of my son every second weekend – and just once during the week. And even then it's only during the day. Sleepovers are out of the question. Caroline says that I live too irresponsibly,

222

and my lawyers can't do much about that bit. When it comes to rights of separated parents in England, it's the women – and only the women – who wear the trousers.

If I were only thinking about my own career, Juventus would clearly have been the top offer, but Crystal Palace'll do. That's what I tell myself…

Evening falls on my last day as an Arsenal player. I'm at The Westbury, still my favourite hotel in London, waiting for the fax with Wenger's signature to arrive. At my side are my agent Tom Brookes, Crystal Palace chairman Steve Parish and the manager Ian Holloway. We've spent most of the day there and I'm impatient just like in the old days. The restless version of me is in full force. I can't sit still and I pace back and forth in the lobby. I begin to care less and less about the whole situation. About waiting. Why can't they just pull their fucking fingers out at Bell Lane so that I can get on with my career?

It's after 8pm when Wenger calls. He gets straight to the point.

'I'm afraid your transfer isn't going to happen,' he says. 'We've not been able to buy the striker we wanted. So you're our backup. That's your job for the next year.'

I hang up. I look at Tom who shrugs his shoulders. Then I call back. And I say a bunch of pretty ugly, disrespectful stuff. Like 'arsehole' and 'wanker'.

'We can't stand each other any more,' I say, ending my tirade. 'It'd be best for us all if we parted ways.'

I really try hard to break free.

'Well, okay – that's quite possible,' Wenger replies in his heavy French accent. 'But it's not going to happen. See you at training.'

After a sleepless night, I drive to London Colney early the next morning. I go straight to the gaffer's office and knock on the door.

'You'll have to forgive me for the stuff I said yesterday,' I say by way of greeting.

I really don't want to be Wenger's enemy. He and Morten Olsen are probably the two guys I least want to disappoint. The boss has stuck by me for nine years and knows the score. How it was a big step for me to leave the club I love – especially for another team in England. Something I had to take a long run up at.

'Let's forget about it and look to the future,' he says.

I'm not that naive. My chances in an Arsenal shirt have never been smaller. The next year is an uphill slog unlike anything else I've experienced in my career. And there's no one supporting me. Well, the lads on the first team do. When I move my stuff into locker 23, I'm welcomed with open arms.

In the press, on Twitter and in the stands it's another story altogether. I'm condemned big time. Everyone thinks it's me who won't move. That I've stayed on to milk Arsenal while I run down my contract. And no one does anything to disabuse them of that misunderstanding. Nobody stands up and says:

'We cocked it up and never found an extra striker – so that Nicklas could move on and get a fresh start. That's why he had to stay.'

It's just how it is. I've no longer got the benefit of Wenger's protection – I'm no longer a priority. And when I finally get a few minutes on pitch, it's like turning back time to eight years ago. I make my seasonal debut in October in the Carling Cup…

Turin seems a million miles away and London – the city to conquer all cities – suddenly feels like a crap deal. I curse the rainy weather, miss the sunshine and the sun-ripened tomatoes, the pasta, the espresso and the crafty smoke by the open window in the toilets. My desire to train. It almost physically hurts to get into the Ferrari that I bought down there. It doesn't belong here, so I sell it on.

In October, my involuntary break from national duty comes to an end and I get called up for the decider against Italy – who else? – and a handful of my old teammates from Juventus. We need to win at home if we're going to the World Cup. Otherwise it's over. In the whole of 2013, I've got just less than two hours of match time under my belt, yet I still get the chance to start. I'm not quite ready, my groin hurts, but my urge to pull on the red and white shirt outstrips the pain. I have to make my comeback at Parken Stadium. My last stand.

Morten Olsen has been counting on all this – of course he has.

He understands me and can read me like no one else. It's a risk on his part – but it's not a crazy gamble. Because what's the alternative? Unlike most other people in my position, I thrive when under pressure. This feeling of Danishness – which I simply didn't have in my teens – pumps adrenaline around my body and gets me into a higher gear.

From the beginning of the match, we apply pressure deep inside the Italian half. I do my best to help, but I also know that I need to save myself for chasing down the ball. Otherwise I'll run out of juice.

We're playing against the world's best counter-attacking team, and after 28 minutes when Thiago Motta finds Pablo Osvaldo, it's the perfect expression of their spirit: they deliver a world-class counter-attacking goal.

MAYBE THE HARDEST thing to pull off in football is the header. If all you need to do is head the ball out of your own box, then it's not too much of a challenge. But as a way of finishing from a distance, it's a tricky discipline. Even for the most talented strikers.

My heading skills have always been really good. Something like a 9 out of 10, if 10 is the rating for perfection on that scale. No one is perfect in football. Messi and Brazilian Ronaldo come pretty close. But this is something I've got figured out. I don't think I've ever been on a team where I was anyone's obvious inferior, not when it comes to that part of the game. I don't just do headers to hit the goal.

During the final minute of the first half, Michael Krohn-Dehli and Christian Eriksen play a one-two before whipping the ball in. It's obvious that the defensive giant from Juve – Giorgio Chiellini – has been set on me. But Martin Braithwaite manages to distract him, leaving me alone with Balzaretti, their little left-back. I get so high up that I'm able to bend my upper body over the top of him. That makes it possible to direct the ball down. Buffon is crouching on the goal line. The ball bounces up so hard that he gets caught out. Exactly as I hoped he would. If there's one place he's got weaker over the years, it's his flexibility – springing from one position to the next. The sort of thing age does to everyone. Buffon is still on his arse when he plucks the ball out of the back of the net.

Ahead of the match, the man who is probably the best goalie of all time was asked about me.

'He was a good player who was unfortunately very unlucky and got hit by injury,' he said. 'He always brought good banter and he could make people laugh. I especially remember his unique dress sense.'

He was also asked about my chances against him. He didn't think much of them.

'But if he had hit top form at Juventus, he would have hurt his opponents.'

Now only one thing matters. I need even more to hurt my mate from the fag breaks in the Juventus dressing room. In the middle of the second half, Eriksen and Krohn-Dehli race away down the left wing. I hurry to make a course for Balzaretti.

Krohn-Dehli's cross is maybe half an inch too high, because even though I jump, I only just catch it with the top of my head. Still, the ball goes down enough to bounce off the ground in front of Buffon. For the second time he tumbles backwards into his goal. The whole of Parken is celebrating and dancing in ecstasy. Watching the goal back on YouTube, you can almost hear the Italian commentator putting his head his hands. 'Fotocopia!' he cries out.

It's not exactly bad luck that my second goal is as unstoppable as it is. But I don't care. The endorphins course through my blood. This beats a good night at the casino. Beats sex. Beats *everything*. I pull off my shirt and happily take my booking. With five minutes to go, I'm clapped off the pitch. My only true home pitch.

We throw away the win during stoppage time, which bursts my bubble of euphoria. I got to show them what they'd been missing out on in Serie A, but that's not what consumes me. It's the disappointment of missing the World Cup in Brazil. That should have been my tournament. The one that kept my motivation going. My carrot in a season with no other prospects.

Equalizing to make it 1-1 against Italy at Parken Stadium, October 2013.

(Photo: Claudio Villa/Getty Images)

THE ARSENAL SQUAD no longer looks like its old self. Over the past year, van Persie has been sold up front, while two Frenchmen – Olivier Giroud and Yaya Sanogo – have come in.

I guess Giroud is my direct competitor. He sort of looks like me. Big and strong. A good team player, good up top, like me. But he's no van Persie and definitely no Henry. The unexpected is not his forte. And maybe it's not mine any more. But I struggle to accept that. If I did what Giroud does and kept it simple, if I followed my orders to the letter…Then we would be evenly matched. But he's way ahead of me in the boss's pecking order – no doubt about it.

In midfield, Spaniard Mikel Arteta is leading the charge. He's been at the club since 2011. What he lacks in terms of stature, he makes up for with his piercing, almost scowling gaze and an iron will almost unlike anything I've encountered before – making him near impossible to get around. Like Wenger, Arteta is a true club man right down to the soles of his feet. He wants to do everything to carry his team forward, and you can see it off the pitch too. Even though he's deeply serious and professional, he doesn't create a bad atmosphere or give anyone a bad conscience just because their heads are screwed on differently. No way. He's helpful, a leader by nature and you can tell he's headed straight into coaching as soon as his body gives up the ghost. I don't think I've met many teammates with greater managerial potential than Arteta.

The Germans Lukas Podolski and Mesut Özil have also arrived. Özil is a playmaker who supposedly fell out of favour at Real Madrid for partying too much. Of course, he stubbornly denies that – at least in the media. On his second day at Arsenal, he comes and finds me after training.

'I've heard you're the go-to guy if you want to see some of the nightlife around here?'

'That's not a million miles off,' I say.

Without going into detail, you can safely say there's at least a grain of truth to the gossip. Özil is a bachelor, and during his first week in London we go out three times. He doesn't act crazy or like an attention seeker when we go out, and alcohol doesn't seem to be his thing. I don't buy all the talk about him being an unserious sportsman. He doesn't lay waste to himself or his surroundings.

But yeah, he knows how to have a good time. And like so many others, he's a ladies' man.

A lot of people think the guy is a bit arrogant, but that's not my experience. If he really was arrogant it wouldn't be that strange, because during my time at Arsenal he's the best offer there is of an heir to Fàbregas.

First and foremost, he's different. He does his own thing and he's quiet by nature, which confuses people. He can take both sides. I quickly spot that. I recognize the feeling.

Now Özil shouldn't be made to sound any wilder than he is really. Plenty of guys like him make use of my local knowledge. I pretty much end up being some sort of concierge for my teammates. If they can't get a table at a restaurant, I call and conjure up a couple of spare spaces. If they want to get on the guest list at a club with strict membership requirements. I call and make it happen.

I also shake things up on the home front. Having a butler in Turin was such a positive experience that I get Julie's PR woman to advertise a job. She shows me the three best-qualified applicants. An ex-commando, a slightly older guy and Jan-Ole Herfurth, who she spotted in a feature on a breakfast show on Danish TV. Jan-Ole is a graduate of an international butler school. We're pretty much the same age and I can picture it right away. He'll fit right in. Even when I'm out on the town, he can come along and sort everything. Order bottles and stuff.

My gut feeling doesn't let me down. Jan-Ole truly is a class butler. Really friendly, super service-focused and really hugely thorough. If it's raining, he gives me a brolly when I'm heading out to the car. He puts everything in the right place, polishes the silver, and god knows what else.

There's also something nice about having him around. The apartment doesn't feel like some empty void when Julie's in Denmark and I come home from training or get up in the morning.

Julie and I still aren't living like most boyfriends and girlfriends. We each have our own career to take care of, so she stays in Denmark if she's appearing on stage, doing a film shoot or starring in a TV show. When there's less for her to do she comes to hang out with me. It's a bit like being in a part-time relationship.

I train harder than I did before I went to Juventus. I stay in the clubhouse gym for longer and that begins to bring playing time with it. On a couple of occasions I get the chance to equalize. Including on New Year's Day when I come on as a sub in the middle of the second half. With a minute left to go, we play through Cardiff's back line. Everyone except Koscielny is involved: Szczęsny, Mertesacker, Rosický, Wilshere, Arteta, Cazorla, Walcott and Monreal all use just one touch each before Sagna heads into Marshall's parry. I'm first to the rebound and put the ball in the back of the net.

The goalkeeper lands on my ankle just as I throw up my hands in the air. I know it's bad. At the very moment I make a crucial difference – something I've been waiting to do for so fucking long – I go and get injured. And I notch up another first: being brought on as a sub and being taken off again in the same match.

While I'm recovering from injury, Wenger says to me:

'You need to keep training with the squad. But on match weekends you're to do whatever you like for the rest of your contract.'

Unofficially, I'm already past it – and the goal against Cardiff ends up being my last one as a true Gunner.

THAT'S MORE or less the last time we speak. I have absolutely no doubt about the fact that I've disappointed him. Deeply, in fact. He saw a budding global superstar precisely because I was more than just a finisher; because I had that sharp eye and could be used creatively despite my lofty stature. I was meant to carry on the glory days at the club. Contribute to the Arsenal way. I was an important part of a development plan that was about more than just buying players at the top of their careers. And I failed because I let other things get in the way too much. All the stuff on the other side of the touchline, off the pitch.

Wenger didn't approve of me having a girlfriend who was way older than me and from an entirely different world. A world where it was important to socialize and be seen. He also didn't approve that I was suddenly going to be a dad at an age where I barely had my own shit together. In some ways, I still haven't.

That's the kind of thing churning around in my head while the other lads are knuckling down in the league and winning the FA Cup – the first trophy at Arsenal for nine years, and the first silverware they've won since I made my first-team debut.

I think about it in Madrid and Barcelona and Paris and in all the other cities I visit on my weekends off. When I'm away, but not just partying, he often pops up in my thoughts. Arsène Wenger. Everything is about to come to an end. It consumes me more than anything else.

I try to forget about my son. One day he'll be old enough to make up his own mind and then he'll hopefully choose to see me. I also try to forget about my own dad. I try to forget how my family is breaking apart.

SIX MONTHS earlier in November 2013, I couldn't be bothered to talk to the Danish hacks. I was fucking sick of them – a bit like Jon Dahl was when the Denmark team boycotted the press back in 2008. The only difference was that to me it felt personal. Sometimes it was fair enough for the media to take an interest in my life off the pitch, but sometimes it was just a witch hunt. As if I always had something to apologize for. Like I owed some extraordinary debt to the nation.

No other footballer has had to be held to account quite as much as I have. And I couldn't take it any longer. My life was dark enough already and when the fake stories began to show up, it all got too much. One outlet wrote that I'd poured a drink onto some woman's hair. Another said I'd chucked a pint glass at a car. None of it was true.

But the Danes didn't give a fuck about that. It said it had happened in the papers, and for everyone who had ever been pissed off with me that shit stuck. 'Of course he did that, the absolute dick' – that kind of thing.

So I ended up behaving a bit like when I was a teenager and got a bollocking in front of the rest of the team at KB, at school, at the U21 Euros or at home. I pretended not to give a toss. Next, I refused to answer questions from one journalist. And in another interview I just said a lot of arrogant shite:

'Not even the smallest bone in my body has been moved when I've read what you've written and heard what you've had to say about me,' I said.

Comments like that rarely get a positive reaction – that much I know. So I should have known better. This time it was a sports editor from one of the Danish nationals who was gonna blow up. He claimed that I no longer wanted to talk to the Danish people. That I was insulting the whole of Denmark when I refused to speak to a couple of selected journalists.

That's total bullshit. The Danish people aren't the same as Danish journalists. And, for that matter, I don't have a problem with all Danish journalists. I've got a problem with the kinds of people who write entire stories using some half-baked source. I owe them fuck all. I'm not employed to feed the media with quotes that just dig myself a deeper hole. If I comment on lies in the first place, that means I acknowledge they exist.

I'm employed to deliver on the pitch. Off the pitch, I'm only accountable to myself and the law. And when I step outside the law, I have to pay. I also understand that much in hindsight.

Eventually as part of this whole shitshow, the sports editor addressed my dad directly in the paper. Encouraged him to step up as my role model. He wrote that my dad should raise me until I learned to behave better.

It's completely insane for a total stranger to get mixed up in this. But it also tells you a lot about so-called experts. How little they actually know most of the time. Because my dad is no longer in a position where he should even think about trying to raise me. Certainly not.

THERE ARE some things I can defend. At least to myself. And there are some things that are completely brain-dead. Once upon a time I would have explained it all away. Even the brain-dead stuff. I would have called it boyish pranks. But my innocence is long gone, and of all the stupid episodes in my life, the Nørrebro taxi incident is the stupidest by far. Why? Because it's all about a man who hasn't done anything to me first. He's in the wrong place at the wrong time. And I act how I do because I'm so frustrated on so many levels but don't say it out loud. Instead I say it'll all turn around. That it's not too late. But in reality, I'm a wild animal at the zoo. A caged tiger. Aggressive and angry that everything isn't going the way it should.

It's a Tuesday night in March. Arsenal are playing Bayern Munich in the Champions League. As you know, I'm off duty on match days, so I've come to Copenhagen to hang out. We head to the Nørrebro Bryghus pub where they're showing the match on a big screen. We drink plenty while Guardiola's team play my team off the park. Afterwards, I want to move on, so we hail a cab outside. While the driver is putting a bike on the rack at the back, we fiddle with his cab radio. He spots us doing this and we end up having an argument. When he threatens to call the police on us, we get out of his taxi. But something snaps in me. Who the fuck does he think he is? I leg it and catch up with him at the traffic lights. I take my belt off, unbutton my trousers and stand at the back of the car grinding against it – doggy style. Spanking it with my belt.

Even though no one gets hurt, I can understand why the driver might have been shocked. It wasn't a smart stunt to pull.

The next day I'm in a white tuxedo at the Hotel d'Angleterre for a fundraiser. We're raising money for myself and Julie's charity, the Rich Without Money Foundation, as well as the Make A Wish Foundation, which helps make dreams come true for kids with life-threatening illnesses. It must look confusing just a day after I was pulling off stupid boyish pranks while out on the town. It's confusing for me too. So much so that I get dizzy. The contrast is so great, that I feel beyond confused.

Seriously, who am I? And who is the person other people want me to be?

With Julie and Elkjær at our fundraiser in Tårnby for our Rich Without Money Foundation, June 2013. (Photo: Liselotte Sabroe/Ritzau Scanpix)

BY THE SUMMER of 2014, my jewellery company has been around for three years. A designer has helped me shape the bracelets that I want to brand as the Noble by Bendtner look, and as the director my dad is in charge of getting them into shops and sold to distributors. But he hasn't made any sales of note. He's spent and spent so much that it doesn't make sense any more. I say as much to him a few times, and whenever I do he promises that the big breakthrough is just around the corner. All the trips to every single jewellery expo on the planet are about to pay off.

I talk to my mum about it. She begs me to keep the company going. If I close the shutters on this shit, he'll have no job whatsoever. And they need the cash. After all, it's not just me who has dialled up the lifestyle – my parents are living a completely different life to ten years ago.

But there are some limits. To date, I've pumped in over three-quarters of a million pounds into the company, and things just can't stay that way. First, I hire one of Julie's friends to take a closer look at things. Charlotte's her name, and she's at uni. Which sends my dad off in a huff. He's not going to have some slip of a girl – especially not my girlfriend's friend – show up and snoop through his accounts. Overnight, he resigns. After stringing it out almost indefinitely, he's suddenly had enough. Instead, he gets a job with a mate. The mate happens to own a construction company. Which one? The one that's going to do up my new apartment – a penthouse on the corner of H C Andersens Boulevard and Christians Brygge. It goes without saying it was my dad who introduced me to him.

All the while, Charlotte carries on digging. It's impossible to make head or tail of the accounts in that tiny jewellery company. She's out of her depth, and Jan-Ole and I agree to get some heavies on the case. So we contact Plesner, one of the biggest law firms in Denmark.

'I need to know what's happened,' I say to these pretty venomous lawyer dudes.

'Just relax. If anything irregular has occurred, we're certain to find out about it,' they reply.

GERMAN LESSONS

2014–2015

WHILE THE BEST players have gone to the World Cup, I let loose behind the mixing desk with Tiësto. My Dutch DJ buddy, who I originally got to know in London, is passing through Copenhagen – and this symbolizes the high point of my summer.

I reach the low point a couple of weeks later at the d'Angleterre, one of the swankiest hotels in Copenhagen. I don't witness it myself, but I get to hear about it. Medina – Julie's so-called best friend – has been screaming down in reception:

'I'm going up to Nicklas's room – the cheating bastard!'

She's heard I've been up to no good, and now she needs to set the world to rights.

It's typical behaviour for people who end up being friends because they're celebs. It's all about attention. If Medina really cared about her friend, she wouldn't be there causing a scene in the city centre. She would just take care of her.

Oh well. Julie and I talk things over and head for the cabin in North Zealand. While I'm soaking up some rays on the terrace, she takes a photo of me with her mobile. My pecker is covered with a bra, but I'm otherwise 100 per cent naked.

'Remember to protect yourself against the sun,' I write as I post it on Instagram.

It seems pretty innocent to me. I could have been wearing a pair of Speedos instead, but people are so eager to be pissed off. There's nothing they want more, and the pic goes viral all over the world.

My potential agent-to-be is far from impressed.

'Nick, you're not making it any easier for me,' he sighs.

There's only ten years between me and Ivan Marko Benes, but he's been in the game for an unbelievably long time. His dad comes from Croatia and is also called Ivan. He trained up his boy.

Ivan junior was born and raised in Amager, and he's a chain smoker with Mediterranean good looks who gets straight to the point without any bullshit. When he got his international licence in 2001, he had just turned 23. That made him the youngest FIFA agent in footballing history. Not just in Denmark – but in the world. He's been a legit success and has represented a number of Denmark players. Internationally, he helped launch the career of a young Zlatan Ibrahimović.

Tom Brookes is still in the picture. But we still haven't renewed our contract, and I'm not all that keen on the cards in his final hand. It's still Eintracht Frankfurt who seem most interested. We visited the city last summer together and to be honest neither the team nor the money are anything to shout about. The same goes for Málaga in Spain. Eager, but skint.

So I agree to talk to Ivan and his partner, Henrik 'Håkse' Risom. Just to see whether there's anything they can do that Tom and his connections can't. After blowing them off on more than one occasion, we manage to get a meeting set up. I like them right away and give them the green light to search their part of the transfer market.

'But I can't be arsed hearing about anything that won't go anywhere. If you've got a club, we can talk about it,' I say.

Ivan's bra worries turns out to be more on the money than I'd reckoned with. The British papers make a big fuss about my stunt. David Walsh at *The Sunday Times* – the reporter who revealed Lance Armstrong's doping regime – goes particularly hard on me. Previously, he's been a real fan, and when the fuss about the thing with Adebayor reached its zenith, Walsh did a profile interview with me in which he said I was 'cool', 'funny' and 'blessed with remarkably good technique'. Now Walsh is unable to come up with anything positive at all. Nothing except that I apparently remembered Clem Cattini's 70th birthday and turned up in Winchmore Hill with a present, even though I had long since moved on to Birmingham.

Of course I did. I love giving presents. Especially to people who have earned it and aren't constantly begging for something.

Walsh says I've become a symbol of everything that's gone wrong for Arsenal. That I've been given too many chances for too long and that I've only stayed to claim a heavy pay packet.

It's the same misunderstanding all over again. As far as I know, I looked to move on in 2011, 2012 and 2013. And I sacrificed my own earning power in the process. And before that Wenger didn't want to get rid of me, no matter who showed an interest. Whether it was Bayern Munich, Manchester United or Inter, the answer was always thanks but no thanks.

Walsh totally fails to mention my injury hell. Nor does he mention the formation change at Arsenal that suddenly made it really tough to be number two or three in the pecking order for strikers. Nor the fact that I scored nine times in just two months during the spring of the 2009–10 season when I finally got a regular spot in the starting eleven. Nor how the season after I was the fifth highest scoring, assist-creating striker in the Premier League based on minutes played. And I still had to make do with coming off the bench.

It's fair enough I've let Walsh down, fair enough to give me a bollocking for my unquenchable optimism and tendency to over-inflate my own ability when I was young. I've let myself down too. But turning me into the actual problem is just way too cheap.

Listen: I made my first team debut at 17, and since then I've scored 47 times and made 22 assists in 8,552 minutes. That's the equivalent of a goal once every two games of a full 90 minutes, and equal to an assist once every four games. You don't need to be a model pupil at school to understand those figures. Or to see the positives in them.

Walsh mentions Eintracht Frankfurt, Burnley, Crystal Palace and Aston Villa as likely suitors for my services. But that's not what ends up happening.

JUST THREE DAYS after our first meeting, Ivan calls me with something interesting. He's got through to VfL Wolfsburg, who Brookes contacted without any luck. Wolfsburg finished fifth in the Bundesliga, which isn't quite enough to qualify for the Champions League, but is good enough for the Europa League. Given the team they're putting together, only Bayern Munich and Dortmund will be stronger.

The city is a couple of hours' drive from Berlin, and the club is loaded. Volkswagen makes sure the club's coffers are kept topped up, which is why my financial demands can be fulfilled.

But they've heard the stories and make all sorts of demands in relation to my behaviour. The Director of Football and the coach draw up a long list of terms that I have to fulfil to keep the club and their main sponsors satisfied. It's all set out in black and white. Volkswagen requires my respect. And that's not the only thing they put down on paper.

I'm not allowed to be drunk anywhere others can see me. I'm not allowed to behave violently. If I'm going to dick about on the roads, the worst permissible offence is a parking ticket. I must not offend or threaten others. I must generally behave with decency. And last but not least: No more bras for me, I guess.

I am also told I have to live within a certain radius of Wolfsburg, a condition that applies to everyone in the squad. If they didn't include it in the contract, all the partygoers would end up moving straight to Berlin.

It sounds strict to me. But most people I speak to about it are surprisingly positive.

'Germany's where it's at,' is the overall analysis.

The crowds flood into the stadiums, the national team just made winning the World Cup look like a piece of piss, and the German approach will clearly do me some good. Why? Because in Germany you train for longer and more often, but on the other hand you play fewer matches. Not only should it minimize my injuries, but it should help me get into far better shape.

They also mention how the English footballing culture has been unhealthy for me. That my talent is so big it will only come into its own if I learn to live life more seriously off the pitch.

It all sounds spot on, so I end up running into their arms. After having my fate determined on the closing day of the transfer window for three years in a row, it's suddenly resolved in the middle of August. Not exactly early on, but it's not desperately late either. And it's much needed, because after five months off from matches I'm not as sharp as I ought to be. Far from it.

I ARRIVE SINGLE. In the long run, things didn't work out between me and Julie, so now I'm here on my own – but only until I find a house and Jan-Ole can join me.

Everything's incredibly neat and tidy here in Wolfsburg. And it's small. You can drive through the city, where half of the 120,000 inhabitants work at the car plant, in just a couple of minutes. Fortunately, there's nothing wrong with the Ritz-Carlton or the hotel's three-star Michelin restaurant, so of course I indulge myself.

I can no longer be bothered playing with a high number on my shirt, and it doesn't take long for my mum to get involved. She talks to her friend who recommends I try number 3. Normally that belongs to a central defender, but if 3 is my new lucky number then that's that, I think to myself. Fuck what the others are thinking.

The squad are good – even better than I had dared hope. Wolfsburg have bought Kevin De Bruyne from Chelsea and also have the Brazilian Luiz Gustavo and the Croatian Ivan Perišić on their books. Quality players on a par with what could be found at Arsenal and Juventus.

Up front, the star of the team is Ivica Olić from Croatia, who is almost 35, while Dutchman Bas Dost is returning from injury. I simply have to topple one of the two.

The person I like least right from the very start is our head coach. His name is Dieter Hecking and he's an ex-police officer. Hecking is notorious for demanding extreme amounts of work, but fortunately he has less sway than he would have done in the Premier League. In Germany, the power is split between the head coach and the director of football, and at Wolfsburg the latter of the two – Klaus Allofs – is a way more easygoing guy.

Hecking is borderline militant in his style. In the morning we have to shake hands, and he's always barking out orders. On the pitch, he demands deep pressure play from his attackers, and when we've got possession we're expected to stay inside the box. There's no expectation that we track back and participate in the build-up. I come to understand that I've not been hired to create assists. I've been signed to nudge the ball the last few inches over the line.

By the time we reach November, I've still not scored. The goals are coming from midfield. Olić, my direct competitor, has managed three, so it's not like I'm a long way behind. But then Dost is match-fit and goes straight into the starting eleven. Judging by our level on the training pitch, it doesn't make much sense. I'm dealing with some groin issues, but still.

Maybe it's a form of punishment. There are journalists and fans everywhere in Wolfsburg and, unlike in Italy and England, they have free access to the players. You need to get used to that quickly, because otherwise you learn it the hard way. One day I get asked about my start at the club. What I think about the whole thing. I reply that it's hard to score goals if you don't feel like you're being played or used right.

It's intended as a homespun philosophical statement, but Hecking and Allofs react straight away. I have to come in and be told off in front of them and it's only then the penny drops. They think I'm criticizing my fellow players.

'You just don't do this. The team always comes first,' says Hecking.

But I'm not criticizing my fellow players. I'm criticizing him. It's him who ought to know which foot you take the ball on when a striker is running forward. The kind of really basic thing that we learned at the Arsenal academy is simply out of his grasp.

I'M LIVING through the longest goal-drought of my career, but after 309 days redemption comes. We're playing a Russian team, FK

Krasnodar, in the Europa League, and I come on to replace Dost with a quarter of the game to go. In the 89th minute, Aaron Hunt gets brought down and even though he has a shot at a hat-trick, I demand to take the penalty. Josuha Guilavogui, the French midfielder, immediately backs me up and I get my way. I need that goal more than anyone else on our team.

I safely put it away and during stoppage time, De Bruyne wins the ball in a tackle. It comes to me and after feinting my direct opponent I find the far corner of the goal with my left boot. Aaaah, finally. There it is. The kick I get out of playing football. And hey, two goals in two minutes after 309 days off…Talk about getting my fucking arse in gear.

On Twitter, Gary Lineker takes the piss out of my success:

'Nicklas Bendtner has just scored 2 goals in the last minute for Wolfsburg. This is not a joke. I repeat, this is NOT a joke!' he tweets.

Now, of course I know that Lineker is a Spurs old boy. He's probably the kind of guy who lives in the past and is bound to hate Arsenal players like me. But still. It's also easy for him to say. The internet and social media have made it extremely easy to get personal and vicious.

When I was bullying the kids in the years above me, I didn't get off scot-free. Sometimes I would get confronted – my rudeness being thrown right back in my face. I had to stand eye to eye with the people I'd taken the mickey out of. But there's 53-year-old Gary with his smartphone getting a hard-on from all the likes he's getting.

So I answer him back. Praise him for the great tweet. Right away he backs off and tries to smooth things over. Of course he does. It wasn't aimed at me – it was just taking the piss.

Gary's just acting like everyone else does on Twitter, Facebook and Instagram at the time. I've become a useful idiot for people. Kids and adults alike. How else can it be explained? It's been impossible for me to post anything on social media all year without thousands of people writing 'Lord' in the comments.

And I reckon it's not meant in a fun way or with a twinkle in their eyes either. Not like when my friends called me the Baron.

So when it starts I'm tempted to give them a taste of their own medicine. But I know full well it's a battle that can't be won.

They say the internet never forgets. But I hope it does a bit anyway. Because it's not exactly nice.

I GET A VISIT from a girl who calls me Lord to my face. Philine. She likes to tease, but that's easier to live with. She takes the mick out of the people she loves, and I know because that's how it was when we met – in a big, long-lasting slanging match.

It was summer and we were at a party at the STAY hotel by Islands Brygge in Copenhagen. I fought my fucking corner and she didn't let herself be intimated. Told me how smug I was and how unbearable I must be in a relationship. When we parted ways, she gave me her number. Well, I asked for it.

After moving into my house – a white boxy villa covering more than 3,500 square feet, she keeps me company for a few long weekends. Right now she's making us pancakes. Actually, it's for me and my German teacher. I have to learn the language – the club expects it – but to date it's been an uphill struggle. I can't remember a thing from school – of course I can't.

Heinz, or whatever the fuck my German teacher is called, tells me that '*guten Tag*' means 'hello'. If it were up to me, I'd prefer to say '*auf Wiedersehen*' and slam '*die Tür*' behind him. But I can't. Instead, Philine serves him homemade cakes, pancakes and whatever else we can think of. That way, I run down the clock before we have to start our lesson. Half an hour of cake and half an hour of German is my limit.

It's a trick I've picked up at the clubhouse. As you know, the Germans love to train. But if there's one thing they love just as much, it's cake. And no one loves cake more than Dieter Hecking. As soon as he's done barking at us, he's back inside at the cake table to scoff some sachertorte or lemon drizzle. His two assistants are the same – it's clear to see. They're all on the portly side and while I have nothing bad to say about it, I might feel a tiny bit provoked.

The espresso I could understand. I eventually understood the cigarettes. Ditto afternoon tea in England. But a cake table while you're supposed to train like you've never trained before?

Julie and I find ourselves getting back together. I've missed the stability of having a girlfriend who knows about the skeletons in my closet. Juggling truths and lies constantly is not something I'm good at. And I kind of feel like I need to do that with more recent acquaintances. With girls like Philine. Julie says I'm forgiven. That we should draw a line under the past and look to the future together. She's good at that – the forgiveness thing.

To begin with, all three of us live there in the house at Sandweg 34. Me, Julie and Jan-Ole. We had a pretty good time when it was just Jan-Ole and me, because we share several interests. He also loves the fast lane, and if you get your kicks from rushing down the autobahns around Wolfsburg then that's *kein Problem*. There are no speed limits meaning there's nothing to piss off the club.

As we drive back and forth between Wolfsburg and Berlin, we get up to at least 140mph, and sometimes my heart is in my throat. I'm diehard – no doubt about it – but I need the adrenaline rush I've been cheated of on the pitch.

Unfortunately, Julie and Jan-Ole can't quite figure each other out. They both like being in the kitchen and I've become a big fan of Jan-Ole's food. I guess Julie feels like he's taking her place. As a result, she ends up bossing him about. Make no mistake. Jan-Ole is my employee and my employee alone, and he won't put up with just anything.

The eventual solution is that they take it in shifts being here. When Julie arrives for a fortnight, Jan-Ole goes to Denmark. And when Julie leaves, Jan-Ole comes back.

I'LL BE the first to admit that I'm no stranger to the delights of the ladies. My dad was a cheater too. He still is. Shortly after leaving the jewellery company, he also left my mum. They'd managed to sell the house on Otto Liebes Allé and had moved into the penthouse in one of the new high-rises on Amager Strandvej before he told her it was over.

Not long after, Mum found out that he wasn't just having the midlife crisis he had been banging on about loudly for so long. He'd just gone out and found himself a younger model.

The infidelity isn't something I'm going to denounce. But the way he left his wife of 30 years…It doesn't exactly impress me. He ran away with the lot. Mum's big heart let him do it as she didn't know he had found someone new. Now she's been left with nothing – not so much as a cutlery set – and that upsets me. She's always been there for us all – even him – and this is the thanks she gets.

In the New Year, I hear from Plesner, the big law firm. Those lawyer dudes are done with their investigation and are keen to present the results to me. But the club won't give me permission to go, so I send Jan-Ole instead. When he returns, he's deathly pale. He has no idea how to break it to me.

It turns out that almost no jewellery has been sold – even less than I thought. In contrast, cash flow in the opposite direction has been heavy and rising. Out of the company. The money has been spent on all sorts: hotels, restaurants, luxury goods, plane tickets. Some was deposited as cash in safe deposit boxes at the bank. Boxes that have since been cleaned out. But a lot of it – and we're talking about a pretty big six-figure sum – is simply gone without trace.

It looks shit, and the lawyers say that if I want to, I can bring charges and win my case. But I don't give them the go ahead. I hesitate. If I take that step, my family will be broken for ever.

It's all out in the open now, but that doesn't mean my dad comes crawling back. It's this thing about how he never does anything wrong. The attitude that's infected me. I don't hear a peep out of him and I don't confront him either. But I hope deep down that he'll change. That he'll turn up with the money and a big, fat apology, even though that's just wishful thinking.

We end up passing it on to a smaller law firm. People that Jan-Ole vouches for. It's their job to get some cash out of the jewellery designer. She's been having a good time of it too.

I begin to beat myself up about it. Why didn't I see it coming? My dad has never held back. I suddenly remember episodes from the early years at Arsenal when I would pass off my spare tickets to Jannick, so that he could sell them for a little extra cash for himself. When he made £100, my dad would take £50 without asking permission. He just did it. His attitude was very much 'I'll have that thank you very much'…

Who does that? Who takes money from their own sons? Seriously, I don't get it. And I promise I'm never going to forget it.

IN JANUARY, Olić leaves for Hamburg. The old goal-poacher misses his old club – probably the city too. Now there's just two of us battling it out, because the winter transfer window budget has been blown on the winger André Schürrle. He's joined us from the bench at Chelsea, but is a newly minted world champion and is anything but cheap.

At training, Hecking calls me and Dost over.

'You're the ones who need to score goals – I'm placing my trust in *you*,' he says. 'And you're starting on an equal footing.'

I have a hard time believing the man. He didn't like me before, and over the winter break I've only landed myself in more hot water. It all begins with the death of our Belgian central defender Junior Malanda in a car crash on 10 January. It's deeply tragic – he's just 20 and everyone in the squad is floored. That subdued atmosphere is dominant in the cabin a few days later when we take off for a training camp in South Africa. Several of us have the urge to drown our sorrows on the flight down there, and we end up gathering in a big gaggle around the back rows. Alcohol is knocked back and cards are played, seemingly without the coaching team noticing a thing. When the others fall asleep, I still can't sleep. So I take some more sleeping pills – a few more than they say you're meant to – which is a bad idea.

It's not something I can remember clearly, but I'm apparently wandering around whacking people with my neck pillow. Including Aaron Hunt, who I've just wiped the floor with at poker. We have a reputation as the two bad boys on the team, and maybe there's some truth to it.

Aaron's eyes open wide. He snarls at me:

'Don't do that again!'

But I do, so he gets to his feet. We scrap about between the seats until Diego Benaglio, our goalkeeper and captain, pulls us apart. No one bears a grudge afterwards – Hunt and me have always been cool – and luckily the episode is kept on the down low. The team doctor comes to my defence, saying it's so tough to get through to me that it's impossible I could have known what I was doing. And he's right about that.

However, it'd be very strange if Hecking consigned it to oblivion. And sure enough: in the first match it's Dost who gets the chance.

Okay, I think to myself. That means it's my turn next time. We're third in the league and hosting the mighty Bayern Munich at home. In advance, Hecking says he's happy with a point, but that's not how it goes. De Bruyne, this young, ginger Belgian who didn't really make his mark in the Premier League until he later returned with Manchester City, is seriously flourishing. He's serving up one golden assist after another. Sweet set-ups of the kind I've only really seen coming from the feet of Cesc. On the other end of those sweeties is Dost. He scores twice and we're 2-0 up. During the second half, De Bruyne doubles the tally himself, and the German champions are dispatched south after a 4-1 thrashing.

Naturally, I don't even get a sliver of playing time during the next game. Instead, Dost maxes out his spree. In the course of five weeks, he scores 14 times in nine matches and is the highest scoring player in Europe. It's absolutely insane – it's almost surreal to witness it. This footballer, who lacks a formidable shot, good technique and is hardly lightning quick…he puts them all away. He manages to score with any and every opportunity, from every angle and vantage point, and is incomprehensibly efficient. Hats off to him.

So, I have to wait for my chance. And I have to wait a long time, because once Dost is no longer banging his chances in, he gets let out on a long leash.

He runs up ten starts without a goal before it's my turn. For three bracing months, all I can do is watch. I score a couple of goals in the meantime, but whether I get to come on as a sub on any given matchday is seemingly down to chance. And I feel sorry for myself, as I have a tendency to at times.

At no point does Hecking attempt to reach out and explain his decisions to me. Instead, he comes down hard when an opportunity arises. Like the day I've put on my cap. That's definitely not allowed. He totally flips out and bans me from the next game.

Another time he promises me a start because I scored midweek against Napoli in the Europa League. We're playing Schalke 04 at 5.30pm on Sunday, and for whatever reason I get the impression that our training session on Saturday is at the same time. 5.30pm. It isn't. It's scheduled for 3.30pm, so I arrive two hours late. My punishment: a fine and a ban from the Schalke game.

I don't get that man. Morten Olsen would have asked me to take the cap off, get better at German and to knuckle down. Wenger would have been deafeningly indifferent about the cap. Conte too. But here I'm excluded, while the only other striker on the team is going through a major goal drought. If I didn't already know, I do now. The feeling is mutual. Hecking can't stand me either. He sees me the same way David Court did at Arsenal. He's provoked by my very presence. If he could, he'd jump up and down on my fucking cap.

AS ON SO many previous occasions, I find solace of a kind in playing for Denmark. It's become my sanctuary. The place where I most frequently deliver the goods. For example, my two goals against Serbia mean we can still squeeze into the Euros in France next summer. If we do manage to pull it off, it'll be by the skin of our teeth.

Almost nobody knows about my dad. Just Julie, Jan-Ole, my mum, my brother and some of my closest friends. Up here at the Marienlyst hotel, only Agger falls into that category.

It's the last day of March 2015. We've come together to play a couple of friendlies. The last ones before the deciding qualifier. Even though times have changed, I enjoy being back. The old guard have disappeared from the squad and the replacements are pretty different. They've grown up with social media, camera phones and over-cautious advisers. That means less partying. And almost never when we're not allowed to.

There are still some social bright spots. People like the two Nicolais – Boilesen and Jørgensen – who are phenomenal guys, always a guaranteed laugh. In a world where more and more people are forgetting about camaraderie and being strategic instead, there's something about those two.

It also warms the cockles of my heart when the newbies do things I might once have come up with – without Morten Olsen giving them a bollocking for it. He's getting a bit softer in his old age…

Ahead of the match against the USA, I kid around a bit with Boile. We tell ourselves that if he delivers the set-up and I score to run out 1-0 winners, that'll be good enough. Things don't go the way we expect them to. The Americans get themselves 1-0 ahead before Lasse Vibe, a new, strong running strike partner, totally screws up his backheel on his first touch. From there, the ball tumbles all the way into the centre of the box where I'm able to poke it over the line. It's my easiest goal for Denmark ever.

The Americans get ahead again, but a high cross is headed on and I smash a volley into the net for 2-2.

The final goal is even better. Christian Eriksen sends a deep pass to me. His delivery soars halfway down the pitch and is absolutely perfectly placed. He's developing the kind of vision that I've been missing since Cesc's heyday at Arsenal. I bring the ball down, let it bounce and half-volley it into the far corner. It's not just a class goal. I've scored a hat-trick for my beloved country.

I'm on 29 goals. The record jointly held by Jon Dahl and Poul Tist Nielsen suddenly seems within reach, so when a journalist asks about it I can't help but dream big. I should have learned my lesson by now – keep your mouth shut about that sort of thing. But instead I say:

'Jon Dahl has an impressive goal tally for Denmark. But I've been doing my sums. If I score seven times a year for the next three years, it's definitely realistic.'

The next day I get praised by the American head coach. A German called Jürgen Klinsmann. They say he was pretty sharp back in the nineties.

'Sometimes it goes well and you score and gain confidence, and three goals is the right medicine for Bendtner. I wish him the best in the future,' he says.

But his countrymen at Wolfsburg aren't listening. Not even after our 3-1 victory in the cup final. I don't make it onto the pitch.

Things look better on paper than they feel: in my first season in Germany, we come second in the Bundesliga and win the cup. But I find it hard to find much to celebrate. Don't get me wrong – I'm obviously chuffed for the lads. But it's Hecking who should feel lucky. He's been blessed with several players who are at the top of their game simultaneously. People who leave for Manchester City, AC Milan and Inter. It's not his achievement. It's the players' achievement. Unfortunately the other players', not mine.

WIEDERSEHEN

2015–2016

I'VE NOT really felt the way people wished I would. Not always. When I was expected to be sad about something or other, I'd struggle to be seriously sad. When I was supposed to be in love, I rarely was. When I was meant to be happy about something, I had already moved on. And when others talked about homesickness, I had no clue what they were on about.

Right up until today. I'm 27 and on a scheduled flight from Germany when I catch sight of London through the window on approach to Heathrow.

It's the end of July 2015 and it's only been a year since I packed my things and left for Wolfsburg. Nevertheless, I sense that I've changed. When I lived here, I didn't appreciate things enough. All the opportunities I had. The status I enjoyed. What others would have given to be in my shoes – in my football boots. What a big deal it was to get that far. And how much I should have looked after it…It just didn't sink in.

I know that full well. I should have prioritized football 24/7. I didn't – and now it seems as if I'm a step or two further down the ladder. It went wrong because I let my discipline slip. Had it depended on talent alone, I would have gone up in the world. To clubs more powerful than Arsenal.

I'm sitting there on the plane, and I feel like turning the plane around or, even better, going back in time. I want to find that young lad and bang him on the head with a hammer. Something so heavy that he won't be able to ignore it. Yell into his thick skull like the worst, shittiest German coach: 'Pull yourself the fuck together!'

Whenever I think about my younger self, my mood goes off a cliff. That's true right now, as the plane prepares to land. I'm on a flying visit. Wolfsburg are playing in the Emirates Cup – Arsenal's pre-season warm-up tournament. I had hoped in a way that my new club would draw my old one in the Europa League the season before, but this is better than nothing.

I'm trembling a little ahead of the reunion. What will the crowd say? The spectators I've been through so much with? Will they remember me for the good times, or will they remember me for not scoring even though the chances were there? As a greedy player on the margins who wouldn't move on? I hope that's not what they've hung on to. It shouldn't be. Because it's not true.

When the wheels hit the tarmac, something magical happens. In a split second, that insecurity is transformed into sort of feeling at home. I can't describe it better than that. It feels right being here. Safe. The grey weather, the bobbies, the black cabs with tonnes of leg room.

During our first friendly, we play Villarreal from Spain. Bas Dost is carrying a knock, but I'm not allowed to start just on that account. When I finally come on during the second half, it's back. That feeling of being in the most important place of all the places on the planet.

In the stands, the Gooners are truly bored. I step up to the touchline to come on for Max Kruse when I hear it:

'Super Nick, super-super Nick!'

It's the highpoint of the game. And I'm not just saying that because of who I am and because of the self-confidence I sometimes have. The media noticed it too.

In spite of all the speculation and lies, in spite of my own mistakes, the crowd still remembers the good times. What once was. It's a relief, but it also hurts a bit at the same time.

Just think what we could have experienced together…If only I'd, well…For fuck's sake.

I TAKE that feeling with me back to the German Super Cup. It's the final match ahead of the opening day of the Bundesliga, and we're playing Bayern Munich. Who else? The champions. I have to settle for the bench once again, but it must be tough for Dieter Hecking, because Dost has shown fuck all since the glorious golden month back in the spring. Still nothing.

Even though we have home advantage, no one seriously expects us to threaten Guardiola's men. I come on with 20 minutes left to go. We're 1-0 down, but I'm not doubling up alongside Dost – I'm relieving him. I really do think we could've created some havoc together, the two of us, especially late on in a winner-takes-all match. But Hecking is no great improviser. He can't even do that.

There's one minute of normal time left when De Bruyne shoots from away on the right. He's got better and better over the 12 months we've been playing together on the same team, and in training we understand each other. I know that he often goes for a flat cross, so I put on some pace to get to the near post. Jérôme Boateng pushes me so far out to the right that I do something I don't usually do. I open my body and let the ball pass to my left foot. I use it to angle my finish up above the head of Manuel Neuer. It's a complete surprise – and fabulous. It's a top-class passage of play and the Volkswagen Arena erupts.

Not much happens during extra time, so it comes down to penalties. Hecking calls us together. To my great surprise, I'm not only taking a penalty: I'm going last. It's one hell of a vote of confidence from a man who looks at me on a daily basis like I'm a child molestor or some junkie.

When Xabi Alonso misses Bayern's second penalty, they're in real trouble. This is what I've always dreamed of. A really big adrenaline rush. It's 4-4 when I position the ball. I take a long run up and pick a point to aim for. I don't camouflage a thing. There's no point. If Neuer guesses it, then Neuer guesses it. But if I carry out what I have in mind he can jump and manoeuvre on his line all he wants.

I hit it just like I want to. It feels right, and *yes sirree,* it hit the roof of the net, a metre above his glove. Almost in the corner.

Everyone celebrates and for the first time ever I've been the decider in a high-level final. A match that actually mattered. It's incredibly satisfying – exactly how that kind of thing is meant to feel. And it leaves me hungry for more.

My old mates have come to watch the match. It's basically the old gang from Amager, but we call ourselves something different now. 'The Fathers'. Because we've all brought children into the world. The Fathers are triumphant, totally high in the proverbial skies, and after I've showered off and sung victory songs with the team, I opt for their company and a night out in Berlin.

It's as if I just can't settle into the Wolfsburg dressing room. I haven't tried to before – not properly – and that's probably down to a lot of things. How I struggle to be completely present. How I don't really believe I'm there to stay. How it's too much of an investment forming new friendships.

They're actually a good group of lads, and I've been out with several of them, but we can't quite find the right tone. The exception is Perišić. Perišić is class. Including on the pitch. This season is going to be his – not mine – because when we get back to normal, Dost is still first pick. I manage to score on two out of my four appearances as a sub during August – first in the cup and then in the Bundesliga. But it doesn't make any difference that I take less time to score my goals. I'm the second choice, maybe even third behind Kruse since his arrival from Borussia Mönchengladbach.

WE ENTER September without De Bruyne. The team's creative focal point has been sold to Manchester City and it's a sale that will prove fateful in more ways than one. Not just for me and the team, but also for Hecking.

Without De Bruyne's ability to open up space and service his fellow players, Wolfsburg become easier to deal with. It seems pretty apparent that we're not playing for gold or silver in the league this time around. Last season was a rare success story. But our coach doesn't realize that. He clings to his formula, even though the players he has don't fit it. When I finally get the chance to start against Hertha Berlin on Saturday 19 September 2015, the league has been in full bloom for a month.

Caroline has invited me to her 40th birthday party at Valdemar's Castle in Denmark – the invitation is a bit out of the blue. Royalty will be there, A-list celebs will be there, the gossip columnists with all their cameras and shitty questions will be there. Everyone will be there – and I see it as an opportunity to regain some of what I've lost. If we can put on a good show for the whole world, then it'll be easier for me to get access to my son when the whole world isn't watching. I've only seen Nicholas a couple of times since I moved to Germany and things can't go on like that.

In my head, I'm already at the airport, and I don't cause much of a headache for Hertha Berlin. My thoughts are off the pitch, and Hecking takes me off halfway through the second half. Understandably so. A minute later we're awarded penalty. My replacement – Dost, who else – takes it and two minutes before time he puts us 2-0 up.

I know full well that it's back to square one for me. It's such an unbearable thought that I push it away and resort to my old companion. I sip on my drink in the chartered jet, and when I reach the island of Funen and Caroline's ancestral castle, I'm tipsy. After the main course, I can barely string a sentence together. I sneak in to join the kids to sleep it off, and later on Caroline joins us. Like an inseparable little family.

At god awful o'clock the next morning, I'm shaken awake. It's my driver, who has been waiting in the car park. I had given him a clear instruction beforehand: No matter what excuse I came up with, he had to stand his ground and ensure I was back in Wolfsburg by nine o'clock.

You never know with Hecking. Even though there's nothing scheduled, he can call a training session at just a few hours' notice. It's one of his methods for keeping his squad in check. That's what he's like.

I fall back asleep in the car. So deeply that the pilot and driver have to carry me on board at Odense Airport and settle me down at the back of the plane.

IN OCTOBER 2015, it comes crashing down. I'm frustrated like never before. This recurring stunt of dangling playing time on the horizon which then never appears as if it's the most natural thing in the world…Arsène Wenger never pulled shit like that. We might disagree, but he never did that. He was a man of honour. Hecking is not. He punishes me when he can, while others get away with exactly the same thing.

Like when people arrive for training a little hungover. Granted, it happens to me, but I'm far from the only one. The sort of thing you typically see if there are five or six days until the next match and you've got friends visiting. You don't feel like drinking mineral water on a Saturday night. Not even if Hecking might spontaneously call training on Sunday morning.

In my case, it ends up with a bollocking in front of everyone else. Ten minutes of yelling and then I'm banned from the next match. When the others pull the same move – arrive late, stinking of sleep deprivation – Hecking does nothing. Chats bullshit that we can all see through.

'That's okay Bas, we discussed it. We knew you would be coming in later today.'

Sometimes I hang out with fellow Dane Leon Andreasen, who plays for Hannover 96 and has been in German football since 2005. We've long ago put our conflict behind us from our days on the Denmark U21s. Leon has a German mindset, and when I complain about the many unreasonable rules, he shakes his head a little.

'Nick…You just need to grit your teeth,' he says.

I get what he means, but I can't grit my teeth if I don't think it'll be of any use. After all, I don't trust my coach. Eventually, I get so desperate that I fly in Ivan and Håkse for a meeting with Allofs and Hecking. And once again Hecking holds that carrot out.

'If you can give 60 minutes at full steam ahead against Leverkusen, then that will stand you in good stead for the Champions League game,' he says while everyone is listening. He even looks me in the eye and everything.

Afterwards, I'm still sceptical. He's said it before. But I notice that Ivan and Håkse believe him. That I will be rewarded for putting in extra effort.

Match day comes around. I'm dreaming of the Champions League and run my lungs ragged. I put us 1-0 up and provide the assist for 2-1 as well. The winning goal. It's more than Hecking demanded and I should be the first name on the team sheet when we fly to Eindhoven to play PSV. But no. He starts with Dost up front and I only come on when we're behind with 20 minutes left to run. As a replacement for Dost – not alongside him. Sprinkles on top of the shit sundae.

Back at the hotel, I call Ivan.

'I can't hack it any longer,' I say. 'I can't deal with his behaviour.'

This time my agent has less to answer back with. He also knows what was said in that meeting. And he knows that I find it hard to trust people. If I feel they've betrayed my trust, it's more or less impossible to regain it later on.

FOR THE SECOND time in a row, we're beaten to the punch by Portugal and we end up drawing Sweden in the Euro 2016 qualification play-offs. It's November 2015, and I'm suffering with pain. But it's not something the Denmark team doctors can help me with. I need Thomas Jørgensen from ProTreatment. Thomas is a physiotherapist who specializes in professional athletes. When he started out with me and a couple of others, it was on a couch in a shared building. That was in 2006. Now he runs a big place in Dragør and has branches in several other locations in and around Copenhagen.

I tell Morten Olsen about my situation. I explain that I want to be treated by hands that know my legs inside out. Otherwise there's no point. Officially, we're only allowed to be treated by the Danish Football Association's own physiotherapists – they've made a big song and dance about it – but my coach leans towards me and says:

'Take a taxi once we've had lunch. No one need know.'

That kind of thing tells you a lot about Morten Olsen. People think he's more unyielding than he is. He is first and foremost reasonable. The opposite of all the shit I'm dealing with in Germany.

I'm ready just in time for the two deciding matches. We lose 2-1 in Stockholm, but it's all to play for at Parken. It's a freezing cold, drizzly night, and even though we put our best foot forward, it's Zlatan Ibrahimović who shines. He half-volleys a corner and creates a second before I come off to be replaced by Duncan. Zlatan is already 34 years old, but he's still at the top of his game. You could say he's stayed there. It's enviable. I can no longer compare myself with him nor believe I'll achieve the same things he has. Nobody else can believe that about me either. Not while retaining their grip on reality.

I don't hear it myself, but afterwards the journalists claim that I was booed on my way off the pitch. Sure, I didn't play well and wasn't fit enough to play two matches in four days, but seriously? If that's true, then my last home pitch is no longer mine. As if that wasn't bad enough, Morten Olsen quits at the press conference after the match. It's a crude farewell after 15 years in the job. We've nothing to show for it and I feel more alone than I've ever done before. Morten is the only person who has continued to believe in me. Even when he was totally sick of me.

Perhaps that's the reason – this feeling of isolation – why I can't keep my trap shut when *11 Freunde* asks me some questions. *11 Freunde* is a serious and well-regarded German football magazine, but the hack doesn't just want to talk football. He's looking for conflicts and asks about me and Hecking. Why didn't I get a chance to play after my performance in the Super Cup? That kind of thing. I tell him what I think. For the first time in a long time, I say it as it is.

'I scored two goals against Bayern Munich, and there and then – a year after my arrival at Wolfsburg – I thought: "Now! This is going to be my season!" But all of a sudden I was back on the bench, and then I wasn't even in the squad any longer. As you might well imagine, I'm frustrated about that.'

Needless to say, but I may as well say it for the sake of thoroughness: the interview doesn't make my club feel any warmer towards me, while for the Denmark team it's neither here nor there. The new national coach – the Norwegian Åge Hareide – was the head coach at Brøndby at one point. I don't know anything else about him.

They're guessing that Hareide will hire a Danish assistant and Jon Dahl's name keeps coming up. If that's true, then things look even worse.

Recently, there was a big group of ex-Denmark players at a dinner at Bistro Boheme in Copenhagen. The restaurant is run by Per Thøstesen, who used to be the cook for the Denmark team. Things got boozy, which they often do, and in the days afterwards people wrote to me. They said that Jon Dahl had been totally hammered. I've seen that plenty of times, so it's nothing special. But all of a sudden he had begun talking about me. And it hadn't been nice things. That I was a moron, a tosser and fuck knows what else. And that everyone should know.

I don't really get it. There's things we share, him and me. And to be honest, I thought we were cool. Occasionally we've run into each other at a party and there's never been a problem. I've only uttered his name once. And that was just after the hat-trick against the USA, when I showed him loads of respect – but also officially declared that I wanted to beat the joint scoring record held by him and Poul Tist Nielsen.

Jon Dahl must have been faking it and I should have been more vigilant. That's what you get with alpha males. They want to keep the limelight for themselves. He's not been able to let go of his irritation about me and the way I burst onto the scene – but it's been nine years. He should really have moved on instead of feeling threatened.

I END UP spending Christmas in London with Caroline and the kids. It's a gigantic mistake and not fair on anyone. I've let myself get carried away playing happy families. It goes on for a week, because I so badly want to be part of something stable, so badly want that security, so badly want bigger helpings of my son.

We come up with all sorts of plans. That I should leave Wolfsburg and find a club in Dubai and start over. Together with her. Together with them.

But my heart isn't in it. I was *so* infatuated with Caroline, but it never managed to become true love. I don't love her. I love the thought of a united family. And I think that's how Caroline feels too. That's the reason why she can't make it easier for me to co-parent Nicholas. It's not out of malice – it's because I've hurt her, just like she's hurt me.

Things are over with Julie too. This time for good. She's been generous and probably also craved my love, just like I craved my dad's love. When that's how you feel, it takes a lot for you to put your foot down. But she's finally done it. She's issued an ultimatum that I can't agree to, because I'm not ready to start another family – especially not given how things went the first time around.

When I get back to my house on Sandweg in Wolfsburg, I can't feel anything at all. Instead, it's all churning around in my head. Nicholas, love, career, my dad. And a new one: my finances – and my spending.

My brother says I've always loved giving presents. That it ran riot when I came into money. It wasn't just him who got a car in 2009. My dad got a bright blue 1964 Corvette as a toy, my parents got an SUV, and my mum got a hefty diamond ring.

My friends got stuff too. Holidays, wine, champagne. If we were heading to MASH in Copenhagen for steak, word would always spread and suddenly there would be ten of us there. Of course, it was always all on me. That cost £1,000 alone. Then we'd go for a quiet night out. Another £1,000. That's a conservative estimate. I can hardly begin to describe how much money I've spent on stuff like that.

And finally, there were the girls. The girls got bags and shoes, a one-night-stand got her boobs done, so did a girlfriend, and family members got whatever they asked for. It was a bit like the Janis Joplin song: 'Oh Lord, won't you buy me a Mercedes-Benz?'

It's insane to think about. But I haven't given it much thought until the day Ivan loses his patience and gets involved. We're talking more and more often – including about non-football stuff. And while it can piss me off, I really like his directness. It's refreshingly different – he dares to engage in the uncomfortable confrontations. I'm used to people paying me lip service so they can stay close to me and enjoy the good times. How they're scared of losing what they get by being on good terms with me. But not Ivan. Ivan gets to me.

'But can't you see? That it's a bit weird? Why is it always you who has to pay?' he asks. 'Have you thought about who you hang out with and why they're there?'

I haven't. I've not wanted to. But now I begin to. And yes, it's definitely clear to see. There are true friends who would be there no matter what. But there are also false people. People who never invite me over, but always invite themselves round.

I feel angry. It's not like those with much less than me have to spend like I do – but a beer, a coffee, a home-cooked meal, or something else low-key would be fine. It's the thought that counts. Just like when I was a boy giving presents that I had made in woodwork at school.

It's still like that. I don't really mind what I'm giving. I just really like to give, and I've always been scared of people thinking I'm tight. I could never stand owing anybody anything. Just having a loan from the bank bothers me massively. No one should feel that I'm freeloading.

And the longer I mull it over, the more I understand. It's about something bigger than myself. It's also about my dad. How I've wanted to avoid ending up like him. I didn't want to be the man lying to and cheating his own kids. I'm not that guy, even though we have so many other traits in common. The cheekiness and the womanizing and all that.

I can't do it any longer. I've been too generous and reckless. In addition to the gifts and holidays, there's the partying and gambling. Those things alone must have cost me £5 million. That's another thing it's insane to think about.

I have to stop. My career won't last for ever and the money isn't necessarily going to improve beyond what I'm getting now.

Especially not if I keep warming the bench.

So take Ivan's advice and end up setting up a trust for Nicho. A trust is a fancy savings account for kids. An account that no one except my son can get their hands on. It's a reassuring thought.

I know that he'll hear and read a lot about me. Some of it won't fit, but some of it will, and when that happens, I don't want him to see me as a fiasco or a loser. I want to put him in a situation where he can say: 'Dad made some mistakes. And yes, he's been in some crazy situations. But do you know what? He's fixed it. He knows what it means to be a man. He's learned from his mistakes.'

Nicho wants for nothing. Quite the opposite. He's living a sheltered life – a life of luxury. And I'm helping to make sure that continues. I'm not only paying his school fees and other expenses, but I'm providing for when he's an adult. Why? Because it eases my bad conscience. Because I feel more responsible.

I also establish some friend-rules. A user fee of sorts: if we go to a gig, eat out or hit the town, they have to pay an amount – maybe £50 or £100 – and I'll cover the rest. That way they show that they actually want to hang out with me even though it may actually cost them something.

Most people welcome the new era. Many of them invite me to dinner and so on, but there are also people who fall by the wayside. And it's mad to think that's all it took. Everything I shared with those people wasn't worth more…it was 'fake love', as Drake puts it.

WOLFSBURG IS A city with a lot of green space. Woods, parks and so on. There's also a canal running through the middle. The Mittellandkanal. It carries on for ever. '*Gerade aus!*' as Hecking's assistant says – straight on!. He presses a stopwatch into my hand and straps a heart-rate monitor to my chest, and then I've got 70 minutes to run 14 kilometres. As far as the bridge and back again. When they're feeling in particularly high spirits, I get dispatched on a second trip after lunch. There are days where I run 20–24 kilometres and don't play with the others at all. This is despite the fact that Dost is injured and that I've not violated any of the special conditions attached to my contract.

When I join regular training, it doesn't seem to count either. I simply don't understand the success criteria Hecking is operating with. You can kick the ball into the top corner of the goal three times in a row without hearing a word of praise. But go into a sliding tackle and you're immediately the best player in the world. What kind of sick vision of football is that, really?

It's a war of attrition. I've got another eighteen months on my contract and they want me to move on as quickly as possible. Well, Hecking does anyway.

Everything I don't like is turned into points of conflict. Like when the team has to do gymnastics and I say how much my body hurts. I explain that my legs can't deal with a lot of the stretched positions where you lie on the mat and work on agility. There is no understanding, no alternative. Our head coach just gets even more stubborn and sets the fitness staff on my back. Now I need to get fucking agile.

One day I dig out my contract. I go through it line by line to find the loopholes. Without any joy. The Germans are a thorough people – so what exactly had I been expecting? But anyway… There's this bit about the primary sponsor and how I have to honour them through thick and thin. I should place them on the same high level as the club and all that kind of shit. What if – I think to myself – what if I happen to show my love of Volkswagen's biggest competitor? Once the seed of the idea is first planted, I can't drop it.

And one day I do it. I upload a picture to Instagram. Of me in front of a Mercedes. One of those that all Bundesliga players can lease for 1,000 euros a month. In other words, a completely legitimate car.

'On the way to yet another training session,' I write in the caption.

The uproar is gigantic, and so is the fine. Here in Germany, it's worse than playing in Paddy Power's pants. Worse than spreading hatred. Worse than skinning your opponents with the deliberate aim of injuring them. I've done the unthinkable. I've shown the world that I don't exclusively drive around in a Volkswagen – there's no coming back from that. It's only a matter of time before I leave here. I put the house up for sale and move back into the Ritz-Carlton. Ready to roll.

Negotiations begin. Allofs tries to mediate. He suggests all sorts of stuff. Including that I take three months' leave. But I just can't picture it. I'm never going to be happy here and if Hecking hangs on, then we'll still be stuck in the same position.

In the middle of all this, Åge Hareide calls. He's just hired Jon Dahl as his assistant coach. The rumours were true.

'I've decided to try some other options. As soon as you've played a bit more, the door is open to you,' he says.

I could cry when I end the call.

I don't want to cry. Crying is cracking. I'm too weak to handle it. I agree with my PR agent lady that we'll announce it ourselves. Better to make it sound like a decision I'm happy with.

I message a few friends. It's just like at Birmingham ten years ago. We start partying on weekdays. It's not pretty – it's destructive. Every day after training ends up being more or less the same. We hit the supermarket, buy beers and take them back to the suite. That's the only thing I feel like I have figured out. I'm drowning my sorrows.

ROCK BOTTOM

2016–2017

FOR THE FIRST time ever, it's happened – the alcohol isn't working. It just isn't having any impact. All it does is make me more sad and miserable.

It's June 2016. We arrived on Wednesday and have been here for three days already. Here being a ten-bedroom mansion in West Hollywood.

My days begin at around noon. Then the first guests turn up. They swim in the pool, drink the bartender's cocktails and dance to the sick beats. Obviously it's mostly white people, but apart from that it looks like a scene taken from a nineties music video with Snoop Dogg, Dr. Dre or Ice Cube.

Rumour quickly spreads. There's a flock of European footballers in town and anyone is welcome to the party if they're a someone in the worlds of music or movies – or if they look fabulous.

It's a Saturday afternoon and I'm sitting watching Rita Ora, Zac Efron and Jake Gyllenhaal from behind my sunnies. They're here, I'm somewhere else. I'm depressed like never before.

One of the other boys – one of the Premier League lads – digs for more info.

'What's happened to you?' he asks.

'I don't know. I can't feel anything. And not in a good way,' I answer.

He drags me inside and says he wants to show me something.

All I'm thinking is, Oh no, not coke.

I've only once come into close contact with cocaine. The real deal – not crushed caffeine pills like back on New Year's Eve in 2004. It didn't last long. I wasn't all that old – still a teenager – and I hated the substance right away. But I know loads of people who really love it. Acquaintances – new and old – who just can't do without a line of white powder if there's been even a sniff of booze. But footballers take it as well as all sorts of other shit in the off season. It's not for me. People who are born with bagloads of self-confidence don't need that kind of shit.

It's not that I've begun to doubt myself. It's everyone else I've got problems with. I no longer trust people. Don't believe what they tell me. Can't tell whether they're being honest or just want to get something out of me. That's why I'm so depressed – and why I'm in pieces and have been now for three or four months straight.

My pal has no hidden agenda though. He just wants a chat somewhere people can't overhear us. He says that no one can really understand it – what's really going on inside my head.

I don't fancy explaining. I've never been one for opening up. And definitely not to other footballers. I can count my genuine mates in football on one hand. The egos are too big and there are too many vested interests in this world of ours. We can have fun together, but the being vulnerable thing…I'll leave that to the others.

We agree to give it an extra shot. Agree that we only live once, and that I should drink my way out of depression. So I give it a go. And it helps a little. But afterwards, I must have drunk so much booze that my body protests and brings my head down in punishment. Especially the next day. It's a rough start.

I think that's where it's all buried. My body is trying to talk sense into my head.

After ten days of getting wasted, I stumble into the departure lounge at Los Angeles International Airport. I'm sitting by the gate when I plunge into the darkest hole. Seriously, I've never been in a worse mood, and I have to bury my face in my backpack and just cry.

Eventually, I panic. My gaze lingers on the airline counter by my gate. They're boarding in 20 minutes. The flight to JFK in New York City. I get up and walk over. I hand over my passport and credit card.

'Can I buy a ticket here?'

I can. I call a Dane I know in Manhattan. He's a banker.

'Do you have time to go and play if I land tonight?' I ask him.

He does. I buy the ticket. I extend my escape from reality as I've extended my holiday. I refuse to face reality back home.

People are beginning to worry about me. My mum calls. Ivan and Håkse call. They basically threaten me.

'If you don't come home right now, we'll come over there and get you,' Ivan says.

I've no clue what to say. We've not spoken much in the last few months. I mostly just let his calls go to voicemail. And when we eventually have spoken, we've been in such disagreement that I've had fuck all interest in listening to him.

People usually only manage to disagree with me once or twice. Then I cut the connection. Either that, or they change tack. Most of them change their minds. They have too much to lose by dropping me as a friend. But not Ivan. Ivan is ice cold. He's the first agent I've had who would rather lose me than keep me, if our relationship is going to be solely on my own terms.

'Don't you dare threaten to sack anyone' he says, granted half-jokingly. 'If anyone is going to sack anyone, it's me!'

I MOVE into my apartment on H C Andersens Boulevard in Copenhagen. Even though I've owned it for three years, I've preferred to stay in hotels whenever I've been in the city. It was more comfortable while it wasn't finished. Something I mostly blame on my dad and his mate. Of course I do.

I'm literally earning nothing right now. Wolfsburg's goodbye payoff all came in one big helping and I've no longer got a pay packet to look forward to next month. Because no one's turned up.

Nothing but tumbleweed. No clubs – none of the interesting ones – have been in touch, and I'm still hitting the bottle. In the last four or five months I've maybe been sober a couple of days, but not more than that. When you drink that often, you're pretty much a semi-alcoholic. It's miserable. The thing I hate about my own family.

I tell myself stuff to make it seem less bad.

'The difference between them and me,' I say, 'is that I can stop whenever I fucking well want to.'

I really mean it. I've always been able to stop whenever I wanted. I didn't end up being a compulsive gambler even when people claimed that would happen next. I stopped. Overnight. Not gambling – but gambling to the bitter end. Now I need to repeat the feat, but I can't yet. I've not yet hit rock bottom. I've not had my wake-up call.

That arrives on a Sunday in July. On the Saturday I attend an old friend's wedding and it's only late into the evening that it occurs to me. Caroline is in town and I've got Nicholas for most of the Sunday. I'm meant to pick him up from the d'Angleterre. By the time I get home it's past 8am. There's no point sleeping. Not now. I have to stay awake – so I sit on the sofa with the iPad and binge on Netflix.

I'm woken up by a text message – all in a tizz. It's from Caroline. Nicho and the au pair have been waiting for me and Nicho is upset. I write back to say I'll be there straight away. She replies and says it's too late. They've already made other plans for the day. And that's fair enough. For once there's no taking my own side. I've fucked up. Big time.

It's the first time I've not kept a promise to see my son, but it's one time too many.

Later that day I call Ivan.

'What next?' he asks.

'What can we do?' I answer. 'I need to get away from here. I need to get back on the pitch. I won't survive another month without a club.'

Ståle Solbakken lets me train with FC Copenhagen. It's decent of him, because I've not always been able to repay his hospitality. Two or three years ago he was in the media saying all sorts of stuff about me. How he would get the most out of me if I decided to play for FC Copenhagen. It was lost on me, because I couldn't picture myself in the Superliga. I still can't. Not yet. The city of Copenhagen has been unhealthy for me when taken in longer doses. Everyone here knows me, everyone associates me with something. And there's not enough money in Danish football.

In the dressing room after training I look at my reflection in the mirror. My cheeks are chubby, and where I've pissed away 10 kilos in muscle, I've gained 15 kilos in fat. I've got man boobs and get puffed out doing nothing. It infects my feel for the ball. I'm less assured – less natural in my interactions with it.

Before the summer holidays, back in May, I was also training at FC Copenhagen's Peter Bangs Vej complex. After a week, Åge Hareide stopped by. He was about to name a squad for a friendly tournament in Japan, and it was a golden opportunity to show off my stuff. He'd been there all of ten minutes when I twisted my left ankle and had to stop training. I literally got injured right before the eyes of the new national coach. What are the odds? It wasn't serious, but still…It was pretty shit. A double helping of shit if the national team is the only thing you're dreaming of.

August arrives. Ivan and I fly to London. He's set up meetings with a couple of English clubs. The Queens Park Rangers manager Jimmy Floyd Hasselbaink, Brentford's manager and a representative from Nottingham Forest. Three Championship clubs. The Premier League doesn't seem to be an option. The issue isn't really the minor scandals – they're worried about my match fitness.

That evening we go out for dinner at Novikov – one of the best Italian restaurants in the city. To my horror I spot Frederik Fetterlein a couple of tables over. Fetterlein was a truly great tennis player who partied his talent down the drain. Now he pretends to live the jetset lifestyle, but in reality he wants to do anything he can to be seen and remain in the spotlight. It's pretty tragic to witness it. People have forgotten about his breakthrough. He's famous for being famous – and for hanging out with all sorts of reality TV stars. That's exactly how I don't want to end up. And maybe I fear that I actually will one day. In the swamp of the fake-reality world.

Those people don't inspire me. They have no extraordinary talents.

Fetterlein spots us and comes over to say hi. He's got a cheerful mate in tow.

'Can I get a picture with you?' Fetterlein asks.

'Yeah, of course,' I say.

'But you can't post it anywhere,' Ivan interrupts. He's even pointing and everything. 'It must in no way look like Nicklas is in London to party. We're here to work.'

'No, no. Of course not,' says Fetterlein. 'It's just for my son. He's a massive Bendtner fan.'

Then he looks back to me.

'You absolutely sure? You could come with us…We could go out together.'

'It's just not possible,' I say. 'We've got an early start in the morning.'

Two hours later – at one o'clock in the morning – the picture of me and Fetterlein appears on his Instagram.

'Always really lovely dinner hygge in the UK,' says the post.

It's obviously meant to look like we're best mates.

When Ivan finds out, he almost explodes. He goes totally bananas and talks about heading out to find him and that kind of thing.

'He's a bastard. A total bastard. Fuck me – some people are tacky.'

Now the penny finally drops for my agent. When you're as famous as I am, people can always use you for something. It doesn't make any difference whether we know each other. Whether we spend an evening together in London or not. If Fetterlein can attract some attention then he's happy. He has no shame.

There's a lot of people like him and I don't have anyone to shut down those kinds of stories any more – not since I split up with Julie and her entourage.

NOTTINGHAM FOREST are keenest. But not so much so that the manager Philippe Montanier and the Director of Football Pedro

Pereira want to buy me sight unseen. I just need to be examined in further detail during a trial. It's my first trial in 12 years. I've not done one since I was 16. It goes well enough, although my weight still continues to be a serious problem. Montanier is impressed by my abilities on the ball. He says things I've heard his countryman Wenger say too. Things like:

'You're a very different tall striker. You can improve us in a lot of different areas.'

But he still needs some answers.

'Do you want to do this, Nicklas? Is this *really* what you want?'

He emphasizes 'really'. I'm embarrassed to lie to good people like this. But I do it anyway. I say I really want to join Nottingham Forest. That I see it as my big chance to get back to the top. It's not true. If there's one thing I want, it's the money. And being an hour on the train from London and Nicho. I don't give a shit about the rest. Me – the guy who has always loved playing football. Loved being great at football…I can't find my desire. Not at all. It feels like I've lost myself.

Armand Traoré, my mate from the first senior year at Arsenal, arrived here earlier in the summer and he has good stuff to say about me. Maybe it's him who makes the difference – maybe it's my own white lies. In any case, they offer me a two-year contract. It's a good one. Incredibly good when you consider Forest's situation. The club has been languishing in the bottom half of England's second-best league since 1999. Its Kuwaiti owners must be desperate for promotion when investing as heavily as they are in a gamble like me. The money in English football has only grown while I've been away. Make of that what you will.

I live life very unprofessionally. I don't stick to my bedtimes and only fall asleep at two o'clock in the morning. Six hours later, I get up and drive to training, where I fail to sacrifice myself for the cause. As soon as we're done in the clubhouse, I drive back to River Crescent Waterside Way – an apartment complex by the River Trent – to have an afternoon nap. When I wake up, I head out for dinner. As a rule, I'm usually accompanied by a couple of Danish mates or a woman. Apart from Jan-Ole, I've always got people visiting. I'm seeing a handful of different women all at the same time and begin to call them my 'weekend girls'. They get flown in to London in turn and then I have a driver bring them the last stretch. There's one from Australia, a couple from Copenhagen, one from Milan, one from Los Angeles and one from Sweden. I've found some of them via Instagram. The rest of them have come from a dating app that I also use when I'm on holiday in the USA. None of them knows about the others' existence and they generally stay for about four days at a time – Thursday to Sunday. That lasts for a few months. Then the demands begin. How I should tell them where I'm at and stop seeing other girls. That kind of thing. When that happens it's thank you. Next! The partings don't bother me. I'm pretty much emotionless.

When I smash my ankle in October, I head home to Copenhagen for some treatment with Thomas Jørgensen. My body just wasn't ready for that much game time after such a long break from playing and I should have been relieved about getting injured. But that's not how it feels to me. The injury feels like an inconvenience. My mood has improved thanks to all the games in September and now the downturn is galloping towards me. Everything is whirling around my head: my family crisis, the lost Arsenal dream, the ugly face of my alcoholism that rears its head when football is missing. I feel devastated. As a player and a person.

One night, I end up at Lusso – a nightclub just round the corner from the d'Angleterre. From my table up on the balcony I spot her in the crowd. She's young and fit as fuck. We make eyes at each other for a bit, then I go down to say hello. Her name is Natasja. A gaggle of other girls forms around us – they also want to talk to me. Things aren't that crazy in England any more. Eventually, Natasja has had enough.

'I can't be arsed watching this. I'm off,' she says.

I make sure I get her number and we spend the next couple of weeks basically messaging constantly. She's in no rush to meet up or anything. That only turns me on. Brings out the trophy hunter in me. The day before I'm heading back to Nottingham, I go for broke. I message and say that this is the final call.

We meet up that afternoon, and say our goodbyes at one o'clock in the morning. Five hours later, I pick her up on the way to the airport and she stays with me for the next week. I'm not in love – yet again – but she's sweet and she says the odd surprisingly wise thing. Negatives include her age, she's a bit like me back when I was 19 or 20.

I end up inviting Natasja to stay on a more permanent basis. Why her? It's hard to explain. Maybe I need her different approach. Her perspective on love. In a way, it's nice to be with someone who looks at life ahead of them through slightly naive eyes. A person who hasn't been ruined by bad experiences.

PRETTY EARLY on in my stay at Nottingham Forest, we're up against Arsenal in the EFL Cup – formerly the Carling Cup. Whenever the two clubs play each other, journalists usually write about their shared history. Players from Forest founded Arsenal originally, and they played in old Forest jerseys because that was the cheapest solution.

This time it's about Nicklas Bendtner instead. In a TV interview, Arsène Wenger gets asked about me. What does he think about my status as a Championship player. He can't hide that he's a bit taken aback.

'It was a surprise to me. But at some stage he needs to restart his career,' Wenger says, giving the interviewer a grave look. 'We know he is a top-quality player, but he needs to play.'

I don't know whether he can hear himself speaking. But he might just as well be talking about my years at Arsenal. Under Wenger, I simply didn't get enough playing time, even though I scored an okay amount of goals whenever I did play. I wasn't allowed to develop.

It's not the best experience in the world to sit at home watching your ex-boss on the flatscreen. And I know full well that it should fire me up. I should use everything I've learned. Show him that I'm too good to be running around down here. But I do the exact opposite.

The only missed penalty kick of my career against Newcastle United in December 2016.

(Photo: Laurence Griffiths/Getty Images)

I can barely do anything. Can't even motivate myself to do extra training ahead of the big showdown.

Even though I publicly say that I'm looking forward to the encounter with my old club – and reiterate it over and over – it's not true. It's way worse playing at home against Arsenal and representing a second-tier club than it is to visit with the Wolfsburg team. After all, Wolfsburg were at least a big team with big players in a big league.

It's so obvious that even a diplomat of Wenger's expertise can't talk his way out of it: yes, I could have stayed as a bit-part player at Arsenal, but I ended up going to a mediocre side. A tremendous talent that shone all too rarely and faded far too soon. So no. It doesn't feel at all cool to draw the Gunners in the cup. It feels like defeat – long before we lose the game 4-0.

It's a weird thing. When the will and motivation is there, you can see my muscles growing. When it's gone, everything feels like wasted effort. What the fuck is it all for?

When I end up with ankle problems, I'm pleased in a way. For as long as I'm not match-fit, there's no demands or finger pointing. I enjoy not being able to perform. That's a new feeling too.

When I come back, I've not played for six weeks. It's December and we're up against Newcastle. Pretty early on in the match, we win a penalty which I step up to take. But their keeper sees straight through me. It's the first time I've been denied from the 12-yard spot in an official game, and even though I score later on following a goal-line scramble, it's hard to shake off. My invulnerability isn't what it once was and in the next game I manage to score the third own goal of my career. Against Derby to boot. Forest's number one rivals.

My shattered family come to visit for Christmas. It's up to my brother to generate a festive atmosphere, because my mum and I aren't helping to lighten the mood. It's really long odds and I'm slipping further and further into the darkness. When we're not playing, I head into London to visit Nicho. If Caroline asks whether I want to stay and eat with them, I say no. I've no intention of sitting there and playing happy families again – I'm not going to get myself into any more stupid situations with her. Instead, I hit the town and rush back to Nottingham the morning after.

The darkness of night falls and becomes my permanent state. It's pitch black in London, pitch black in Nottingham. Pitch black everywhere in between. My brain isn't working. Even less than before. It's as if it's wrapped in a greasy, sticky mass. Completely numb and exhausted.

I've had everything and got nothing left. So, of course, things have to get worse. Even worse. In the middle of January, Montanier is sacked. Now both the manager and the Director of Football are history. They say the owners want to dump the club – that it can't happen soon enough. In the meantime, they rustle up a temporary coaching solution from the academy. If he wants to make an impression, he has to give it his all and find cheaper solutions than his predecessor.

I'm called in to see Gary Brazil – that's the name of the replacement. He gets straight to the point.

'I've got huge respect for you. Both for what you've achieved and for what you've struggled with. But I want to go in a different direction with the team. I want youngsters on the pitch. I want them running into the corners – I want to go out wide. I can't use guys who seek out the ball.'

'So what now?' I ask.

'I want to move you on. But I want to do it properly. Find yourself another club, son.'

We shake hands and that's more or less it. I'm not even pissed off. Unlike Dieter Hecking, he says what he thinks. And he does as he says.

But that doesn't change the cold hard facts. I've got no future in the Championship. I've hit rock bottom and back home in Denmark, Preben Elkjær is asked about my situation in an interview. He says I've never had a career.

It's over. I don't want to do it any more.

CLEARING MY MIND

2017

I'M STANDING on a lawn in Marbella. The sun is shining, but there's a storm raining down – of questions and camera flashes. I'm surrounded by press photographers. Everything has been turned upside down.

It's Tuesday 7 March 2017 – first thing in the morning. Ivan posted the photo on Instagram last night. It shows me, him and Stig Inge Bjørnebye, the former Liverpool defender. We're sitting in Ivan and Håkse's office at Nørrebro in Copenhagen – all of us looking into the camera – and I'm putting a biro to a piece of paper with a dopey grin.

That piece of paper is a contract with Rosenborg BK, the Norwegian champions, who I'd only just heard of three weeks ago. Since then, I've been hearing about little else. Rosenborg's board have completely ignored our rebuttals and continued to push.

I didn't see it coming. I'd reached a point where I had given up. Football was a closed chapter in my life. I wanted to put my stuff into storage and travel the world. See a bunch of stuff I still need to see. But Ivan, Håkse and my mum asked me to cool it. They said I should think it over before doing something I couldn't undo.

'Start over,' they said.

Not start over like going to Nottingham Forest. Start over *completely*. I needed to start from scratch and build up slowly. It sounded tough, but I listened.

And then Åge Hareide started sticking his nose in. He came

to a meeting with me and Ivan at Ivan's office.

'If you move to Rosenborg, you'll get something to work with. Loads of crosses and chances,' he said. 'And once you're a regular at your club, you'll be my first pick too. You're my preferred striker as soon as you're match-fit.'

It tipped the scales. So now I'm a Rosenborg player. I'm going to play in the Norwegian league – I don't even know its name! And it feels good. Weirdly good.

I can't really explain it, but I can point out who has paved the way. Director of Football Stig Inge Bjørnebye and head coach Kåre Ingebrigtsen. Two class guys who've shown a confidence in me that I thought was no longer possible. They've given me something to get out of bed for.

'If you have any special requests – anything at all – that will make you feel happy and comfortable, then we'll make it happen. If you want to go to London to visit your son midweek…that kind of thing. We'll make it work,' is one thing that comes out of Kåre's mouth. Completely out of the blue.

Even when I mostly laughed at them, they stuck at it. They repeated how good it could be. How much potential I had. How badly it had been utilized. How patient they would be.

But it was their perspective on professional football that rekindled my desire. Kåre and Stig mention things that no one else talks about. About unity. About understanding each other's differences. About making space for individuality so that the collective can flourish. I've never heard anything like it – it sounds like a family in which there's room for everyone. That's the kind of thing I've been dreaming of. About space. About being allowed to be myself while also contributing to a team at the same time.

So now I'm in Marbella with my new club. Out of the starting blocks to shake off the cobwebs. My first training session is far from impressive. I've got a long way to go – and the same goes for my teammates. There aren't many technical players in our midst, but we've still got a month until the start of the season.

A camera crew was hot on my heels at the airport this morning.

Watching from the sidelines, there are as many members of the press as you get for a Champions League match. Danes, Norwegians – even some Brits – have all flown in to catch a glimpse of me.

I'm still fed up with journalists. But I can live with this. Somehow, it feels like the slate has been wiped clean. No questions about my past mistakes, no attempts to trip me up one way or another. Not for now. Just curiosity, and a little bit of disbelief. Positive energy, as my mum would put it. Maybe it's a Norwegian thing.

I GUESS Trondheim is about the same size as Wolfsburg – maybe a little larger. Apart from that, the cities have *nothing* in common. This place is wild and untamed. There's no massive car plant, no straight canals. Instead, there's a surf-covered coastline and one hell of a river running right through city. We're surrounded by mountains – or fjelds, as they say in Norwegian.

The club's amazing fixer is called Harald and he must be in his 50s. He doesn't show me where to eat or where to go out and have fun. He takes me on a sightseeing trip in the fjelds. Even though it should be spring by now, he gets some winter tyres fitted to my SUV – a leased Volkswagen, would you believe it. I didn't have a problem with the brand – just Hecking.

While we're hiking, Harald tells me about the flora and fauna. About the changing seasons and how the lakes freeze as the clouds waft across the sky so that you never see the same thing above you twice. Although this place is basking in peace and quiet, everything is in motion. I like that. It appeals to me. Me and my restless soul.

But there are also some things I'll have to swallow. Like the fact that we train on artificial grass. When you're over 6ft 3in and weigh going on 15½ stone, AstroTurf is bad news. My knees don't care for it at all. And when the temperature in the morning is below zero – which still happens in the middle of March – they hurt so much that I feel old. Old before my time.

The squad gets along. It's not like at most other clubs where the players zoom off from training – each one in their own sports car. Here we squeeze into the back seat, pack the flasks, food and a few lagers into the boot, and then head out to go fishing. It's hard to spot the cliques. Everyone is invited.

Mike Jensen – my childhood rival, the gruff lad from Rødovre – has been working on his angling skills since he got here in 2013. He's still to catch something. Seriously, he's been standing there in his waders with water up to his hips for hundreds of hours. Absolutely zero catches. It's crazy – but he seems bizarrely happy just to be trying. Mike isn't the Mike I knew when we were kids. Nor is he the Mike who became infamous for shouting in the face of an injured opponent. Mike still has the winning mentality of old, but he's a more easygoing version of himself. Something has changed.

I realize pretty soon it's all Trondheim's doing. Life up north in Norway has left its mark on Mike. He wants the same thing for me: turns out it was his idea to tempt me here.

It's not always important to catch first, most, or biggest when you're out fishing. What really counts is being there with the others. Side by side in the ice-cold water with a pouch of snus tobacco under your upper lip – almost silent. You don't want to be the guy who scares off the salmon and trout.

When night falls, the Milky Way shines above the city. Instead of staring at the TV like a couch potato in my hotel room, I put on a thick winter jacket, pull the hood down over my forehead and head outside to explore. I stroll through windswept neighbourhoods with names like Kalvskinnet (Calf Skin), Bakklandet (Hilly Land), Brattøra (Steep Confluence), Lademoen (Loading Moor), Steinberget (Stone Mountain) and Nyhavna (New Harbour). And the small bridges that cross the river. I follow its course towards the port and stare out across the fjord that leads out to the Norwegian Sea. On the horizon there are ships – their lamps beaming.

Few people recognize me in the dark, but when they do they stop to talk. I don't understand everything they say – to my Danish ear, their cheery, sing-song Norwegian isn't always the easiest to catch – but it's nice enough. When I'm allowed to carry on, I go back to my mental training. I visualize. My mum's soothsaying friend got me started on it eight years ago – just before the motorway smash

– visualizing things I wanted to happen. I've not tried it in a long time – but I give it another go now.

I visualize it in front of me: ending up as the top scorer with at least 20 goals in the league. Scoring the winner when we're playing in Europe. Making my comeback with Denmark. Celebrating when scoring my 30th goal wearing the red and white strip. Us qualifying for the World Cup.

It makes it all tangible, and it clears things up in my mind. Now I know what I'm dealing with. The peacefulness and the fresh air are seeping into my head. The fog is providing relief to my brain. The fat is dripping away. It's a slow process with small steps, but it feels like I'm having a really serious clear-out in there.

THE SEASON in Norway is based on the calendar year and our opening match is against Odd Grenland. It seems like a fucking weird name for a football club to me, but what do I know? I know that it makes no odds who our opponents are. We're always the massive favourites.

Since the start of the millennium, Rosenborg have won the Norwegian championship ten times. On just six occasions the team has had to make do with anything less, and this year expectations are bigger than ever. Mostly because of me. I haven't played a single minute of football yet, and I'm already being described as the highest profile player in the history of Eliteserien – Norway's top flight. The sale of shirts has gone through the roof and there are welcome banners hanging all over our home ground, Lerkendal. Sixteen thousand people have made their way to the stadium, and while that might be fewer than I'm used to, it's almost a sell-out and still early days in the season. I'm psyched. From the first whistle, I can feel how hungry I am to get going.

So I do. After 56 minutes, Pål André Helland whips in a cross towards the back post. I outpace my marker, raise my head and direct it across goal. The goalkeeper doesn't even make an attempt to jump for it. 1-0. Right away, the team are chasing after me. It's an incredible feeling to be so appreciated. Everyone wants me to succeed. That's how it works.

In the next match, I reach a hard cross first. Another goal. With goals from my only two chances in my first two matches, my potential should be proven. That should be enough to keep everyone happy while I iron out the final issues. But I'm mistaken. Not all Norwegians are as easygoing, and after a couple of so-so performances, the so-called football experts start asking questions.

The biggest fool of the bunch, some nobody from Norwegian TV2, claims I'm simply not good enough to make Rosenborg's best starting eleven. If you've attended training for a mere three minutes, then you'll know that's a ridiculous claim. Completely, utterly ridiculous.

It's something I'll get used to later on. The commentators up here – generally a bunch of pretty unimpressive guys without much experience of top-level football – can get completely hysterical. I think they must be bored. There's not enough going on and they get paid per click or something. They do nothing but speculate aimlessly, evoke fantasies and scaremonger. And it goes without saying that they are usually exceedingly poorly informed about pretty much everything. If only it were that easy to be a footballer.

Of course, Kåre and Stig are cool as cucumbers. They get hold of me at lunch in the small clubhouse where my face is filling every wall and screen imaginable. If there's a poster, it doesn't matter whether there's one, three, five or eleven players on it – or the whole damn squad, even. I'm guaranteed to be on it.

'We have patience. This isn't something that's going to happen in half a season. It's going to happen over one, two or maybe even three seasons,' is what my new bosses have to say.

They're generally pretty quick on the uptake. Trondheim is so small that you can't break wind without everyone having an opinion about it. So when I end up chatting to a couple of Trondheim's self-proclaimed nightlife kings, word gets around fast.

'They just want to use you to make themselves important. They'll make up their own stories,' Kåre warns me.

He need say no more. I don't want any Fetterleins in my life. That's not going to be what gets in the way of my comeback to top-level football. One thing leads to another, hey presto, I've made yet another big decision. I'm on my way out of the city centre. Away away. Out of the danger zone and into nature.

NATASJA FLIES in and we go house hunting together. Harald is squiring us around and we're also escorted by Ivar Koteng. Koteng is the club owner and he's loaded. But he doesn't show off his millions. Not one bit. He looks like he lives off junk food, and he's always dressed in tatty jeans and his rotation of zip-up jumpers. Probably because they're easy to put on and take off. Although I might have different tastes in fashion, I like his unostentatious approach. If you've got unlimited money, it's quite the statement. Between the lines, Koteng is making it clear that he's not been changed by wealth. If our club owner went fishing, he'd do it the same way as Mike does. Not to catch anything – just because he enjoyed doing it.

I end up buying the most expensive cabin for sale in Trondheim. Well, it's a bit more than a cabin. It's a super-modern villa – even for my tastes – and it's hidden away behind the mountains. You have to go through a long tunnel and drive up the fjeld from the other side. £1.6 million seems like it's a little on the pricey side for a temporary house, but then Koteng steps in.

'If you can't get rid of it for that price, then it's no problem. I'll take it,' he growls. It's a quick aside, but it doesn't make it seem any less decisive. The support feels total.

After training, the usual bunch of journalists are waiting and want to talk. They ask about my accommodation situation. Can I confirm whether I've bought a house in Jakobsli? I tell them yes I have, but they can't write about it. They need to respect my private life.

Wouldn't you know, true to form I'm hot news in the local paper – *Adresseavisen* – the next morning. They've slapped a big picture of the house on the front page and described it as the 'star striker's functionalism palace'. When I see what they've done, I'm really pissed off. Stig and Kåre notify *Adresseavisen* on my behalf that I'm done giving exclusive statements. We can only talk football from now on.

And the peace is over. My house becomes a destination for daytrippers. Every afternoon, when I come driving up the narrow lane there are people waiting with cameras. Little kids, young girls, older folks creeping right up to the windows, looking inside and ringing the doorbell.

That's definitely not okay. It's too extreme for my tastes.

Even though it was worse in London – paparazzi waiting for me at all hours of the day – they usually stayed away from my home. And there were far more of us celebs sharing the unwanted attention. Right now, it's as if there's one celebrity in all of Trondheim. Everyone's eyes are on me. All. The. Time. At least that's how it feels. Like I'm under surveillance. It's too intense.

AT THE MIDPOINT in the season, I've scored six times in sixteen league appearances. It's not flashy, but I've put in some good performances and there have been glimpses of my past top form. For the first time in eight years, I've been injury-free for eight months in a row, and I can feel it in my body. Everything is beginning to work in harmony. My instincts can take over.

I score a brace against Kristiansund on 5 August, the second comes out of defiance. Even though I'm standing there shouting for it, Jevtović goes for it himself. Luckily, the rebound bounces in my direction. I smash it resolutely in the back of the net but don't celebrate afterwards. Instead, I school my strike partner. Granted, I no longer play for Arsenal, but when you're in front of goal you do what's best for your team. You don't leather the ball into three opponents blocking your way when your partner is in space an arm's length away. End of.

Masses of column inches are written about the blow-up. But to be perfectly honest I don't give a fuck. I'm happy with my own reaction. It shows I'm hungry. For the first time in forever, things are on the up in my soul and the game of life. I forget about everything except winning.

And I'm on fire. During our next game against Molde, I score a goal that they'll never forget about in Norway. It's shown all over the world as an 'and finally' segment at the end of the sports news. It's kind of 'look, he's *still* alive, that Danish Lord Bendtner.'

But if I'm honest, no one should laugh when they watch that goal. It happens quickly. Molde's goalkeeper fluffs his goal kick, and it's collected by Matthías Vilhjálmsson, our Icelandic number ten. Matthí is caught off-guard by a tackle, but then Mike gets possession of the ball. He knocks it to the right – towards me. I'm on the edge of the box, almost with my back to the goal. Even so, I hit it with my first touch using the outside of my right foot. It's an instinctive kick. Like taking aim with a pool cue at such a quirky angle that the shot spins round the obstacles in front of you.

If the ball had followed a straight line it would have ended up by the corner flag. But it doesn't – it arcs in the air like a boomerang, and it just manages to find its way inside the far post. Right in the top corner.

This time I know for sure. It's the goal of the year. At any rate it's a goal like no other. I have to remember to enjoy it.

THERE ARE always people trying to invent conflicts, and some of them have pretty wild imaginations. Like how I'm at odds with Matthí in the dressing room. That we're fighting for the same spot in the team, and that it's somehow got personal. Nothing could be further from the truth. While they write their crappy gossip about us, we've become such good friends I've even babysat for him and we have several barbecues together every week.

Like I said, the Norwegian pundits don't have enough to talk about. Which is why the question of my sponsorship contract gets blown out of all proportion. In short, Rosenborg have a contract with Adidas that requires the whole squad to play in German football boots. That kind of thing would be unthinkable in more southern latitudes, but up here it's the collective that is acknowledged as the star – that's how it's been until now. Things don't look good for my Nike contract.

When it emerges that another player had to bin his Nikes while I was given permission to carry on playing in mine, it's front-page news.

I figure I might as well be proactive and personally approach Stig with a solution. Adidas should buy me out of my Nike contract and match my old terms. Of course, it'll mean a farewell to my bright pink football boots, but after nine years it's high time something new happened on that front.

Rosenborg agree to the plan, and since none of the press and no one in the squad cotton on to the fact that I'm not only part of the team contract, but I also have a personal contract, everyone is happy.

It's not something I've been accustomed to – playing problem solver. But I could get used to it. It gives me a bit of a kick.

I'M EXCITED. For the first time in two years, I'm checking my mobile the day before they announce the Denmark squad. I wonder whether Hareide is going to call with an invitation to the matches against Poland and Armenia. He doesn't. Hareide prefers Nicolai Jørgensen, Andreas Cornelius and Kasper Dolberg, who can all play up front. I'm on more of a goalscoring streak than they are and I have way more experience to call on. But they're playing in stronger leagues, so I guess it's fair enough. Maybe I need to show even more. Maybe Hareide exaggerated how easy it would be if I just headed north to Rosenborg. Or maybe there's someone whispering in his ear.

I tell myself it's all to play for and I've got plenty to prove. Our final fixture ahead of the Europa League group stages happens to be against Ajax Amsterdam. Ajax are a way bigger football team, and I'd be chuffed to knock the Dutchmen out. The team is packed with people being bigged up as the next big thing. That includes Dolberg, who has some indisputable qualities that he's still failed to show in the very biggest matches.

We depart from the Amsterdam ArenA with a victory. In the return leg, the Lerkendal is full to bursting: 22,000 spectators and flares in the stands. This is something that Rosenborg's fans care about. It's something quite different from beating opponents on the domestic front.

Early on in the game, the Dutch toy with our back line, and it's more luck than skill that I'm able to put us ahead in the middle of the first half. Ajax dominate so much – they're completely devastating after their home defeat – that they forget their markings at their own end of the pitch. All I have to do is park up by the back post and direct the ball in.

We end up knocking them out 4-2 on aggregate. We're going to play in Europe – properly. The first of my ambitions has been fulfilled. But I don't say it out loud. I don't want anyone to know what my dream is. If it gets out, I'll only draw flak for everything perhaps being unsuccessful.

Three days later I get a call from Hareide. Yussuf Poulsen has picked up an injury, so a spot has opened up for me. Even though it's the result of a withdrawal, it still feels good to be back at the Hotel Marienlyst. Measuring myself up against the best players in my own country gives me much more than when I only wanted to compare myself with the best in the world. Less is okay. Especially when you come directly from a league where you're at the centre of everything all of the time. Things have most definitely changed on the Denmark team. I no longer have the biggest profile. That would be Christian Eriksen. At least on the pitch.

Training sessions under the new coach aren't all that different to what they were like under Morten Olsen, and I put in a good performance. I'm really switched on and in the kind of mood I've not been in since the early months at Juventus.

Hareide and Jon Dahl have hatched a plan of sorts. Organized chaos. We're going to defeat the Poles – the supreme group leaders – by playing the opposite of polished football. Cornelius is dispatched to the right wing, but not to break through the back line. He's there to create havoc with his monstrous physique. The idea is for our midfielders to capture the balls that Cornelius wins in the air.

Our plan catches Poland napping, and the mighty nation fumble in vain for a counter-response. Suddenly it's a question of by how much – rather than whether – we can win at all. With 15 minutes to go, it's 3-0. Cornelius has run himself ragged – he's totally shattered.

All the subs are warming up, but it's me who gets the chance. It's a fair call based on our performances in training, but I just haven't seen it coming. The chaos tactic has Jon Dahl's fingerprints all over it. Jon Dahl isn't a creator, he's a toiler. And I'll give you this – he's good at it.

As I approach the white chalk line, the rhythmic clapping begins. All around the stadium. And when I finally step onto the pitch – there it is. The roar. It's the Emirates times ten. It's as if everything is forgiven and forgotten. Well, maybe not forgotten exactly. They still remember, but I'm being recognized for still standing.

I'm treated like the prodigal son returned home. The punishment has been served, I'm still loved. I'm filled with a warmth I've been missing and longing for, more than I've wanted to admit to myself. My whole body is glowing. It's the biggest moment in my footballing life.

'Friday, 1 September 2017, 22:15' should be tattooed onto my skin. But there's no need. It's etched into my memory.

I slot in nicely and make it hard for the defenders and get a couple of good chances in the 15 minutes I'm on the pitch. There's no goal from me but we ease to a 4-0 win. There is upon my return to Trondheim though. The Danish fans' love has given me wings, superhero powers, and during the three league games in September I score five goals. I also get on the scoreboard three times in the Europa League, all with penalties, though we can finish only third in the group.

It's not really as a result of us playing all that well, but I'm extremely effective, I'm getting sharper and sharper, and making use of every single finish. Suddenly I'm in the running for top scorer, which just whets my appetite. Now I'm on the hunt.

BACK HOME in Amager, my mum has her life back under enough control that she can be a good grandma. She sees Nicho far more than I can, but even on that front things are improving. Nicholas is almost seven years old, and he's become so curious about his dad that he can't be kept away. So I'm allowed to have him to visit accompanied by my mum and his nanny, Cille. That's how Caroline wants it, and to be perfectly honest, it's a reassuring solution from my perspective too. I don't really know him all that well. That's how it's ended up, but it's not how it should be. Not for ever.

It feels good to have my son under my own roof. Feels good to bring him to a match at the stadium. Feels good to share something that's going well. Feels good for him to meet people who think his dad is a decent, talented guy.

In October I get to play a full 90 minutes against Romania at Parken. In the stands a group of spectators have brought a banner with them. In huge letters, it says: '*FRA LORT TIL LORD*' – something like, 'FROM SHITLORD TO LORDSHIP'. They're right in so many ways. Especially when you come from Amager. Shit Island itself. I can laugh about it now – and I don't take it all that personally any longer. The malicious shade around being called Lord has been shaken off and it's become my new nickname.

My feet feel lighter than they should this far into the club season. It's not just a feeling, because against the Romanians I get proof. We're 36 minutes in when Kasper Schmeichel punches a ball up field. He finds Eriksen who passes the ball forward to me. I hold onto it and then play it back to Eriksen who is storming forward. I also set off at a run. Eriksen reaches the centre line where three opponents try to halt him. He wriggles free and fires towards the Romanian box. His pass arcs over the yellow-shirted central defender. I've turned up at exactly the right moment and reach the ball just as it hits the grass. My outside touch works like a charm as I step around the advancing keeper and put the ball away into the empty goal.

The mutual understanding between me and Eriksen on the pitch has never been stronger. We've not just done a one-two – we've done a one-two-one-two, all in the space of 12 seconds. It's my finest goal for Denmark in ages. Top three of all time.

Even though everyone at Parken is roaring, I hear it clearly. The referee's whistle. The flag is up for offside – but it wasn't. I was level with their last defender when the pass was delivered, which can clearly be seen in the slow-motion replay.

At half-time the linesman comes over and apologizes. I'm fucking hurt. A class goal like that could be the be-all and end-all for my position in the attacking pecking order. It was almost too elegant, almost too effective.

During the second half, I'm being pushed and shoved over five metres, but I still manage a finish of sorts with my head. This time I'm not sent off, and Eriksen puts away the subsequent penalty. The goal secures a point and sends us into the play-offs to face Ireland.

The winner over two legs will be going to the World Cup. At Parken, I watch most of the game from the bench. I'm clearly still behind Jørgensen and Cornelius.

It ends 0-0 and our offensive strategy doesn't seem all that convincing, especially when we fail to take the initiative. It's as if everything has to go through Eriksen, which is a flimsy tactic. Especially when he fails to rise to the challenge.

I've got to say that he does manage it in Dublin though. The Irish make it 1-0 after just five minutes, but that's almost a good thing because it forces us to throw caution to the wind. It suits us. Shots and assists are bubbling out of Eriksen, and there's loads of others who want to get in on the action. They include Pione Sisto, who will take a shot from anywhere and has probably never even heard of the Arsenal Way. He must be absolutely desperate to score his first goal in the red and white jersey. Understandably. I'm hungry too.

I come off the bench when we're 4-1 up. Eriksen has scored a hat-trick and the match has been decided. So when I earn my second penalty kick in a month, I want to take it myself. Of course I do.

For the sake of the team as a whole, I kept a low profile against Romania, but otherwise it's always been a tradition for me to demand to take the penalties. It was basically a running joke between me and Agger who always ended up pushing me all the way out of the box again. That was what happened against Turkey in 2014 and Serbia in 2015. And doubtless on a few occasions before that. I've been in similar situations at Birmingham, Arsenal and Wolfsburg.

Denmark needs strikers who score and will score no matter what. I tell Eriksen and Delaney as much when they get involved. Eriksen hesitates for a second, but then he agrees to let me have it. Of course he does. Eriksen ain't Agger. He's a friendly guy.

I put it in the top corner and act like it was the winning penalty kick in the World Cup final. It's a huge relief.

Back in the dressing room, we're cheering and singing. I don't notice any irritation or anything. If I've pissed people off by taking the penalty, then they're hiding it well. Everyone is happy, and most of them want to head out into Dublin to celebrate securing their ticket to the World Cup. But personally I'm not really up for it. I'm no longer Bamm-Bamm from my early years in the Denmark squad, and I don't want to be either.

If I head out into the Irish capital, I'm risking everything going wrong. I can already picture it. The local lads hassling me until I can't stick it any longer, and the whole thing ending in some massive screw-up. It would spoil other people's big night. I've seen it happen too many times, and it's not worth it. So instead I have a couple of beers on the way to the airport and I catch the last flight home.

Now all I need to do is finish the job in Norway. I want to get back to Trondheim. I want to nab the top-scorer title. Then everything – all the things I dared to visualize on my walking tour of the city back in March – will have been fulfilled.

I can feel it. I'm reacting like Mike did. I've aired out my mind. I'm reading the game faster. Spotting the gaps that might appear. It's Maths with Gregers all over again. And for the first time I understand how important it is to have my head screwed on. It's good to be strong, but the power of my brain and the way it thinks…It's just a completely different beast. It needs special treatment and the perfect diet.

It's all connected. Because off the pitch I no longer need to escape. It probably sounds corny, but I've found something that quells my fear of missing out on things. It's the opposite of alcohol and nights out on the town. It's nature itself.

COUNTDOWN

2017–2018

YOU CAN overdose on anything. Don't get me wrong – I still love the fresh air, going on walks, the view of the snow-capped mountains, sliding around on the ice that's set on the Baklidammen lake like a layer of concrete. But I don't love the Norwegian winter. Not unconditionally. It checks in early and outstays its welcome. Dark, cold and unbelievably long – that's just how it feels by December. By the time holidays come around, I can't rush quick enough for the taste of paradise in the Maldives.

Natasja and I are going away for a fortnight and when we touch down in the land of bounty everything is lovely. I'm not planning to laze around and drink all day long. That era is over. Instead, a physiotherapist has issued me with a rock-solid training programme. For the first time in my career, I want to report back for duty and be fitter than the others – stronger than ever. Packed in my suitcase are swimming trunks and dietary supplements – that's pretty much it. The pills have been bought online after I got advice from an expert on building muscle mass. I'll be sticking on the right side of the doping regulations, but only just.

I know it full well. I'm looking for ways to keep the fire inside me burning. I need to. Otherwise the temptations will become too much. My comeback can't stop here. I need to get even better, need to keep building on what I've already got. The way I'm feeling right now, I'm 90 per cent Nicklas. A year ago I was maybe 20 per cent Nicklas. So there's still 10 per cent to go. And that 10 per cent will not only make me indispensable to the Denmark team, it'll also make me impossible to ignore when the transfer window opens in the summer.

I wrapped up 2017 with a total goal tally of 25 – the vast majority of them scored between August and November when I seriously hit form. I put away 19 in the league, which wasn't quite enough. I had planned to score at least 20, but because I didn't say it out loud to anyone, it seems as if for once everything is going well: league champions, league top scorer, goal of the year, team of the year, comeback on the national team and a son who proudly ran around Lerkendal clinging to our championship trophy.

It's best to keep my cards close to my chest, so that's what I'm going to keep doing. But my goals for 2018 are pretty easy to guess. I want to be Åge Hareide's first pick for the World Cup and I want to secure a transfer to a big club in a big league – preferably in Spain or Italy. It's not too late to prove myself at the top level. I need it. For my own sake.

BACK IN Trondheim, the winter transfer window is open. There are some enquiries for me. It's been surprisingly quick to drum up some interest in me again. From the beginning Ivan, Kåre and Stig have had a plan to sell me at the end of the season. But by mid-January there's a steady stream of bids. Many of them are pretty exotic – from clubs in China, the Middle East and the USA, which I just don't feel ready for. That adventure will have to wait a little longer, I tell myself. And then in the midst of all that, Gus Poyet turns up. The former midfield star from Uruguay has just been hired at Girondins de Bordeaux – a top-five club in Ligue 1 in France. It's not at all unattractive.

He and Ivan go back and forth, and I've got to say I like his newworld style. He's no cake-eater, and he sounds like the kind of guy who will get my temperament. That's what I need if I'm going to seriously perform. There's the prospect of playing in Europe, and the salary is pretty good too. But Rosenborg aren't having it. Then want more than the £2.3 million that Bordeaux can afford.

'We can sell you for twice that. And we want to qualify for the Champions League. We're going to use you to get there,' Stig tells me.

It's hard not to feel flattered. Maybe it's more than that. Maybe I feel relieved too. After all, I'm more of a Burgundy man than a Bordeaux guy.

All jokes aside, you never know what's going to happen. Especially not in mid-season.

What if I don't fit into the team? Or Poyet gets the sack after a month? There's a lot of what ifs, and I don't want to jeopardize my World Cup chances. That's the most important thing for me. More important than money, more important than next season, more important than my relationship. More important than anything.

I didn't get enough out of South Africa eight years ago. I won't make the same mistake again. I simply can't afford to.

MY BREAK-UP with Natasja is one of the ugly ones. I feel like I gave our relationship a fair shot, but the age gap – she's 20 and I'm 30 – feels like it's getting bigger and bigger. She's at a different life stage and I can't see us starting a family together.

Natasja is anything but happy about it, and calls me some awful stuff in the messages that are buzzing in several times an hour. But things are going to get even feistier. Some girls from Trondheim have DMed her on Instagram. They claim they got with me while the two of us were still together. Or their mates did.

Far from all of it is true. But no smoke without fire, so I let Natasja work through her tantrum. Just a few days later, she's writing to all sorts of people – not just me and my mum. She's also got into the papers. She gets hold of Denmark's *B.T.* tabloid claiming she's got proof of all my bits on the side. The sports editor goes wild and seriously considers publishing the story. He wants to bring me down. Show the world I don't deserve my upturn in fortune. That's how it feels.

'If it's not true, then you'll just have to issue a denial,' the gossip mongerer says when I won't play along.

It's a lose-lose situation. I can't win. If I respond it'll gain more attention. If I keep my gob shut, it'll still be out there. It's totally insane. Like those times in England. Has it become the task of the Danish papers to act as the mouthpiece for a 20-year-old girl who's pissed off with her ex?

Ivan gets involved and eventually *B. T.* drops the story. But only just. So Natasja rinses me on Instagram instead. Calls me a bastard and all that. One of the gossip magazines spots it and prints everything she wrote about me to her followers. The rag also features a couple of nudes of her. To be quite honest, I would rather have done without this. Especially for Natasja's sake. It's not nice to be used like that. Once the media have chewed you up, they just toss you away. I could have told her that.

SoMe has made it both easier and harder to be a playboy. You can get in touch with basically anyone – and they can all get in touch with you. But they can also abuse your name and blackmail you. I've tried both.

Later on in 2018, an awful case involving Cristiano Ronaldo turns up. He's accused of raping a woman in Las Vegas. He strongly denies it and no charges are brought against him.

The only thing I know with any certainty is that Ronaldo must be under an insane amount of pressure. Given that girls have been keen to hang out with me over the years and score cash, fake boobs or fame from our relationship, things must be way crazier in his case. He has to take every possible precaution when getting intimate with a new lady.

There's a lot of points where it can come off the rails. Superstars can easily end up feeling a little superhuman, which is less strange than you'd think. They're used to being worshipped, used to being considered some kind of gift by their fans. They're so rich and glorified that they can get anything they ask for.

Football is more than a sport. As players, we can be sold overnight. We're in the middle of a tough market and that rubs off on the goods. On us. And the way we think. How could it not?

I'M CALLED up for international duty in March and really feel like I'm finally back. No one is surprised or asks questions. It's taken for granted when Hareide reads out my name, Bendtner is in – naturally!

The best pitches we can use are in Malmö, across the water in Sweden, which is a long way from the Marienlyst Hotel in Helsingør. We switch digs to the Clarion Hotel by Copenhagen Airport. The one that used to be *that* Hilton.

It's noticeable that Jon Dahl only retired a few years ago. A few things have been done to improve our conditions and get them up to the thoroughly professionalized outlook now typical in every football club out there. One afternoon we test mattresses. In three months' time when we're staying in Russian hotels, it won't do to end up in just any old bed. What if the mattress is too soft or too hard for your liking? It'll affect your sleep. It might sound over the top and five years ago I wouldn't have given a shit. But it's different now. Sleep matters. A good night's shut-eye can be crucial if you need to get up and perform the next day. Even I've finally recognized that.

Preparations on the pitch are going less satisfyingly. We've drawn Peru in our World Cup group, so we've scheduled friendlies against a couple of South American teams. Panama and Chile. We narrowly beat the former and the only bright point is Pione Sisto's first goal for Denmark. It's clearly a relief for a man who can be hard to figure out. One moment he's walking around wearing sunglasses inside, the next he won't lace up his football boots. Then there's the stuff he won't eat. He's a bit different to the others, but he's an excellent dribbler.

I start against Chile. I find out on the way into the dressing room. Nicolai Jørgensen is struggling. I don't deliver like I did back in the autumn. It's just my third game since the winter break in Norway and I'm still not all there. That's true of everyone, because we manage to deliver next to nothing – and my replacement after the break – Martin Braithwaite – doesn't turn it around. Our defence hangs on though – as it should – so it's not all shit. Especially not if you ask our coaching duo.

If I'm going to get cracking, it has to be for Rosenborg – but two and a half months of playing on artificial grass has suffocated the drive I came back with in January. You might say I've gone cold before spring takes hold.

Playing at home to Molde on 8 April 2018, Kåre wants to try something new and sends me out to the left wing. Instead, Alexander Søderlund gets to play up front. Søderlund has come back from France, where he didn't exactly make it big. And to be perfectly honest, his willpower and self-image are greater than his finishing prowess. He beats me when it comes to his running stamina – no doubt about it – but otherwise he's not very intimidating. Which is why I don't consider it a downgrade. There's no competition for the top spot.

I score twice while Søderlund gets one, meaning Kåre's gamble pays off. Mostly because everyone's passes get through. As I say to Norway's *VG* newspaper afterwards:

'Today we played the way we agreed we would. I think it's the first time this season we've stuck to the plan we agreed.'

Not long after, we face Lillestrøm in the Norwegian Super Cup. Mike is having some health issues, so I'm made temporary captain. Who would have thought it? Irresponsible Nicklas Bendtner captaining the national champions? It's the first time in my career and I'm absolutely thrilled. Downright proud.

From a new position in our offensive midfield, I direct my teammates. It's still goalless when we reach the second half. I decide to take matters into my own hands when I receive the ball ten metres inside their half, with four opponents in front of me. I get past the first, nutmeg the second, and the last two don't get there in time. I finish with a gentle arc well beyond the reach of the goalkeeper. It's enough to secure victory.

KÅRE IS STRUGGLING with injuries in the squad, which means I'm being used constantly in positions that aren't my favourite. It results in some glorious assists, including a couple with my heels, but back home in Denmark Ivan is – to put it mildly – sceptical.

'You need to score more goals. Åge needs to see that you're dangerous up front. You can't lead the front line for your country when you're playing in midfield for your club.'

He also claims I've shown my face in Copenhagen a few too many times and I keep documenting it on Instagram.

'Stop showing up to parties, ice hockey games and gigs. It's so easy to spin a yarn. You need to stick to the story about serious Nicklas.'

I've had enough of hearing the latter. At its worst, I feel like I'm being advised to be someone completely different to who I actually am. After all, I haven't completely changed. I've just got older and wiser as a result of all the tumbles I've taken. A little less wild. But it's all part of me. My baggage makes me the person I am.

I ask Ivan to knock it off. My World Cup isn't in danger. Impossible. None of the other strikers are scoring at the moment, and during the autumn – against Poland, Romania and Ireland – I generated more chances than any of them.

When you also take into account that I've scored twice as many goals for Denmark as all my competitors up front put together – even at major finals – it's just a given...

IT'S A HECTIC time. There's always something happening. Not so much on the football pitch as off. The whole thing feels like a countdown. The only thing that matters right now is the World Cup.

In April I fly in a New Zealand mouthful. Reanin is trying to break into Hollywood and Norway doesn't quite cut it. Anyway, she gets bored up at the house straight away. And that means I spend less time at home than I did with Natasja. And I spend more time going out in Trondheim and Copenhagen.

In mid-April, Arsène Wenger makes an announcement about his future. After 22 years as Arsenal manager, he's decided to call it quits. I sit down to write a few words about him. A tribute of sorts. I post it on Instagram. I'm not angry at him any longer. Instead, I'm grateful for my time under his wing.

I remember all the times I ended up in his office to explain myself. His desk was right at the back of the room, but we always stayed by the sofas – there were three of them – where he liked to sit and watch back match videos.

Our relationship never really got that deep. I think that was true for a lot of guys on the team. But he had a good feel for his players, including me. It's really hard to think of anything negative to say about him. Apart from that Carling Cup final in 2011, a couple of slightly incomprehensible appearances on the subs' bench and the transfer-that-wasn't to Crystal Palace, I've got nothing but praise for him. The punishments and fines he issued me with were deserved. He was exceptionally talented – no doubt about it. And it definitely can't be his fault that I wasn't more obedient. For someone to successfully grab that version of me by the scruff of the neck, they would have needed to be right on top of my private life. Wenger wasn't, and nor was it his job to babysit me. He had loads on his plate and I wasn't his most important piece in the jigsaw of our team. Most of the time, I was on the periphery. So naturally I got away with stuff if that's what I wanted. And I wanted to.

But if I had been living life the way I have for the last year, Wenger would have picked me. If not every time, then at least much more often. There's absolutely no doubt about it. I'm too good for the Norwegian league. Stig himself has even said as much to *Euroman* magazine. That I'm the best player to appear in Eliteserien. EVER.

In late April I'm invited to the tennis at Parken. It's an exhibition match between Caroline Wozniacki and Venus Williams. We go way back. Caroline is a Liverpool supporter – a true Red – so in the early days we mostly saw each other through Agger. Later on, we began to hang out in both London and Miami – sometimes with Rory McIlroy, sometimes just the two of us. She's a really sweet girl. During a break, a bunch of flowers is handed over right there on court – in honour of her grand slam title. Mads Mikkelsen, Brian Laudrup and Bent Fabricius-Bjerre are also in the crowd, but it's suggested I give her the bouquet. I'm eager to.

My bad-boy image has been more or less erased. Even the

Injured at Lerkendal, May 2018. (Photo: Ole Martin Wold/NTB/Ritzau Scanpix)

sponsors are coming back, and I say yes to Copenhagen Airport and a hair product. I've told myself I have been numb to the opinions of the world at large, but it's obviously not that simple. It's really nice to lower my guard a bit, to be back in from the cold after years spent as the black sheep. But it also makes it harder to keep my eyes on the ball.

In Trondheim I get involved in an anti-bullying project. As a role model. I don't tell the school kids that I was a bully myself. I tell them that I got bullied. How much it hurt and how wrong it is to bully. It's just one side of my story, but I don't feel like they can get much use out of the other side. I don't want to inspire them to do something wrong.

Maybe Ivan's right. Maybe I say yes too much. That's just what I'm like. When something gives me a rush, I keep doing it, keeping looking for it, until I go off the rails or I begin to get bored. But eventually I can see it for myself. Two league goals in two months isn't the best, and take my concern to Kåre. I tell him I need to get back to the top.

'Of course, Nicklas,' he says. 'We don't want to play you out of the World Cup team.'

Demoting Søderlund to the bench pays immediate dividends, and I'm up to three goals. I figure I'll give it my all in the final match. Score a couple more. We've got Brann Bergen at home on Sunday 27 May, and then I need to report to the World Cup training camp in Copenhagen. It can't happen quickly enough.

After 61 minutes we're behind. We're playing so poorly and uninspiringly that it's almost beyond belief. We're meant to be the champions, and I'm meant to be the sharpest player up front. I notice the frustration simmering – I want to kick someone to the floor. Obviously, I don't. Throwing punches has never been my style. I give a little extra in the melees. There's half an hour to go. It's still within reach.

And then…I feel it straight away. The tear in my inner thigh. I'm injured. It's my groin again. But fortunately it's my right-hand one.

CAUGHT

2018

IT'S THE STORY that won't die. For a week after I'm cut from the World Cup squad, the Danish media cover it as if nothing else is worth talking about. I'm a permanent fixture in the TV bulletins several nights in a row. My fate reaches foreign shores too. *The Times of India* writes about my injury. As does Germany's *Bild*, *The Australian* down under and *USA Today*. You name it.

Eventually, it all ends up being too much for Åge Hareide. During a press conference, he loses his temper and yells at one of the reporters.

'I'm sick of talking about players who aren't here. I made myself perfectly clear on that at the last press conference. This is the last time I'm going to say it. Do you understand?'

There are quite a lot of people who don't really understand. Especially in the squad.

One of our biggest stars messages me from the training camp in Helsingør to say, 'What about our plan B? What do we do if we're behind with 20 minutes to go? Who else have we got to bring on? Who else has got experience of big games?'

Of course, that's how I see it as well. I've got form when it comes to rising to the occasion. Just think about my two goalscoring headers against Italy. On that occasion I hadn't played for ten months.

Most of the guys send messages, including a couple who have made it there at my expense. That almost makes things worse. It would be easier to swallow if Hareide simply thought the others were more cool-headed up front. Or better suited to the task. I would disagree – I mean, it's my job to believe in myself – but it would also be tough to argue against. Taste is a difficult thing to debate. But dropping me due to an injury that I'm almost over… It just doesn't make sense to me. There's plenty of people who've had issues in the run-up to the World Cup – way bigger issues – and I'm still match-fit. Soon I'll be pain-free too.

Today is 9 June and in exactly a week I'd be ready to come on against Peru as a sub. In the following match, I would have been able to play the full 90 minutes.

There must be more to it than meets the eye. And I can't let go of that thought. So as I struggle to fall asleep, I lie there and wade through the explanations.

Maybe it's the thing with the penalty kick, how I took the ball from Christian Eriksen when we were 4-1 up in Dublin. I can't believe that's true. If it had been such a major issue, Hareide should have said something. But no one pointed any fingers, and two weeks ago he was busying lauding my good influence. How important I was for the atmosphere in the squad, even when injured.

Then there's the thing with the flip-flops. When we posed for the sponsor photo the other day – all wearing our Matinique suits – I had forgotten my leather dress shoes up in the room. Instead I posed in flip-flops. I was the only one. Of course it looked stupid, but they were going to retouch the photo anyway, and it was another thing that everyone could laugh about. Even Jon Dahl.

Jon. Now that I think about him…I find it hard to let go of the things he's said about me in recent years. But then new information emerges. Again, my info comes from sources close to the horse's mouth. And the truth is perhaps a little more complicated.

It's long been an open secret that Thomas Jørgensen and ProTreatment are a thorn in the side of the DBU's physical team. And now there's speculation that Andreas Bjelland – the only defender to have played in every World Cup qualifier – and I have been sacrificed because we did our rehab with people who the DBU would prefer to be shot of.

Why do they have such a problem with a private medical team? Because most members of the squad prefer ProTreatment and their methods ahead of the DBU's own. Even our captain.

Under Morten Olsen, we used them in secret – but now the Players' Union that represents us has forced through a set-up where two therapists have access to the players' hotel. Just so long as Thomas doesn't show his face.

In the days after I'm dropped from the World Cup squad, it becomes clear that the DBU's physical team have been calling up Rosenborg to ask about my condition. Their reason is impossible to misconstrue. They've been cross-checking information to make certain that Thomas is providing the same information to the club as he's giving to the Denmark team. Whether I'm as ready as he claims.

It's the same story with Bjelland and Brentford. It looks like they've been searching for cracks in our health checks. Anything to make our deselection more palatable to the press and fans. Something to stifle criticism. In other words: someone at the DBU doesn't trust us players.

Maybe the old boys on the national team are right. Maybe it's all about politics. Maybe I've been sacrificed because the DBU's doctors and physios want to bury ProTreatment. Maybe Hareide is being advised by people with their own agendas. Maybe it's a combination. One big hotchpotch.

No matter what, it feels fucking unfair. And it gives me a gigantic desire to show the Danes that I've not been feeding them bullshit. That I could have turned out for the national team and given it my all for the red and whites.

I tell Bjelland about this. He feels exactly the same way – understandably given his contract expires at the end of the month. He was going to use the World Cup as a springboard to find another club. Now they say he's too injured to play or sit on the bench for most of June. Stuff like that isn't particularly attractive to potential new employers.

So we knuckle down during training out at Dragør. After a couple of sessions, I've sweated out the dregs of my solitary booze-up on wine at the penthouse at H C Andersens Boulevard.

We're exactly where we should be. We can sidestep, side jump, turn on the ball, control it and shoot for goal – without any pain. And Bjelland can deliver his long crosses that they claimed he couldn't do any longer when they dropped him.

I SHARE our progress on Instagram as a story for my followers. That way everyone gets the message – I was always going to be fit in time. I'm used to documenting my sessions at Dragør – why stop now? I don't feel like I owe anyone anything right now.

When Ivan sees it, he's bothered.

'There's no point pissing off Åge,' he says.

I know what he means. But for me it's not a war against Hareide. It's a question of my credibility. Credibility that I've struggled to regain. My fellow countrymen can't be allowed to think that I tried to steal a World Cup spot from someone else more deserving. But that's how it ended up looking. And it's the national team coaching staff who are to blame for that. They kept their options open, and when it turned out I was recovering fast enough to squeeze into the squad, they threw it back in my face.

Stig and Kåre hear how well my rehab is going. They're in no doubt: of course I should line up for Rosenborg in the final match ahead of the summer break. Their master plan to get me ready for the World Cup and sell me on for a fat fee during the summer transfer window has gone up in smoke too.

I fly back to Norway and train with the squad. On Monday 11 June – five days before the Peru game – I'm able to come on for the final 15 minutes against Tromsø. We're so far north they have to clear snow off the AstroTurf before the match. AstroTurf – smooth as glass – in the middle of summer. I can't imagine a bigger anticlimax. Ten out of 16 teams in Eliteserien use artificial pitches, and it's one of the things that's bugging me more and more. They should make it illegal to play on that shit. My knees hate it, and it doesn't let you play proper football. Still, I'm fucking doing it. I'm playing, and I don't notice anything in my groin. It's a massive boost.

Two weeks later – as my country struggles to take their chances in Russia – the summer break in Eliteserien reaches its end. By now I'm so well-recovered I am able to start at the Lerkendal. We bulldozer Vålerenga in a 3-0 win and I deliver my best performance of the year. I set up the first, miss a self-made sitter and score the last. Back in the day, my focus would have been gone. But I've got better at playing the small matches, while missing out on the big ones. Kåre is pleased, but also worried that I'm going to be sold to a big club down on the continent:

'Bendtner is enormously important to any team,' he says in what might be read as a cheeky sarcastic jibe at his compatriot, the Denmark coach. 'If he keeps playing like he did today, I'll have to lock him up.'

It's classic Norway. Either I'm to be denounced as a flop, or I'm a genius beyond comparison. There's never any middle ground, but then again there's no one to split the attention with up here. Even that gets tiring after a while.

A couple of days later, Denmark crash out of the World Cup in the round of 16 against Croatia – after going to penalties. I watch it from my sofa. I'm mostly standing on it. I can't make myself sit down and I'm shouting and screaming at the screen.

Schmeichel is outstanding in goal, while our own penalty takers blow three out of five. I think they looked scared. And that's just not good enough. You can't be scared when approaching the ball. Better not to be one of the takers. That kind of thing is infectious.

Ugh…What I wouldn't give to be in that situation… In a penalty shootout at the World Cup… Wearing the red and white… Oh Lord… It's just horrible to think about. It's a nightmare not being there.

I'm about to get plenty of excitement on the penalty spot too – although not at quite the same level. We're facing Valur in the Champions League qualifiers, and we lost 1-0 away in Reykjavik. During the first half at the Lerkendal, the highlights are few and far between. That lasts until the Bulgarian referee steals the show. He blows the whistle for three highly dubious penalties – two for us and one for them. The final one is awarded to us well into stoppage time when we're 2-1 up. I have to score if we're to go through. If I fluff it, then we're out of Europe. For my first kick I put the ball in the roof of the net. The second time around, I'm less sure. The goalkeeper has been eyeballing me and gets his hand to it, but the ball makes it over the line thanks to the crossbar. It's all so close to being pissed down the drain that I barely get it.

Back in the dressing room, we know full well our play was no good and we've got off extremely lightly given our awful team effort. It's another matter entirely for Kåre. The match against Valur ends up being his last one as Rosenborg head coach. The board no longer believe European success is possible with him at the helm and the next day he gets the boot. It's brutal. And a long way from the tale of a close-knit team spirit I bought into once upon a time.

KÅRE DIDN'T see it coming. Nor did I. We're talking about a man who has brought the championship trophy back to the club three years in a row. And right now we're in second – two points behind Brann Bergen with half the season still to go. It's not exactly a total fiasco.

But, on the other hand, there's not much left that surprises me any longer, and I guess the club have got greedy. Instead of being pleased with what they have, the board want even more. They want a return to the nineties when Rosenborg over-performed in the Champions League. The playing squad seems secondary. But to be honest, it's stumbling a bit – especially in creativity.

We stand together as a squad and demand Kåre's reinstatement. We even refuse to train, but there's nothing to be done. The mighty Ivar Koteng is completely immovable, and even though I like our talent coach Rini Coolen, who has just been promoted to head coach, all I really want to do is leave and move on. It was Kåre who brought me here, and without him I've only got Stig left. Everything else is much of a muchness.

I'm sick of my house. Over the summer, I've had a constant stream of uninvited guests – some aggressive little beetles in the walls. In order to get rid of them, an exterminator sets traps along the panels in all the rooms in the house. It doesn't exactly help make the place feel homely.

When Hareide calls up his first Denmark squad after the World Cup, neither Kasper Dolberg nor Nicolai Jørgensen are fit. But that doesn't change anything. I'm still out in the cold. It's hard to see it as anything other than a punishment of sorts. Maybe it was for the Instagram thing. Bjelland, who's been lucky enough to wind up at FC Copenhagen, isn't in the squad either. Mike is, though. So it's not the Norwegian league that's a problem.

Now it's beginning to seem a bit personal, given there's still no explanation forthcoming. Not even when there are a couple of late call-ups the day after I scored and set up another against Strømsgodset in Eliteserien.

I've read a couple of interviews in which our national coach makes a big song and dance about how he communicates closely with his players. He seeks them out and explains his way of thinking so everyone feels they're in the loop.

'Too many leaders talk far too little with their employees. I know people who have never once spoken to their boss and after 25 years they get a gold watch and "good job" pat on the back. They need praise every day! And criticism – when things aren't going well,' he says in an article about being a good leader.

I know that Hareide is still talking about me. He even admitted to Mike that I was missed during the World Cup. Especially in the penalty shootout against Croatia. And yet, our final exchange of words was in a hotel corridor almost three months ago.

I would have been happy with a phone call. Either a month ago or this week. With an explanation – or anything – that I could work with. Instead, I'm treated like some random reserve. Not like a player who has been on the team for 12 years and has sacrificed himself for the cause and the Danish flag. Definitely not like a player who has scored 30 goals in the process.

My pride is hurting in a way it hasn't before. Not being on the national team. And I invest my pride in the national team.

I write a text on my mobile. A farewell from the red and white jersey for as long as Hareide and Jon Dahl are running the show.

But I can't bring myself to send it because other stuff gets in the way. First there's a pay conflict between the players and the DBU. The DBU again. The DBU is an awkward dance partner.

Philine and I give things another go. We head to a Guns N' Roses gig in Oslo, and we spend the rest of the summer in each other's constant company. I've got my hands full. I'm infatuated with her in a way I haven't been with many other people. But it goes deeper than that. I love her too – because we've known each other for as long as we have. Something has blossomed inside me.

The combination of infatuation and love is unfamiliar territory for me. We've always pushed each other's limits, and sparks often fly between us. It's as if we're constantly competing with each other. Including on Instagram. We can be pretty childish. We catch each other in embarrassing moments and then share it with our followers.

Philine's dad, Jens Erik Roepstorff, is a retired world-class handball player, and Philine is not bad either. The whole family are used to having to perform. It shows. At Philine's parents' house, they need to have a really good reason to enjoy a glass of wine with dinner. At my childhood home, there needed to be a really good reason not to.

I talk about my disappointing summer with Jens Erik. I've not only missed out on the World Cup – we screwed up our Champions League play-off against Celtic, and most recently I had to hobble off the pitch in our Europa League qualifier. A pulled hamstring. It strikes on the penultimate day of the summer transfer window. Nürnberg in the Bundesliga were on the verge of signing a contract with me.

I tell it like it is to Philine's dad. How I'm starting to feel seriously trapped. All my plans have gone up in smoke. I'm in a completely different place to 2011, luckily, but I recognize the same frustration from back then.

I start on rehab in Dragør. The pulled muscle will keep me out for at least three weeks. On Sunday 9 September 2018, I have another appointment with ProTreatment. Unfortunately, I never get that far.

I'VE NOT WATCHED many old movies over my life. But I have seen *The Godfather I, II* and *III* several times. In *Part III*, there's the totally legendary scene with the mafia don Michael Corleone. He's become a man of mature years. A family man, greying slightly and determined to make his business legit. But the other mafia bosses are against him. They don't want to let him go.

'Just when I thought I was out – they pull me back in,' he shouts at his family members in desperation.

That's exactly how I feel. Like Michael Corleone. I'm staring at the wall in a cell in the basement of Bellahøj police station in Copenhagen. My night unravelled in a way that no fortune-teller would ever have predicted. Totally awful. But it's not the mafia bosses who have sent me down here. It's my demons. Who are my demons? I don't know. All I know is that they are inside me, in my past, in my bad decisions, and in all the people who think they know Nicklas Bendtner because they read the papers or had access to some free opinions online. The people who take malicious pleasure at the very sight of my face or mention of my name.

The whole evening flickers by. I remember three of us couples were out for dinner. Crossing the street to the nightclub opposite. Finding a corner and ordering drinks. It being half one and me looking for Philine. Her being in the middle of a chat in the men's toilets. Me getting jealous. Me deciding to bounce before I totally kick off. Her catching up with me as I'm getting into a taxi. Us quarrelling. First with each other, then with the driver who has driven off in the wrong direction. Me leaving before things go the way those kinds of things have gone in the past. The meter in the taxi saying 52 kroner. The driver turning the taxi around and thundering after us. Him pulling onto the bike lane next to the pavement and driving alongside us. Him yelling at us through the open window. A lot of fucking times. Him stopping the car and running around the bonnet. Him throwing something. It crashing against the wall behind us. Me not daring to turn my back on him. Me going up against him. Both of us moving forward. Both of us raising our fists and me throwing the first punch. One blow being all it took. Him hitting the car on the way down. It looking violent. A car stopping. Me panicking. The two of us legging it. Getting back to my apartment. My hand being swollen. Me saying the same thing over and over. 'They're coming to get me. They're coming soon.' The ring of the doorbell. Four officers standing in the middle of my kitchen. Informing me that I'm under arrest. That I have to come with them. The ride in the car feeling never-ending.

I'm still here. In a cell in the basement of Bellahøj police station. Staring at the wall. I've got a new refrain on repeat. 'I'm finished. I'm finished. I'm finished.' Other than that, this place is empty – resoundingly empty.

WHEN I'M RELEASED, I head straight round to Ivan's townhouse in Østerbro. Apparently the taxi driver has been badly injured. He's fractured his jaw. That's what the papers are saying online.

The story is already out there. Of course it is. His own boss took it to the press. The manager is horrified on behalf of his driver. He says he's never seen anything like it. At any rate, he can't possibly have watched the CCTV footage that he brags about having turned in to the police. That much is certain.

Everything comes tumbling down in no time at all. A club in Dubai withdraw their totally crazy offer. My private advertising deals are terminated. And of course there's plenty of condemnation too. People seriously believe I would cheat a guy out of 52 kroner – around a fiver in English money. That's what's at the heart of it. In fact, it's the total opposite. At the time what was going through my head was that I no longer wanted to be cheated by others. Whether it's 52 kroner or 5.2 million kroner. It's become a matter of principle. A principle that comes at an unforeseen high price.

Hareide is one of the quickest off the mark. He says that people who are guilty of violent offences can't play for the Danish national team. A couple of days later he withdraws his statement. Someone must have got hold of him. Instead, he now says that anyone who has taken their punishment is considered welcome. In principle. As long as they're good enough.

I don't hear from the man himself. Not a text, not a call. But I do hear from Lars Høgh, the Denmark team goalkeeping coach. The guy who has just received a diagnosis of life-threatening cancer and ought to have enough to be getting on with. Lars asks if I'm okay and whether there's anything he can do for me. He's not just a legend – he's a real sport.

Ivan and I are contacted by someone claiming to be speaking for the taxi company. He offers to drop the charges. But they want me to pay a sweetener. A big sweetener. The guy reckons I'm in real shit and that I've been racist and fuck knows what else. Says my career is in ruins if I don't cough up.

Normally, I'd consider that kind of proposal. It's pretty common. Especially in England. I'm aware of cases where footballers have bought their way out of bad publicity. Not rape cases – but paternity suits, drug cases and violent offences.

The guy looks pretty evil in his Facebook profile pic. He's not the only person I hear from. Over the coming days, all sorts of people who know the driver get in touch for various reasons.

I also hear from Brian Nielsen, the retired boxer. Brian plays poker occasionally, and a week after the clash he's sat at the same table as the taxi driver at a private tournament in Vanløse. They're up all night and the driver blabs on about the case so much that Brian has to ask him to shut it. In the meantime, the press say he's on sick leave indefinitely. On sick leave – but not so sick that he couldn't stay up all night playing for cash in a ten-hour game. It kind of almost reminds me of my casino period at Arsenal…but I don't say that out loud.

Eventually, Philine can't contain herself any longer. She wants to share her side of the story, and writes a long post on Instagram. Everything she says fits with my recollections. Right away, the mood changes. If it's all true – that the driver chased us down, got out of his car and threw something at us while we were walking – then it's definitely not such a clear-cut case. Even if I should have paid him for the 90-second-trip we managed…

I receive hundreds of messages. And every single one of them from Amager says the same thing. That they would have done what

I did. Almost exactly the same. Except they would have thrown more than one punch.

What's the saying? You can take the yobs out of Amager, but you can't take Amager out of the yobs?

In a way, I'm relieved. Things looked seriously grim. Now there's a glimmer of hope. Maybe my career isn't in complete ruins. Maybe I'm not done.

BACK IN Trondheim, unrest is simmering. I have to apologize to the fans, sponsors and club. I'm more than happy to – I shouldn't have got myself into that situation. If I had gone straight home after dinner, it would never have happened. I can't escape that.

Just so long as I don't have to apologize to the driver, I'm up for most of it. I reckon we were just as bad as each other. At least. It was him who put me in an impossible situation. If it were about the 52 kroner, he could have called the police or unleashed his boss on us the next day. Instead, he hunted us down through the city centre .

When I'm called in for questioning and the police officer shows me the CCTV, I have even fewer regrets about the way I reacted. It's quite possible that the taxi driver misunderstood something, but I simply didn't want to pay for being driven towards Holbergsgade when I had clearly requested H C Andersens Boulevard as my destination. Instead you can hear the driver calling up a friend while zooming around searching for us.

'I swear on my mother's grave I'm gonna punch him,' he yells into his phone.

The police have decided to charge me with assault. And the driver is being charged with using his phone while driving. And attempted assault. That last bit seems important to my chances of acquittal.

My pulled muscle keeps me out until October, and when I'm finally back it's on the wing and in midfield. My privileges seem to have been spent.

Lots of weird stuff happens. Several evenings in a row, there's a drone hovering over the house outside Trondheim. It shows up as soon as darkness falls. I can hear it humming when I turn down the volume on the TV. And I can see it when I go out onto the driveway. Turns out it was nicer to have fans laying siege to my home after all.

The club needs to save face. They need to secure the championship. The same thing goes for the Norwegian cup. They need some success stories. The evening before my trial in Copenhagen, we play in the semi-final at the Lerkendal. I end up bagging the matchwinner and afterwards it's hard to cool down. My thoughts are galloping away. I think I'm a little afraid of everything that awaits and when my alarm clock goes off at 4am, I've not slept a wink. I don't manage to get any sleep on the morning flight down to Copenhagen either.

I turn up bleary-eyed in front of the City Court. There's at least 100 members of the press waiting for me and my defence lawyer Anders Németh. They're drinking coffee and loitering next to their broadcast vans.

I've not spoken much to Anders. But I know he's a hotshot attorney in the world of law. He's even pricier than the guys who helped to untangle the jewellery company. When we spoke on the phone, I had a couple of suggestions for Anders. One of them was to call Brian Nielsen as a witness. But he's not keen on it. He reckons it'll be better to maintain a low profile and avoid launching a counter-attack. In other words: it would be a huge own goal if the big footballer retaliated against the little taxi driver a second time.

I don't totally agree. I was provoked into doing what I did. But Anders is the smart one, so I do as I'm told.

The courtroom is packed to the rafters. In the gallery, I spot Philine, one of her friends, Ivan, his colleague and a journalist who has been following me for years – and of course, my little brother and Mum. There's not a single mate. They're probably all at work.

The driver is the first person to testify. He spews out all sorts of things. He says I called him a 'black bastard'. Witnesses said I treated him 'like a doormat'. That kind of thing.

Shortly after, the taxi's CCTV footage – internal and external – contradicts the driver's statement. At no point do I say anything to do with his skin colour or anything like that. At no point do any witnesses mention that I might have trodden on him.

I get more and more optimistic. But things point the other way too. Like the fact that I'm still accused of kicking the driver. There's no kick to be seen in the CCTV either. You can see how I step over him when he first hits the bonnet and then the tarmac. That's got nothing to do with any kick.

But the prosecutor is insisting. She refutes that one single blow can cause a jaw fracture. If I've got the right end of the stick, I'm going to be punished both for throwing a punch and for landing it as cleanly as I did.

The driver isn't done. It was only an empty coke can that he lobbed at us. An empty coke can that whistled through the air and smashed into a wall with a crash – over 10 metres away? It sounds totally unlikely, but no one queries it. Not out loud. They just seem to reckon that if he says it then it must be true.

The thing about the bike path doesn't come up either. How the hell can it not be a problem that the man drove onto the bike path and then followed us yelling? If that's not threatening behaviour, then what is? Fucked if I know.

During the final break, Anders goes through the likely scenarios. If I'm found guilty of throwing the punch, we'll request time for reflection. If I'm found guilty of kicking as well, we'll appeal on the spot. That much I understand.

THEN IT HAPPENS. The lead judge reads out the verdict. It's brisk. My sleep deprivation gives the whole thing a glimmer of surrealism. I can see everything from afar, through a filter and with ear plugs in. It's no use for me to sink down or chew harder on my gum.

First, the driver is acquitted of attempted assault. Then I receive a custodial sentence. For one punch and one kick. Fifty days. Over and out.

Slowly, I come to. How on earth can you lose that badly when you were ahead for most of the match? It feels like a trap. A catch-22, as Ivan says. If I had fought back in court, I would have been punished for being a bully. So I did the opposite and dealt with a shit-ton of bullshit.

That case was lost in advance. It wasn't just the taxi that caught up with me that night. It was my story. All the things that I've messed up in the past – plus interest.

Back in Trondheim, the atmosphere is pretty listless. I'm not the king any longer. Our goalkeeper – Andre Hansen – is the Eliteserien player of the year for 2018. Without him we wouldn't have won the championship, because up front we've never found our harmony. He knows that too. He's settled down in the dressing room and is surrounded by people like Søderlund and Konradsen.

But no one confronts me. They just avoid me as much as they can get away with. If it were up to Stig, the taxi case would have been closed long ago. I wouldn't be appealing the verdict. It's hard for the club given the situation. Difficult to move on. Everything becomes about my sentence. It's all anyone can talk about.

I think it over a bit. Rosenborg could have sacked me, but they stood by me. Even without Kåre having my back. If I lose again in the High Court, the sentence can be increased up to three months. In prison or with an electronic tag. Maybe I should just get it over with. Do the 50 days during the winter break. Hopefully in my apartment.

When I bring up the idea with Ivan, his eyes almost fill with tears. Not that we can see each other – we're on the phone. But I can hear it. He says it was easy to see in court how much I wanted this to be over, and how badly I was affected by the circus around me.

'It's a good idea, Nick,' he says.

I tell the club ahead of the cup final. Relief spreads through the corridors and the squad alike. And onto the pitch. I set up Mike's goal to equalize. It might look like a simple through ball, but who else would have been able to predict that Mike could appear from behind, that he would receive the ball at just that speed and on that particular foot? It's wisdom from my academy days at Bell Lane.

I seal the deal with our third and fourth goals to make it 4-1. Strømsgodset are outplayed and the pattern becomes clear. Upturns become downturns, downturns become upturns. My life is like a roller coaster.

THE ELECTRONIC TAG

2019

I LIKE THEM straight away. A man with a hoarse laugh and a woman who constantly says 'Nicklas'. Not in that preachy way that others do – I think it's more about making me feel safe. A 'no judgement from me' kind of way.

They're the kind of people I remember from the good old days in Amager. People who don't beat about the bush. A long way from the trio of judges I faced in the City Court. It seemed absolutely clear to me that they thought I needed to be brought seriously down to earth.

But this is different. After a couple of minutes, the two officers from the Danish Prison and Probation Service crack a joke about the shirts I've got hanging on display. How they might pinch one to take back to their workmates: 'Y'know, as a souvenir.'

That's how it's always been. I've got lovers and haters.

First, we need to find a discreet spot to fit the electronic surveillance box. After a quick tour, they suggest using one of the lofts in the rafters – the one with the wine coolers. Once it's installed and I've had the electronic tag fitted to my left ankle – a black strip of matte plastic – we sit down at the dining table. I offer them coffee while they go over the rules I'm subject to. The dos and don'ts. Where and when I'm supposed to be.

Every morning I have a ten-minute window – between 10.25 and 10.35 – to leave the apartment and drive to training in Dragør. That begins at 11am and finishes at 5pm. I have to be back at the apartment between 5.25 and 5.35. Otherwise the box will send an alert to the Prison and Probation Service headquarters. And the second that happens I'm already in hot water. Within a minute, I'll be called by an officer, and if I don't have a good explanation ready then I'll be done serving my sentence at home. Instead, I'll be off to Copenhagen's Vestre Prison.

The officers will pop by a couple of times a week. At least. I'll normally get 15 minutes' notice and then they troop upstairs to the apartment at H C Andersens Boulevard or show up at ProTreatment. They can demand blood and urine samples at any time. Alcohol and all other narcotics are strictly forbidden.

The man and woman tell it like it is. They have to keep a particularly keen eye on me, because the higher ups are keeping a particularly keen eye on them. Under no circumstances can I receive any special treatment.

'Nicklas. Anyone else who was heading to training while wearing an electronic tag might be able to get away with eating the odd lunch down by Dragør Harbour,' the woman says. 'But not you. Because someone's going to take your picture, and then we'll have our bosses on the blower. We're under scrutiny too.'

IT'S THURSDAY 3 January 2019. It's 4.45pm. Electronic tags are usually fitted early in the morning. Sentences don't usually begin in the late afternoon. But in my case they do. Ever since my sentence was passed, the Prison and Probation Service have been spammed with enquiries. Along these lines: 'When does Bendtner's sentence begin?' 'Can we accompany your employees for a day while they visit people wearing tags?' and 'What will you do if Bendtner's blood tests show any trace of anything?'

It seems pretty fucking likely there will be one or two paps lurking outside my building's front door, and none of us can be arsed to contribute to that show. So the officers wait until the vultures have lost their appetite.

It's good to get started on my sentence. But I'm also dreading what awaits. Ever since winning the Norwegian cup a month earlier, I've been busy living the good life. Fucktons of good food, fucktons of good wine. The wine club where we drink legendary vintages and eat world-class homemade meals has been active. After all, I was pretending that nothing could touch me. That I hadn't just been convicted of violent assault.

We rounded off the month with a New Year party at the home of Lars Seier and his wife Yvonne in Switzerland. While Philine and the other guests were partying to the max, I came down with the blues. The gravity hit me. I was completely checked out.

I'm still being deprived of my liberty in a way, and even though I'm serving my sentence at home it's still not on my terms. When I feel restless, I can't just open the door and leave. If Philine and I are fighting, I have to stay on the sofa. And if I fancy a glass of something…well, that's out of the question.

Fifty days on the wagon seems a bit immense. Alcohol isn't just my kryptonite. Alcohol has also been my comfort in bad times. A refuge when things hurt. A means of relaxation and to take a break from the thoughts of my dad, my son and my career. The things that are constantly haunting my head the rest of the time.

Now I have nowhere else to escape to. I have to deal with them while sober. There's going to be some long evenings.

Will I be able to handle it? I'm sure I will. If I could stop big money gambling – more or less overnight – then I can do this too.

I STILL NEED to set myself some goals. Things to hold myself to. So I go on the offensive on Instagram. I take a photo of the tag and tell my followers that it's been fitted. That I've made up my mind to use the time constructively. That I want to talk my way through my almost 31 years of life and think through some thoughts. About the ups and the downs. Why things wound up the way they did. For a book to come out of it.

I've also decided that I want to get really fit and pay back Rosenborg. The club's trust in me meant I decided not to appeal the verdict. But I was also sorry for the taxi driver. His behaviour got him fired and that wasn't what I wanted. Our work situations could both have been different if I had got into a different taxi that night. For example, I might have been playing for one of the MLS clubs in America who were making offers for me. But they'll get nothing out of it. You can't work in the USA with a stained criminal record.

Caroline gets in touch. She says that if she pops round, we could take a look at Nicho's calendar and fix up appointments for the next six months. By all means! But when she turns up my son is nowhere to be seen. It turns out he's with Cille, the nanny. As he so often is. Unlike me, Caroline was raised by parents who were very absent, and that part of her upbringing seems to have stuck.

She brings up my book project pretty quickly.

'I've always spoken positively about you to the outside world,' she says. 'Now I expect you to do the same thing.'

There's the woman I know. It seems she's using our son as a carrot to prevent me from telling all about our relationship – or the lack of one. There's never been space for my truth. After she leaves, I'm in a bad mood and keep myself to myself. Philine simply doesn't understand. I'm going to have Nicho more often than I've been used to. I should be majorly happy.

But then it goes as I expected. A couple of the appointments are no good after all, because Nicho needs more time with his half-siblings. And there's also a holiday that he can't possibly come along on.

In the space of less than 12 hours, I'm down to seeing my son four times in the next six months. We'll never get closer like that. But it's classic Caroline. She's showing me who's boss.

The other person who suddenly gets in touch is my dad. He's on a skiing holiday with my little brother. He says he misses taking that kind of trip with the two of us. Wouldn't it be fun to do it again?

Just like that. Out of the blue. He avoids the unpleasant stuff. All the reasons why we haven't talked in five years. His jewellery designer is still paying me back, and he could do the same if that's what I wanted. I don't think it even occurs to him. There are no regrets. He thinks we should draw a line under the whole thing and go on a skiing holiday. At my expense, if he's still the man I remember. I don't reply.

I'VE NEVER trained this hard in my life. When I get home and step out of the shower, I flop onto the warm tiled floor. Completely drained of energy. If there were a fire at the other end of the apartment, I wouldn't be able to do anything about it. I'd just lie there and hope it went away again.

But my graft is paying dividends. It always has done whenever I pull my finger out. My body fat percentage is plummeting and my muscle mass is growing at the same rate. After four weeks at Dragør, I weight 99.4 kilos. That's slightly more than at Juventus, and I should be able to lose three or maybe even four kilos when we really ramp up my fitness work.

It's unclear what it's for. Up in Trondheim a new head coach has been appointed. He wasn't exactly their first choice, if I've got the right end of the stick. Eirik Horneland has been poached from Haugesund, a mid-table club in Eliteserien, and he supposedly stands for the exact opposite of what Kåre does. He's anything but a friendly cousin. Mike tells me about the early encounters. Mobile phone use in the clubhouse has been banned. Not only does it have to be switched off, but it also has to be left in a box for most of the day.

It's not something that puts me in a better mood exactly. It's rules with rules on top. I can already imagine what I'm going to say when they want to take my phone away from me. To be honest, if they want to treat me like a little kid then I'm tempted to behave like one. That's my energy, and Rosenborg sounds less and less like a club I can thrive at in future.

It wasn't too bad being off the hooch for the first couple of weeks. But then the urge resurfaced. Especially during dinner, and when the long talks about my book won't let go of me. I can feel it right now. I've pushed away everything it was uncomfortable to dwell on. I've kept my thoughts from the toughest things in my past at a distance. That's no longer possible.

On the better evenings, I'm glad I can scratch that itch, make an effort and clear out my system. On the worse ones, everything feels like an uphill struggle. I search for distractions. Often in vain. It's no use watching football on the TV. The other day I did anyway. It was Manchester City versus Liverpool and I could hardly concentrate on the game. That's how much I missed standing there against that backdrop. At the Etihad Stadium or anywhere else in England. It was only when I turned the TV off that my brain shut down.

Even though there are big matches in Norway, they're not comparable with the Premier League, Serie A or the Bundesliga. Even a cup final doesn't measure up to matches against teams like Huddersfield Town or Crystal Palace. I need one last shot in the big league. I miss it like crazy.

Adidas write to me. After lengthy deliberations – as they put it – they want to terminate our partnership. The conviction I chose not to appeal is blamed.

I think my luck is used up. When I was 18, I got away with totally incomprehensible stuff. Like the time I'd been playing away with my club team. We weren't going home until the next day and once the hotel corridor fell silent two of us snuck down to the bar. We got talking to some local girls. Suddenly we decided to skinny dip in the indoor pool. It turned out the pool had a slide and before we knew it we'd started our own internal competition. One couple would judge the other couple on the way down the slide – while having sex in every possible position.

At the next training session, my mate showed up with his knees glowing bright red. He'd torn up his skin when he took his girl doggy style.

So there was that time. Since then I've become increasingly unlucky, and there's a good reason why.

Once you've been caught once, it's easier and easier for things to go wrong. You're visible. You're on the radar. And eventually people begin seeing things.

I've seen loads of footballers fucking things up – countless times – where it's not drawn criticism or public shame. If I wanted to,

I could tell stories from now until 2030 all about my colleagues.

I don't want to – but there is one topic that could do with a contribution from an insider who is busy doing more than pointing fingers: the stink around hookers. It's not just Wayne Rooney, the Israeli national team and Brazilian Ronaldo – or even Kyle Walker during the Covid crisis a few years later – who got on that bandwagon. It's a real shame those lads have been portrayed as particularly nasty guys. That's not necessarily true. But they've probably been more careless or unlucky than average. They've only been caught red-handed with their pants down…

Believe me, everyone in my industry has heard of someone who's been at it. Especially in England where it's a grand old tradition to share your cock-and-ball stories with a full audience. People get a high from other people's fun experiences.

You're probably wondering why prostitutes are such a widespread phenomenon in professional football. It's pretty simple. It's because it's less risky than picking up girls while out on the town. And if you're prone to infidelity – I read somewhere or other that this applies to 46 per cent of Danes – then you hardly dare do the deed with a 'civilian' any longer. Not when you're a famous footballer. I know about loads of incidents involving prostitutes. But I know of just as many stories about extortion via social media. We're talking about gold-diggers from the nightlife scene who are up for a fuck and then take a photo of you sleeping it off while you're starkers. With those photos as their trump card, they can demand stuff to keep their mouths shut. And they do.

It's not exactly iron-clad, but at least prostitutes have a business of sorts to protect. So yeah, I've witnessed that at first hand. Even the day before a match when the team were gathered at the hotel in some godforsaken place.

Is it so wrong? Sure it is, and personally I get way more turned on by my own conquests rather than paying someone. But I don't think it's strange that some of my colleagues are that way inclined and let themselves be tempted. Us footballers have been on another planet for a long time. And a lot of us are still there. They've just got better at keeping their heads down because they've been bottle-fed on mobile phone cameras and social media. They know how to be on their guard. They know that each and every person is a potential paparazzo.

Before you condemn willy-nilly and point fingers at amoral and spoiled footballers, remember one simple thing: this isn't a parallel world that we created ourselves from scratch. It's a world we were traded into. A world that was there long before we arrived. A world designed to tear away any sense of grounding possessed by young men. Young men who are programmed to think they can do what they want. And then some.

We're rolling in money and admiration from an age at which our peers are working on supermarket checkouts alongside doing their studies. We've spent less time at school than our peers, but have far more opportunities. And with those opportunities come the risk of being a dick. Unless you hail from the noble lineage of the likes of Christian Eriksen or Mikel Arteta, it's a feat to stay 100 per cent squeaky clean.

PHILINE AND I have Nicho over to visit. Completely on his own. He won't be picked up at bedtime. He's not sleeping alongside his nanny or my mum either. For once, they're not here. Nicho has just turned eight, and for the first time ever he spends the night with his dad and his dad's partner without all sorts of other people hanging out nearby. He's requested it himself. Over and over until Caroline gave in. We hold hands all night and have a really lovely time. Nicho and Philine are a pretty good match.

There's a live wire hidden inside my son – of course there is – and it doesn't take long for him to miss the fresh air up here on the fifth floor. I try to explain to him how my tag works. That Daddy is not allowed to come down to the playground.

Instead he goes through my stuff and pulls out the hat-trick ball from the match against Porto. I tell him to be careful with it. He mustn't rub off the messages written onto it by the lads. Of course, he can't understand that – and it's kind of funny. My boy just wants to kick a ball around. He doesn't care what us grown-ups get up to.

I think to myself that he has the upper hand.

I used to hide my hat-trick balls, trophies and medals away. But now I feel more able to be proud of them. I've not amassed as many as I had expected, and I've not always played a crucial role when the deciding battle took place. But in a team sport everyone counts. That's what people tell me – and it's my own perspective too. Most of the time, anyway.

In football, you can blame all sorts of other people, and maybe for that reason alone I should have played tennis or golf instead. It would have forced me to adopt a completely different level of discipline when it came to work – especially when the going got tough.

My trophy haul includes an Italian championship, two Norwegian championships, an FA Cup, a German Cup, a Norwegian Cup, a German Super Cup, a Norwegian Super Cup and a bunch of other silver and bronze medals from over the years. In addition to that the Danish Player of the Year Award and a couple of goals of the year. It could have been worse.

I've no idea what this Horneland guy has achieved in his career. But I'm guessing he's mostly played and coached up in Norway. Stig and our new head coach are on a stopover in Copenhagen on their way to a training camp in Portugal. They've set up the meeting a couple of days in advance. They want to say hello and talk about the future so that we all know where each other's at. It sounds like a good idea. I'm looking forward to seeing Stig, and I've bought sushi on the way home from Dragør. Philine has promised to leave us in peace to talk.

When I show my guests to the dining table, Horneland looks a little puzzled.

'I've never tried that before!'

I'm still not completely up on my Norwegian after a couple of years in Trondheim, but he makes it sound like sushi is some crazy newfangled thing. And I actually think he means it. He doesn't strike me as being a big joker.

In the meantime, Stig gets to it. He thinks I lack humility. That I should have controlled myself more – including on Instagram.

The whole of December resembled the party that it genuinely was on occasion. And that's out of order. He reminds me about the fine of 50 days' wages. Afterwards, he lays out three different scenarios for the spring:

'You can come back and score 15 goals. You can be sold to a club outside of Europe – a club where the transfer window isn't about to close. Or we can sack you.'

'What do you mean by "sack"?' I exclaim.

'We've looked into whether it's possible in legal terms,' he says.

This makes no sense.

'Then you should have fired me two months ago,' I say. 'So that I had time to find somewhere new to play.'

I remind him of a couple of things. How I didn't pursue an appeal to show respect to Rosenborg. How I would otherwise have fought to clear my name. How the board agreed with my decision. How I stepped up in the cup final a month after the trial. How they all seemed pretty happy with me and my decisions those days.

'You've been involved the whole time. Why did you say you had my back if you're considering sacking me?' I demand to know. 'Is it because there's a new coach?'

Horneland stares into the dish of soy sauce. And Stig quietly backtracks.

'We all prefer option number one – of course we do, Nicklas.'

I explain to them that I'm not doing six hours of training a day for fun. That I'm planning to be top scorer again. While they finish chewing, I get the data from my latest tests at Dragør. The figures are on the way to being good – really good. Apparently they realize that too.

'Were you disappointed by your own performance last season?' Horneland suddenly wants to know.

I confirm that I was.

'But the whole team was off its game. When people can't deliver a pass ten metres forward or do what the coach told them to, it's pretty hard to be a striker or winger. I didn't miss many chances,' I point out.

I ask about their plans. What changes are afoot.

'I'd like to see us playing like Jürgen Klopp's teams,' Horneland says.

I have my own views. It's one thing to have sources of inspiration, but the squad created off the back of it is something else. If you want to play like Liverpool or Dortmund, you need people who can find and use gaps. Firmino, Mané, Salah and so on.

Horneland has warmed up. At any rate, he says a bit more. He wants to hear about my past coaches. What Wenger did, what Olsen did, what Conte did. It's mostly the big guns he asks about. I answer him as best I can. And I exaggerate how much freedom they chose to give me.

Before they leave, Stig has one final request. He wants me to fly back to Trondheim on the very Thursday that the electronic tag comes off. The rest of the squad has the Friday off, but he believes it would be a good signal to send.

I'm not keen. When you've been locked up in your apartment for 50 nights, you want to get outside and see some people and have a taste of freedom before you have to perform. But Stig stands firm.

ONE NIGHT while online, I stumble across the Premier League's latest wage statistics. In 2007, it sounded mad that annual salaries had grown from £77,000 to £960,000 in just 15 years. Now the figure has topped £2.6 million. The 500 or so players in the Premier League earn on average what I earned at an absolute top club just five years ago.

Even if the UK is in crisis, wants to leave the EU, and god knows what else, things are only going one way in football. Every month more young multimillionaires appear. Lads who are living with their foster families one day and in a shag pad the next. I wonder how many will run into the same problems I did…

Once a week, my little brother comes over to eat and play chess. We still can't stand losing to each other, and Jannick always thinks I've cheated whenever I win. I don't. Not very often.

After graduating from Copenhagen Business School, he's

started his own little business. He's landed his first deals and he's doing pretty well.

I've just sold my flat in Bushey. For less than I'd hoped. It was bought ahead of the credit crunch. A bad deal – truly bad.

We agree to undertake a kind of financial overview. What's left? We add it all up, and it turns out I was mistaken. During my wild years – from 2006 to 2016 – I spent even more than I had first thought. On parties, gifts, casinos, hotels and holidays. It's all gone for good.

I'm grateful it's not like that any longer. Consider myself lucky. I'll leave football with enough that I should be set up for life. In any case, I will be if I remain on track.

On 16 February, my mum turns 60. I've planned to attend the big birthday party in her honour. The Prison and Probation Service has granted me a couple of extra hours outside. But shortly beforehand, I get cold feet. I can't deal with my family and all the hullabaloo that comes with it. Not yet. Can't deal with the same stories, over and over again. Watch them come to pieces.

We agree I'll stop by her place instead so that we can take a walk by the sea and go through some newspaper cuttings. She's been collecting stacks of them, filled storage boxes, ever since I was a boy.

The first one I pull out is an article from a local Amager paper. It's about me at 11 years old, and it's not about football. I've just lost the Danish championship final in pool. I came second out of 650 participants aged 10 to 18 years old. I had forgotten all about it, but when I wasn't training at KB, I would head over to Lundø – a recreation club on Tårnbyvej – and play pool with the bigger kids. I was so sharp that only one other boy in the whole country – a lad from Aarhus – was better than me.

Then I happen on a stack of clippings about our win against Portugal in October 2011. I scored the matchwinner and played a pretty decent game, but two evenings earlier I'd had mates round in my hotel room. We got so pissed that I threw up in bed. It's insane to think about it. We had an important match ahead of us, yet still that kind of shit was happening. 2011 was my absolute worst year. That was when the innocence disappeared. When the boyish pranks just got fucking stupid.

I don't have many minutes left. So I have to let newspaper cuttings be cuttings and close the door behind me. It's still too hard being sent back to a time when it wasn't already too late. Where it could still have gone my way – and in grand style. I can't stand the thought. The situation I was in. How lucky I really was. It's so clear. Being good at sport came to me almost too naturally. All sports. It was impossible for things to go wrong. At least so I thought.

THE TWO OFFICERS who remove my tag turn down the case of 12 bottles of red wine. They say they're not allowed to accept gifts. It might look like bribery after all.

That makes me even more stubborn. I love people who don't just make demands, so I drive over to their headquarters in Christianshavn and drop off the case of wine in reception. That way they know I really mean it. I feel like I've been fairly treated. It's been team handling at its very best. The rules have been enforced, but they've also taken into account my situation and the interest that always follows me around. I've not been punished extra for being me.

I continue on my merry way. First I have lunch with my little brother before meeting up with some of the old mates. Stig and I reached a compromise that means I can have one night off, rather than a whole weekend in Copenhagen. In return, I have to be in Trondheim on Friday before noon.

I land with a brutal hangover in tow. My body does not take it at all well when it's reintroduced to alcohol. At the club, the clique around the three As – André Hansen, Alexander Søderlund and Anders Konradsen – has grown bigger. It seems they didn't want me to come back. They were finally the centre of attention and as soon as I show up they were back to being ignored by the journalists. I guess there's quite a lot of envy in that kind of thing. Strangely enough, because I would far rather avoid the attention.

In relation to the trial last autumn, a Norwegian newspaper wrote about the Bendtner coverage in the Danish media. The writer said I was no longer treated as a sportsman in Denmark, but rather they saw me as some kind of entertainment phenomenon beyond categorization. Even when I wasn't injured and was delivering on the pitch, it was still all the stuff off the pitch that filled the columns inches. No matter how big or small it was. Coverage of me followed a sort of vicious cycle. Why? Because people click on articles with my name in the headline.

Now the same story is being repeated up here. The writer's Norwegian colleagues are waiting beside the training pitches day in, day out, even when there's nothing to write about.

Occasionally, they use an anonymous source from the squad. Someone who considers me a direct rival for a spot in the starting eleven up front. It reminds me of my early years on the Denmark team. There was a nameless critic on the scene that time as well.

Ivan explains how it's not just the spotlight that some of my teammates are pissed off about. It's my talent too.

'Try to imagine how depressing it must be,' he says. 'You've got everything they've always dreamed of. Your girlfriend is a model, you've played at some of the biggest clubs out there. And you don't even take things half as seriously as they do. You're annoyed at misusing your talent. Fuck it. They're annoyed that it's you who got that talent.'

It's a long pre-season. After three months of training, everyone is bursting with impatience. I get put with Konradsen and three youth players for a five-a-side game. The others are so poor technically that I spread out my arms in exasperation. I can't hide my irritation. How am I supposed to score goals up front if there's nothing to work with?

It's bad form – I know that full well. But I'm also sick of the whole thing. That we're not getting better with the ball. I'm expected to run through fire, while my fellow players can just slack off and excuse themselves with not making the mistakes on purpose.

We get thrashed by the other five-a-side teams, and eventually both Konradsen and I wander off from training. Afterwards, I talk to him in the dressing room. As I understand it, he's just as frustrated as I am.

The next day, Saturday 23 March 2019, I'm summoned to an urgent meeting with Stig and Horneland. It turns out that Konradsen left training in protest at me. I thought he left because he was playing utterly shit.

'Why didn't he say so when we talked?' I ask.

Stig doesn't give a straight answer. But he talks about the season evaluation from back in December. Some of my teammates aren't happy about what they refer to as 'Bendtner's special terms and conditions'. That I was let out on too long a leash under the old coach and how I spent my days off in Copenhagen and Berlin and that kind of thing. Apparently, where I am in the world on days off affects them.

There's also dissatisfaction about my absence from a sponsor's event and a visit to the children's ward. I'm sorry about that last one too. I misread my calendar and went to the fitness room instead. It wasn't out of malice. I've been an ambassador for the Children's Cancer Foundation for years back home in Denmark and used to stop by the National Hospital in Copenhagen as well as selling rubber bracelets through nicklas-bendtner.com...Every single penny went to good causes.

In the evaluation, several of my teammates said they didn't dare confront me. How I'm such a big star there was no point.

It hits me hard. At least Adebayor was straight up. He didn't hide away – he said what he thought right to my face.

Stig sends me an email with loads of demands I have to fulfil. I have to beam like sunshine at training. I have to post football-related content on Instagram. I have to train and play on artificial turf without complaining.

If it weren't for Mike and his half of the squad, I'd be out of here right now. What's more, Ivan says that Rosenborg shouldn't be rid of me that easily. If I fulfil my obligations until the end of the year, there's a pretty big bonus with my name on it. A sign-off fee that we had inserted into the original contract.

Perhaps the real reason the club are trying to push me out is money. For the first time in years and years, Rosenborg are in financial trouble. The bottom line has gone red, and I'm the biggest outgoing on the player side of things. If the cost of me could be whisked away, everything would look better. And the board would have looked decisive.

I remind Ivan about the match against Valur from Iceland the summer before. How my goals in the final minutes secured them nigh on £5 million of additional revenues. How I got us to the Europa League in both 2017 and 2018. How we won the championship in both 2017 and 2018. How I was league top scorer in 2017. How I scored the matchwinner in the 2018 cup final. How I actually scored 13 times overall in 2018 – despite injuries and despite playing in midfield and on the left wing.

We agree that things can't end like this. There's been too many positives to turn tail now. So I give it my all. I yell 'great goal!' when Søderlund actually manages to get lucky during training. I smile at all the guys who've pulled a Jon Snow on me. That kind of thing. I notice that Horneland always has his back to me. He seems like someone doing his best to avoid eye contact.

I spend a week like that. The day before our first match in Eliteserien, the head coach suddenly calls me over. He's changed his mind after three months of preparation. He now wants to play a completely different system and wants me to start, after having said I was completely out of the squad just a week ago. He wants me at number ten, just behind Søderlund. It's not something we've done in training. Like, not once.

I message Ivan with the news.

'Fuck me, that's a development,' he writes back.

But the time of miracles is over. We get thrashed by Bodø/Glimt. Our opponents reign supreme on their artificial pitch, as if they – rather than us – have won the championship 26 times. The 2-0 defeat is cheaply conceded. We're a very long way from being in contention for anything at all.

I know that already. Now Horneland can say he really tried. That I got my chance. It doesn't matter that the whole team collapsed. Doesn't matter that I was put in an unfamiliar position without any warning at all. I'm not the club's saviour. Not any more. Now I'm the scapegoat.

COPENHAGEN

2019

TIME PASSES. My mum says it would be typical old me if it all still changed. My life in a nutshell.

She's spoken to her friend who said something cryptic. September 2019 is going to be my month of destiny. It could mean anything and my optimism has evaporated.

I'm desperately trying to keep going. I've invested in a racing bike and wetsuit. I head down to the sea at Amager Strand. I pull on my wetsuit and wade out until the water is at my chest. There's a thunder cloud hovering above the Øresund Bridge. The sky also has no idea where things are going.

The planes cut diagonally across the sky. Arriving. Departing. I've been on them countless times. If only I had been on the plane to the World Cup last summer, I wouldn't be lying here splashing about.

I swim for 45 uninterrupted minutes. Front crawl and breaststroke, front crawl and breaststroke. The undercurrents pull at my long body. They come close but don't quite get hold of me. They don't draw me out into the deeps where it gets really exciting.

THE DAY before the transfer window closes, I crash. We're out on a long bike ride somewhere in North Zealand, and maybe it's my English past that makes me quite casually bear left when I reach a roundabout. Whatever it is, my partner is heading right and his front wheel clips my back wheel. I land on my elbow, hip and back. I skid across the wet tarmac, tearing my Lycra. When I had my car crash, my seat belt saved me. This time it's my helmet. It's cracked.

I've got several other deep abrasions. They include a nasty crimson fella just below one of my shoulder blades. It looks ferocious, but to be perfectly honest the adrenaline drowns out the searing pain. I've not seen this much action since the Norwegian Cup final last winter. I'm still here. I'm high.

The next morning on Sunday 1 September, I head to Dragør to get my scrapes checked out. I'm as tender as I would be after 120 minutes of football on full power. Thomas Jørgensen says it feels like my whole body has been sprained. That's just how hard my landing was.

My mood is back through the floor and checking my mobile doesn't exactly help things. There's uncomfortably little happening, and I'm mutinous.

'I've not heard from Ivan at noon on the final day of the transfer window…Isn't that pretty fucking weird?' I ask.

'Yes,' Thomas admits.

I'm restless. It's no use heading home to Philine, because it's guaranteed she won't be able to put herself in my shoes, and it's guaranteed she will try to cheer me up or something. And I'm just not up for it.

I end up at my mum's, sprawled on her sofa on the 13th floor. There's a view all the way across the water to the Barsebäck nuclear power plant in Sweden, but I don't give a fuck. Everything just seems fucking awful. All I can see ahead of me is the end of my career. My Sunday blues run deep, even though I've not had a drink in weeks.

Finally, Ivan calls. I'm expecting him to go round the houses. Something about how I've made things tough for myself. But it doesn't happen.

'Håkse's working on something,' he says. 'Ståle Solbakken might be able to put you to use when it comes to the punch. Isn't it fucking crazy how things can turn around?'

At 4pm, things start to move quickly. FC Copenhagen want

to sign a short-term contract for the rest of the autumn so that we can check each other out. I don't care. If I'm given the chance, I'll seize it. And as long as I can get back onto the so-called research scheme – the one that ensures a substantially lower tax bill – I won't make any big demands. It's actually all up to Rosenborg whether it happens or not. If Stig and the board up there want to let me go with a fraction of the money that I'm owed, we should make it.

At 8pm, I drive over to Ivan and Håkse's office at Nørrebro. The summer nights are drawing in, and no one in the press has caught wind of anything. If they had, it wouldn't be so dark on the street. There would be flashes of lightning. Instead, it's completely dead.

We sign in good spirits. There are jokes back and forth, but when I pull on the white jersey with the lion logo on the chest, things get serious. Goosebumps cover my arms and it feels so right it's impossible to put into words.

We get playful and Ivan and I come up with a prank to embarrass FC Midtjylland. These years, they're FC Copenhagen's biggest rivals and earlier in the transfer window they hinted that I might be on the way to their team. But they were just teasing our fans – because of course it wouldn't happen. Never in a million years. It would be like moving to Tottenham straight after coming back from Juventus. Never in my life. So we make a video of me blocking FC Midtjylland on Instagram. Before long, it turns into a hit on FC Copenhagen social media.

My surprise transfer only gets out just before midnight and then it spreads across the internet like wildfire. By all accounts, people must have woken up to something of a shock, because all the stories are using a breaking news banner and they're all about me. An out-of-shape football player who has been washed up in Norway and is arriving on a short-term contract has taken over all the front pages...the media are strange beasts. They create their own news. But there's nothing new about that.

Obviously the usual haters break out in hives whenever my name is mentioned. But they're in a minority right from the start. The majority of FC Copenhagen's fans seem absolutely thrilled and the Danish media also throw a party. Finally, Bendtner is going to play in the Superliga. Finally, something is happening. It won't be boring, says a pundit.

'The biggest shock of the transfer window,' says one outlet.

'Bendtner can be anything from a nightmare to a dream,' says another.

The press conference in Parken the next day is packed. Among other things, I get asked about a new nightclub down by the Lakes in central Copenhagen, whether I'm looking forward to partying at Lake Pavilion, as it's known. It's obviously intended as a joke, but I can answer with complete honesty that I have no plans to do that. There's no way the journalist can know, but I've just signed an agreement not to drink or party for the next four months. It's a specific requirement from Ståle and it suits me down to the ground. I want to be fighting fit so I can become king of the Lions. That's my only wish. I've not felt this hungry since…I don't actually know when.

When it emerges that my squad number is going to be 32, shirt orders go mad. The fan shop is selling nothing else, and there's speculation that my wages will be earned back within the first week.

I QUICKLY fit into the FC Copenhagen dressing room. Nicolai Boilesen and I pretty much carry on where we left off in the Denmark team camp. He's still a firecracker, but there are also more tender moments. It's pretty rare in the footballing world, but Boile and I both know what it's like only seeing our kids on a part-time basis. We know how hard it can be to put into words in the daily back and forth. I also click with Stephan Andersen, the old Denmark keeper.

I know how much my attitude will matter. It'll be weighed up and analysed down to the last detail. If I do anything that smells like being a spoiled celebrity, it'll result in a harsh backlash. *All eyes on me*, as Tupac would have said. So I do everything I can to seem humble and giving. I joke, I take the piss out of myself, I help move the goal posts around and drag bags of balls about. That kind of thing. And I talk to the youngsters in the dressing room. Give

At 4pm on the final day of the transfer window, Ivan and Håkse called. FC Copenhagen still wanted to discuss a contract. We met four hours later. Here I am captured during the half-time break in our reserve match against Brøndby on 10 September 2019. My first appearance in the white jersey. (Photo: Lars Rønbøg/FrontZoneSport/Getty Images)

them advice and answer their questions. I would do that anyway, but I give it that little bit extra – no doubt about it.

People are pretty welcoming. Even Viktor Fischer, who up to now has been top dog in the squad. On the training pitch, it's clear that he wants to continue being in charge, and he's even more big-mouthed than he was playing for Denmark. But he doesn't grumble when I sidestep him and steal 99 per cent of the attention. He deserves credit for that. It wouldn't have been like that in England.

My sharpness is absent like never before. It's disappeared and is slower to come back than on past occasions when I've been injured. Several hundred fans have turned up for my first training session at FC Copenhagen's Peter Bangs Vej facility. They've never seen anything like it in the history of the club. When I was a boy here, the others were pissing on my clothes. Now I'm almost being worshipped. It's a bit overwhelming if I'm honest.

At the end of my first session, I'm dispatched to practise finishes on the next pitch. All of a sudden the army of camera crews surrounds me with all their kit. I don't get many hits and I miss a bunch, and before long a video of it goes viral. Major international media outlets link to it, so people in New Zealand and India can have a bit of a laugh at my expense. Cool. I mean, how cheap can a laugh get? I've not trained with a ball for months – of course I'm rusty.

I'M NOT BOTHERED about waking up every morning in Copenhagen. Fortunately, because I had feared the worst. But city life exerts less pull on me than it once did. I feel like I can keep the biggest temptations at bay if I've got something else to strive for. Special requirement or not, I don't intend to turn down a good glass of wine every now and then, but Ståle doesn't need to worry about me getting pissed. I'm just not interested in it.

If there's one thing that does bother me, it's my body. Many days, I'm so smashed up that I breakfast on Voltaren. The big 200mg pills – parallel-imported from the UK.

I'm doing what I can to get back in shape so I'm of some use to Ståle. Maybe even a bit more than that. I put in extra time lifting weights and eat healthily on a consistent basis.

There's no way around it. Even though I've cycled, swum and run, they're different from being pushed by others. When I'm working out on my own, I stop when it hurts. It's always been like that. I need someone with a whip – and the infamous carrot – before I jump to it.

And that's how it is. I feel optimistic – almost like the old Nicklas sometimes felt – and I can see light at the end of the tunnel. Apparently, Dame N'Doye is knackered and his knees are ready for the scrapheap. Few believe Ståle's Senegalese favourite can make yet another incredible comeback. And given that the other two attackers in the squad don't bring tonnes to the pitch, there's a use for me. There just has to be.

In the league, FC Midtjylland have made a strong start, but what must be causing Ståle a serious headache isn't so much the table as our game on the pitch. When I get my first substitute appearance I realize it's surprisingly difficult to be an FC Copenhagen striker. There's almost nothing to work with, and I make myself most useful by serving as a distribution point on the edge of the box. On a few occasions I notice impatience running away with me, but I can't do what I did at Rosenborg. My instructions are crystal clear. Under no circumstances am I to move further down the pitch. So I spend most of my time stepping from foot to foot and waiting for something to work with. It's pretty much impossible when crosses from the wingers are in remarkably short supply. On the occasions that an attempt is made, the ball generally sails straight into the first best defender it can find. FC Copenhagen are defending champions, but almost everyone on the team is struggling to reach a borderline acceptable level. Throughout September, we only manage to accumulate a measly four points in the league. And October isn't much better: six out of a possible 12 points.

On 28 October, we face FC Nordsjælland in the cup. It's a Thursday and my turn to start up front. I've tried it once before, but that time I wasn't geared up to the tempo. This time things go better and after 25 minutes the opposition screw up their offside trap. I'm on my own with their keeper and choose not to dribble around him. A trickling shot isn't the way to go either. It's do or die, so I go for the top of the net. My boot smashes against the ball. It sounds perfect, and the same can be said of the roar from the Lower C stand. They've been waiting patiently for this, and for a few seconds my legs tremble like a cannon's just been fired.

FOOTBALL is a head sport. Literally and metaphorically. You sometimes forget how much the stuff on the inside matters. But it really does. With a little bit of a tailwind, anything is suddenly possible. Since scoring my goal, I'm a changed man. I dominate our opponents, win duels in the air, set up my teammates and I'm close to doubling my scoring tally.

I've got a lot more in the tank, so I'm not best pleased when Ståle takes me off. Wasn't I supposed to play my way into shape?

Once I've cooled off, I actually understand his position. It makes pretty good sense if I'm being rested for the next league match on Sunday. If we build things up on a match-by-match basis, I'll hit top form soon. Then I can score another ten goals over the remainder of the autumn. 'The train is about to depart,' I think to myself.

But that's where I'm terribly mistaken. In the next match I don't get a chance. On the other hand, all my attacking colleagues do. Seriously – N'Doye has managed to regain his spot up front in no time, and Sotiriou and Santos also get some game time. They run riot against one of the weakest away teams in the league.

Suddenly it's clear as day. I don't fit into Ståle's plans at all. I'm here because that's what a bunch of other people wanted. And because I can be used as a joker. I'm not here because they're going to build their attack around my qualities. If that's the case they can forget about it. That's not why I wanted to come back to FC Copenhagen. In my dreams, I've pictured myself leading the club to another league title. I've dreamed about being the main man. I've not imagined sitting on the bench and clapping on my teammates most of the time. If I'm going to cheer, I might as well be doing it from the stands instead.

I begin to fill my evenings with things other than pure restoration. I head out with a couple of actors to eat at The Alchemist. I seek out some thrills with the odd game of poker every now and then.

Perhaps Ståle can see I'm losing my motivation. I actually reckon there's a lot he can see. The big moments are few and far between on the turf, but at least I get to sample Ståle's club intelligence. The one that's made it possible for him to remain in power while casting all others aside.

You have to give him that much. He risked very little taking me on for four months, and if I'd had the Midas touch in my first matches, then he would have looked like a genius. Now he can say that Project Bendtner was given a chance.

But was it really? Seriously? Was it a wholehearted chance? No way. In the league, I've racked up 213 minutes of game time. That's too little to learn the team's gameplay patterns – especially during a poor patch. Look at Sotiriou. The Cypriot has been given three or four times as much trust as me, has wasted chances one after another, and is still ahead of me in the queue. It doesn't seem all that logical.

As we sit discussing a possible extension to my contract, the rain falls heavily on Østerbro. I'm slowly being drained.

'It's not been an easy decision,' Ståle says to me. After that, I switch off and don't hear what he's saying, because I've heard it all before.

Afterwards, Ivan calls. He's pretty sure I can get another short-term contract. We just have to ask.

'Ståle hasn't closed the door completely. You can hear that much. But he wants to see you fight even harder than you did before.'

I refuse point blank. Better to stop playing. I'm not going to beg for another four months. It's too shitty. And it wouldn't be honest. I don't want it that much any more. I want to fight, but only if it pays. If the reward is a bloody nose, then why bother?

I remember what all the pundits said when I was unveiled at FC Copenhagen. That it couldn't possibly be boring with me at the club. But that's what happened. No scandals off the pitch, no triumphs on it. The press must feel like I've let them down.

THE BACK GARDEN

EPILOGUE – 2019–2020

THERE'S THE LIGHT. The belief that everything is going to be okay. That you're going to reach the top and make good your failings. The perfect header at the toughest moment imaginable. The noise of 60,000 spectators yelling down at you with joy. A little hand holding firmly on to yours. The feeling of invulnerability. That nothing can touch you.

And then there's the darkness. The disappointments and your reaction when you're disappointed. Your adrenaline fix when football isn't enough. Escape into the gloomy place. Where temptations are lined up, waiting. Bottle after bottle. Body after body. Chip after chip. Bad advice and even worse decisions. The money that makes everyone weak. The past, which just won't go away.

Light and dark. I know nothing else. That's what my life is like. Before it was filled with the light. The good. I was the eternal optimist. I'm no longer that. Not very often.

When did it turn? It happened when I met Caroline and scored my first goals for Arsenal. I felt like one of the superheroes I had once idolized on the posters in my childhood bedroom.

I was in a motorway crash where my car rolled down a bank before being smashed to smithereens against a tree. And I was able to walk away. I didn't learn my lesson – quite the opposite, in fact. It confirmed my immortality.

Then came the collateral damage. In my private life where we crashed – irreversibly. On the pitch, where my body had to throw in the towel.

When I went to the World Cup, I betrayed Arsène Wenger's trust. And when I came back to London, I found out I was gonna be a dad. That summer became crucial. It was then my escape began in earnest. The rest is history. A long, tortuous history.

DURING THE WINTER transfer window, there's nothing that I really want to get my teeth into. Offers come in from Australia, Paraguay and Mexico, but the wages aren't exactly overwhelming and a life in South America immediately strikes me as a little risky. If you end up in trouble in Mexico, things can go really badly.

The window closes and I think once again that's that. That my career is fading into nothing. But then suddenly China comes up. A rich club in the top flight still don't have a target man, and since there aren't that many tall players in the league, I'm likely to dominate in the air.

But is it what I really want? I get caught up in self-doubt. Since Caroline moved from London to Copenhagen, I've seen more of Nicho. Way more, actually. Over the autumn, I've seen him pretty consistently and we've also got a system in place. The idea is for him to stay with me and Philine for four days at a time, before he then does ten days with Caroline. I don't really want to ruin that, because it's worked until now. After nine years, I'm seeing my son on a regular basis, and it would confuse both of us if that stopped all of a sudden.

I still have doubts. The dosh is good and I want to be master of my own fate when it comes to deciding my footballing days are over.

The Chinese send me an impeccable contract, and I take the weekend to think it over. On the Monday, I decide to check it out and see what conditions are like – and maybe even sign it. I let Ivan know and we're both searching for plane tickets when coronavirus shuts down all the Chinese airports. If I had made up my mind three days earlier and put my signature on another piece of paper, it would probably have been legally binding…My life has been full of big numbers and small margins.

I NEED to get away. I invite my little brother to join me on a flying visit to London. For ten years I had my base in the city, but at no point did I take the time to experience any of it. Except the nightlife, that is. That's what we need to remedy.

We check in to The Ritz and eat lunch at The Wolseley. We spend the afternoon in the hotel casino and in the evening we meet up with Ivan at a new Italian place. It turns out he's in town too.

After dinner, we head back to ours and hit the hotel bar. That's the plan anyway, but none of us are up to it. We order cokes, drain them and fall into bed like old men.

The next day I wake up early. I've set my alarm clock and everything. The order of the day is sightseeing. We reach Big Ben and Westminster Bridge on foot, then we take a closer look at the monstrous church next door before we set a course for the City. We also end up standing and staring at Buckingham Palace for ages before visiting the Royal Family's horse stables. It's a really mixed city. So much history, so much high culture, so much self-destruction. So many worlds that are in no hurry to exchange words with each other. Like the booths at the Shadow Lounge. Everyone there thought that their booth – and theirs alone – was the place to be.

We walk around Trafalgar Square and wind up at Tate Modern at a spectacular Steve McQueen exhibition. I own works by Banksy and Damien Hirst, and I'm happy with them – but video installations are just on another level. The constant movement is a good match for me and my restlessness.

We pass a lot of celebrities. I've been to an incomprehensible number of places without actually ever being present. Showing my face but off my face. All of Mayfair and Knightsbridge. Novikov and Annabel's. Nobu, where I celebrated my partnership with David Manasseh. The multitude of hot spots with drinking and debauchery. Several of them have changed names since

I was last here, but are otherwise familiar.

After we've been walking for six hours, we hail a cab. I will always prefer English cabs to Danish taxis. They're beyond comparison. We get caught up in the rush hour. Familiar facades slip past in slow motion. It strikes me how little I've missed it. You miss less than you fear. Perhaps that's the most important thing I've learned in life. Things and places don't change – not that drastically. The only thing that really changes is people. You never know where they are at.

TWO MONTHS LATER I watch the Netflix series about Michael Jordan and the Chicago Bulls. The wildest times – those moments where most was at stake – remind me of a lost era. I well up several times while watching. Seeing how the team didn't punish Dennis Rodman for his boozy escapade in Las Vegas, but instead how they knew they had to accommodate his inner demons is a beautiful experience for a dumbass like me. They knew what they were getting in Rodman – and they treated him on the basis of what they knew.

I think about my own skeletons. I've become less afraid to look my own past in the eye. The biggest breakthrough was visiting my childhood home.

I had said I would never do it, but one day it happens. I'm driving towards Banevænget. It's not as far as I thought. Just a kilometre. As I'm parking, a young woman comes out from number two. I tell her I once lived there and ask whether I can have a look inside.

She's not busy and says yes before opening the gate for me. The fence is the same. My dad built it with his own two hands. And the terrace is just as it always was. My parents held court out here. Barbecuing and drinking G&Ts with their friends.

It all began in a tiny back garden. It wasn't hard to get noticed. I was king of a patch of grass.

I look around. I saunter over to my den. Over in the corner furthest from the house. This was where I could always hide.

I can't do that any more.